Praise for *The Four Factors of Trust*

"Great Place to Work has measured trust by surveying over 100 million working people over the last 30 years. Without trust there is no engagement, satisfaction, loyalty, or happiness. In this book, Ashley and Amelia have built a trust bridge between the employee and customer experience that will create a durable outsized competitive advantage that benefits organizations and humanity."

—Michael C. Bush, CEO, Great Place to Work

"It's no secret that trust is on the decline around the world. Yet trust remains more important, even vital, than ever before. It is, in fact, the one thing that changes *everything*—a force-multiplier for inspired performance and greater well-being in everyone around you. Whether you're in the C-Suite or on the factory floor, you can lead in creating and extending trust to others. Ashley and Amelia's terrific book will show you how."

—Stephen M. R. Covey, author of *New York Times* and No. 1 *Wall Street Journal* bestsellers *The Speed of Trust* and *Trust & Inspire*

"*The Four Factors* has cracked the code on trust. This dynamic team articulates the critical role cyber plays in both securing and recovering trust, bringing to life the challenges faced by cyber alongside pragmatic suggestions to ensure a measurable, predictable, and actionable approach to building trust."

—Dave DeWalt, Founder and Managing Director, NightDragon

"Trust is easy to destroy—and too many of us believe that it's hard to create. But in fact, a deeper understanding of trust shows this to be wrong. *The Four Factors of Trust* provides data-rich, actionable solutions. If you want to build a fearless organization with long-lasting trust and loyalty—for consumers and employees alike—this book will show you how."

—Amy C. Edmondson, Novartis Professor of Leadership and Management, Harvard Business School, and author of *The Fearless Organization*

"Trust is one of the most critical—and essential—issues facing organizations today. With trust, anything is possible. Without it, everything is difficult. *The Four Factors of Trust* reveals a new, research-based framework and measurement tool for earning trust from customers, employees, investors, and other stakeholders. Reading these groundbreaking insights, and showing respect, patience, and commitment, will be invaluable for CEOs and frontline supervisors throughout any organization."

—**Henrietta Fore,** Chairman of the Board and CEO,
Holsman International

"I often say that strong trust is forged from positive, consistent experiences first imagined through high expectations. With the stellar team, deep data, and helpful anecdotes that have shaped this book, I certainly expected to experience a helpful toolkit for evolving trust and I was not disappointed. I trust that any reader equally keen to elevate and evolve their brand will be delighted."

—**Suzanne Frey,** VP of Product and Chief Privacy Officer, Google

"We all know the importance of trust, but few of us really understand how to earn it. Thankfully, Ashley Reichheld and Amelia Dunlop are here to help. In this remarkably readable, well-researched, and actionable book, they reveal what it takes for individuals and organizations to establish reliability, transparency, capability, and humanity."

—**Adam Grant,** author of No. 1 *New York Times* bestseller
Think Again, and host of the TED podcast, WorkLife

"Today's winning companies put people and purpose first. Creating trust within a company is a critical component to being successful in that endeavor. In *The Four Factors of Trust*, Reichheld and Dunlop share with clarity and brilliance the best practices for gaining trust, and even share the methodology you can use to calculate your organization's 'trust score.' This powerful book is an essential tool for everyone working on transforming an organization."

—**Hubert Joly,** senior lecturer at Harvard Business School,
former Chairman and CEO of Best Buy, and author of *The Heart
of Business: Leadership Principles for the Next Era of Capitalism*

"What drives trust, and how do the most trusted organizations earn it from customers and employees? The answer is more complicated than you imagine. Deloitte's Ashley Reichheld and Amelia Dunlop unravel the mystery, and make building trust simpler, in this vital and pragmatic book."

—**Daniel H. Pink,** author of *New York Times* bestsellers *The Power of Regret* and *Drive*

"Read this important new book so you can help your organization measure and manage trust—one of the most vital ingredients for building relationships that are worthy of loyalty."

—**Fred Reichheld,** creator of the Net Promoter® Score and System, and author of *Winning on Purpose: The Unbeatable Strategy of Loving Customers*

"Reichheld and Dunlop have crafted a compelling data-driven narrative that delves deep into the intricacies of trust. Packed with rich case studies, this book breaks down the complexities of what it means to build trust as an organization with wisdom and humor. Don't miss it."

—**Sandra Sucher,** Professor of Management Practice at Harvard Business School, and author of *The Power of Trust*

"Nothing is more important to business success than building trusted relationships with all your stakeholders. Every organization can benefit from reading *The Four Factors*, a thoroughly researched, comprehensive guide for creating a deeply rooted culture of trust."

—**Amy Weaver,** President and Chief Financial Officer, Salesforce

The Four Factors of Trust

The Four Factors of Trust

How Organizations Can Earn Lifelong Loyalty

Ashley Reichheld with
Amelia Dunlop

WILEY

Published by John Wiley & Sons, Inc., Hoboken, New Jersey.
Published simultaneously in Canada.

For general information on our other products and services or for technical support, please contact our Customer Care Department within the United States at (800) 762-2974, outside the United States at (317) 572-3993 or fax (317) 572-4002.

Wiley publishes in a variety of print and electronic formats and by print-on-demand. Some material included with standard print versions of this book may not be included in e-books or in print-on-demand. If this book refers to media such as a CD or DVD that is not included in the version you purchased, you may download this material at http://booksupport.wiley.com. For more information about Wiley products, visit www.wiley.com.

Library of Congress Cataloging-in-Publication Data

Names: Reichheld, Ashley, author. | Dunlop, Amelia, author.
Title: The four factors of trust : how organizations can earn lifelong loyalty / Ashley Reichheld and Amelia Dunlop.
Description: Hoboken, New Jersey : Wiley, [2023] | Includes index.
Identifiers: LCCN 2022024814 (print) | LCCN 2022024815 (ebook) | ISBN 9781119855019 (cloth) | ISBN 9781119855033 (adobe pdf) | ISBN 9781119855026 (epub)
Subjects: LCSH: Customer loyalty. | Employee loyalty.
Classification: LCC HF5415.525 .R447 2023 (print) | LCC HF5415.525 (ebook) | DDC 658.8/12—dc23/eng/20220706
LC record available at https://lccn.loc.gov/2022024814
LC ebook record available at https://lccn.loc.gov/2022024815

Cover Design: Paul McCarthy
Cover Illustrations: Deloitte Development LLC

SKY10035591_090622

For our families

Part I: What You Need to Know About Trust

Part II: The "How-to" of Trust

Appendix

Introduction

Learning to ride a bicycle is an act of trust. We trust that pumping on the pedals will create enough momentum to carry our weight forward. We trust that whoever is encouraging us will hold on to the back of our seat just long enough for us to gain confidence. We transform ourselves into a person-who-knows-how-to-ride-a-bicycle from a person-who-does-not by trusting the people around us, trusting the two-wheeled machine, and trusting our own ability. And then we feel the sweet thrill of accomplishment just long enough to ride our brand-new red bicycle into the rosebush, whose thorns break our fall. Our lives are full of moments where trust is easily given, even more easily lost, and then painstakingly rebuilt, sometimes at great cost.

As leaders, we have seen this cycle play out too often in organizations where trust is quickly given and quickly lost. It turns out that humans are effortlessly good at losing trust and really bad at rebuilding it. We know this from personal experience, but more on that later.

This is a book about building trust. We are passionate about the topic of trust because it creates the types of relationships we want to build, the type of organizations we want to belong to, and the type of world we want to live in.

We are passionate about the topic of trust because it creates the types of relationships we want to build, the type of organizations we want to belong to, and the type of world we want to live in.

1

We aren't going to try to prove to you that trust matters. We *trust* that you get that already from your own personal and professional experiences where you have gained and lost trust—where you have fallen off and gotten back on your own red bicycle. Instead, we want to offer something different. We want to offer clarity about what you can actually *do* to build trust as a leader for your organization, and the impact that can have on other stakeholders in society.

Our goal is to help leaders measure trust, predict trust, and act in ways that build trust because we believe that trust is the path to loyalty.

There are as many ways to measure trust, benchmark it, score it, and put it on an index as there are definitions of what trust actually is. There are measures of social trust, customer trust sentiment, and trust that makes for good public relations campaigns, to name a few. Pew, Edelman, and Gallup are all noteworthy institutions that have studied and written about the loss of trust. We'll share some of their conclusions too. However, much of what has been written previously looks through a rearview mirror to help explain why trust broke down *after the fact, after the bicycle rider landed in the rosebush.* Our aim is to help organizations to move *forward.*

We wanted a measure that was both meaningful and actionable in approaching how trust impacts human behavior—something that would help leaders of organizations not just to understand trust, but to build it leading to positive outcomes. We couldn't find that measure, so we created our own.

Whether you are reading this because you are curious about the topic of trust, you are a leader in an organization wrestling with how to grow trust with your customers or workforce, or you are an academic deeply committed to the field of trust, we hope that you walk away with an understanding of the following:

- The components of trust, what we call the Four Factors, are correlated with measures of loyalty, including Net Promoter Score (NPS), and are the path to building loyalty. You can—and should—measure trust with customers as well as workers.
- Trust leads to meaningful financial outcomes for organizations.
- We can both predict trust based on actual behaviors and predict those behaviors based on trust scores.
- Using these predictions, we can take concrete steps towards building the trust we so badly need in our organizations and society at large.

In the fall of 2018, we were both part of a leadership team that set an aspiration to Elevate the Human Experience (EHX or HX for short). At the time we thought the aspiration was lofty and undefined, but worth striving for. Now we believe that we elevate someone's experience when we acknowledge their intrinsic worth as a human and do everything in our power to help make their experience just a little bit better. We knew from the very beginning that you can't elevate anything if people don't trust you. If we could understand what builds trust, we could create individual experiences for customers, workers, and partners that increase trust and create better, elevated experiences over time.

We have spent hundreds of hours and millions of dollars with our research team studying *one question*:

How do you build trust?

We conducted almost two dozen in-depth interviews with trust experts. We have collected over 200,000 survey responses with customers and workers across nearly 500 brands. We conducted in-depth focus groups with fifty workers—with a particular emphasis on female workers and hourly/gig workers. We have spoken with organizational leaders who have excelled at building trust. We have worked with organizations directly to help them on their journeys to build trust. And we have studied famous and not-so-famous stories when trust was won or lost. We wanted to know: Why do customers trust a brand and become loyal to it? What actions make trust endure through difficult times? How do we build a culture of trust from the inside out, starting with our own workforce? What are the tangible long-term benefits of that trust? But first, before we get to these questions, let's define what we mean by trust.

What Is Trust?

Most people fall back on the "I know it when I see/feel/hear it," definition of trust. Or people cite a specific moment when they felt trusting. Even if you can't "see" trust, its presence or absence drives so much of the difference between a good experience with an individual or an organization and a bad one.

Here is how we have come to define trust: Trust is the promise of a meaningful, mutually beneficial relationship between two or more people. At a fundamental level, trust is what happens, or doesn't, between people and between organizations made up of people. And, critically, trust is the essential bond an organization has with all its humans—customers, workforce, and partners.

Trust is the promise of a meaningful, mutually beneficial relationship between two or more people.

Trust is built in moments of vulnerability. Sandra Sucher, a Harvard Business School professor who has published widely on the topic of trust, describes trust as the "willingness to make yourself vulnerable to the intentions and actions of others."[1] Most organizations and leaders seek to replace vulnerability with contracts, detailed terms and conditions, and other processes and legal vehicles for ensuring target outcomes are met. The less we trust, the less we are willing to make ourselves vulnerable, the more legal replacements we need and the more complicated our lives become. Customers and workers are subject to these contracts, and the balance of power sits with the organization, rather than with the individual. This makes trust for the individual even more important.

In business, trust means people engage an organization with a sense that their interests are being honored alongside the organization's interests. For example, customers believe the software they download from a trusted organization will be safe; when they download software, they are making themselves vulnerable (to malware, hacking, or unwanted apps) but trust—driven by previous experience—makes this choice more straightforward. Workers trust that their relationship with their organization means they'll be respected and appreciated *in addition* to being paid. Thus, they make themselves vulnerable psychologically and financially because they trust the organization to act in their interests as well as its own.

Trust always comes down to a relationship, no matter how fleeting. Some relationships are transactional. Others endure. It can be the relationship we have with ourselves (as in, I trust my future self to make good decisions). It can be the relationship we have with a single person, such as a colleague at work. And it can be about the relationship we have to entire groups of people in an organization.

Because people bring their messy human selves to work, lack of trust in one relationship affects trust in another. In this way, trust in our relationships impacts our general outlook on life. We see this in the effect intimacy has on trust. For example, the data from our research show that workforce participants overall trust "my employer" more than "business in general."[2] It's easier to understand something, and create a positive relationship with it, when you are close to it.

We trust a friend to consider our interests, treat us fairly, and offer respect—behaviors that honor our **humanity**. We trust an organization can deliver its promised products or services—we call this **capability**. We trust someone at work to be straightforward and honest, which means valuing **transparency**. And we trust the brakes on our bicycle will work as well today as they did yesterday, a kind of trust driven by **reliability**. We call humanity, transparency, capability, and reliability the *Four Factors of Trust*. We depict them as intertwined in an infinite loop, because each factor relates to the others and trust overall is only as strong as the weakest factor. (See Figure I.1.)

Taken together, these are the Four Factors that help us build trust before it is broken, and especially after it is broken.

Humanity and Transparency signal intent; Capability and Reliability signal competence

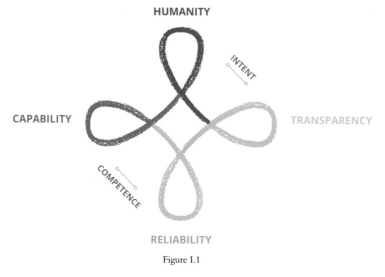

Figure I.1

Who Are We to Write a Book on Trust?

At this point, you are probably wondering: Who are we and why should you trust us? Good question. Ashley and Amelia (the "we" in this book) are trusted friends, colleagues, and collaborators who share a vision and a passion for elevating the experience of being human. We are both principals at Deloitte, the world's largest professional services organization, wives, and mothers. Neither of us are academics. Ashley has a degree in social psychology and gender studies. Amelia has degrees in sociology, moral theology, and business. Ashley's superpower is her curiosity and drive to solve problems, especially in the face of adversity. Amelia's superpower is her authenticity to show up with equal parts head and heart. When she is not at work, Ashley is most likely to be found with her partner and twins, building Lego at home or in her workshop, building the next pirate ship sandbox. Amelia is most likely to be found with her husband and three children on some new adventure or "experience," learning to parasail in Key West or fly fish in the river delta that divides Argentina from Uruguay.

For Ashley, experience is literally in the family, as she is the niece of Fred Reichheld, the author of *The Loyalty Effect* and the creator of the Net Promoter Score (NPS). For Amelia, best-selling author of *Elevating the Human Experience: Three Paths to Love and Worth at Work*, her journey has led her to explore the issue of human worth and love in the workplace. Together, Ashley and Amelia believe that while it is hard to do business without trust, it's *impossible* to elevate the human experience without it.

It's no secret to our teams that we started out on the wrong foot, with what we now would call a "trust deficit." We simply did not see things the same way and had different working styles. Ashley tends to approach her work with unbounded energy and enthusiasm, often back at her laptop at 6 a.m. working on the next challenge. Amelia feels and thinks deeply and needs space away from her laptop (preferably in the sun) to reflect and come back with a fresh perspective. Early on, well before the idea of ever collaborating on something as significant as a book on trust came about, Amelia felt that Ashley would push her too hard when she needed more time to breathe (picture a series of enthusiastic texts and emails in the morning before coffee). Ashley felt at times that Amelia was unavailable and frustratingly disengaged (picture those texts and emails going un-responded to for a day or more). Looking back on it, our working styles resembled a yin-yang or left brain–right brain duality.

While neither one of us can point to the exact turning point, both of us agree that building trust took showing up **reliably**, communicating with each other **transparently**, and demonstrating our **humanity** in ways that showed vulnerability. We never doubted each other's **capability** in the workplace, so there was a base of confidence in our skills as professionals. The story of our personal relationship is one of using the Four Factors of Trust to build a more trusted and enduring partnership and friendship. And while we work on it every day, it has led to this collaboration and this book.

Why Should You Care about Building Trust as Much as We Do?

There are three reasons why we believe you should care about learning how to build trust as much as we do:

- No matter how you measure it, trust is at an all-time low.
- Building trust is one of the most powerful ways to shape human behavior and elevate experience.
- Building trust leads to meaningful, long-term results.

The stakes for understanding trust have never been higher. Trust is on the decline. People today are less trusting of business, government, and brands and their products or services than they were twenty years ago.[3] What's driving this decline? Polarization in politics, social dislocation, changes in economic status, disruption in working life, the toxic side of social media, and reduction in social capital—all these forces have conspired to create suspicion and distrust.

High-performing organizations already know that building trust drives human behavior and leads to better outcomes. NASA focuses on humanity by sending their astronaut teams into the wilderness to struggle together, to be vulnerable together (to each other, to the elements), and ultimately to achieve together.[4] By forcing early and extreme vulnerability, NASA has learned that trust can be forged quickly and deeply, a requirement for ensuring teams work well when orbiting the planet 254 miles away from any other human beings.

And building trust drives results. We have seen in our research that customers who highly trust a brand are 88 percent more likely to buy from that brand again; 62 percent will buy almost exclusively from their trusted brand. And 79 percent of employees who highly trust their employer feel motivated to work (versus just 29 percent who feel motivated when they don't trust), and the majority of highly trusting employees (71 percent) aren't actively seeking other employment opportunities.[5]

What You'll Find in This Book

Part I: What You Need to Know About Trust

Chapter 1 introduces the Four Factors of Trust, including how they impact human behavior. We share a new measure for trust that organizations can use to understand what actions to take to build—or rebuild—trust.[6] We will also share how we tied trust to financial outcomes that matter most to organizations.

Chapter 2 examines some of the questions we wrestled with as we worked to create a more effective measure of trust. We talk about why expectations matter, how trust is fragmented, why trust is difficult to measure, and why it's so challenging to build.

Chapter 3 describes the link between trust and loyalty, and why you need to build trust to earn loyalty. We'll show you how to make choices to build trust, as well as where and when to take action when trust is threatened. We'll also share the story of how *The Wall Street Journal* intervened to build trust with their constituents.

Chapter 4 uncovers *how* winning organizations are winning trust, every day. We reveal the shared characteristics of the most trusted organizations and the relative importance of the Four Factors in different organizations. We illustrate data-based insights with stories of three different types of organizations who prove that building trust into a brand accelerates returns: "Humanity Leaders," like Cleveland Clinic; "Competence Leaders," like Energizer; and "Trust Winners," like Marriott International.

Chapter 5 will look at who still has work to do in the domain of trust. We will share data on the gap between how much brands believe they are trusted and how much their customers actually trust them. We'll also discuss the "Distrusted" cluster (brands with the lowest composite trust scores) and "Ambivalent Neutrals" (those organizations that are neither trusted nor mistrusted). We'll discuss brands in the same categories like the WNBA and Edward Jones, which have been able to build trust while others struggle to do so.

Chapter 6 examines the demographics of trust across workers and customers. We will discuss how lived experience—including identity—shapes trust, illustrated with stories from our own lives. We'll also share which customers and workers are more or less likely to trust, and how expectations and agency contribute to our willingness to trust.

Chapter 7 illustrates the virtuous circle of trust that organizations can create with the humans that matter most to their organizations—their customers, workers, and partners. We'll share stories of how companies, like American Express and Delta, work together to build trust.

Chapter 8 shares what we still don't know about trust, what we hope to learn next, and some of the things that surprised us along the way.

Part II: The "How-to" of Trust

Chapter 9 outlines how you can get started building trust both as an individual and as an organization. We will share how we are personally growing as leaders incorporating trust into our leadership philosophies and how we are applying what we learned to our own organization.

Chapters 10 through 15 are the how-to manual for creating and maintaining trusted relationships. These chapters will address challenges and principles for building trust at select organization domains, including:

- Executive Leadership
- Sustainability and Equity
- Marketing and Experience
- Talent and Human Capital
- Operations and Technology
- Cybersecurity

The **Conclusion** answers the question "How can trusted brands change the world?" It is our ambition to build trust to help organizations grow while also enabling them to elevate the experience of the humans they touch. We discuss who is accountable for building trust, and how trusted organizations can be a powerful force for good.

We know from personal experience that losing trust is easy and building trust is hard. We hope this book will give you practical guidance to help build trust in the individual and organizational relationships that matter most to you.

Part I

What You Need to Know About Trust

CHAPTER 1

The Four Factors That Drive Trust

In this chapter:

- The Four Factors of Trust
- The HX TrustID is born

David Kirby is an Associate Director of Strategy and Business at Ford Motor Company's Enterprise Connectivity group. He has devoted many years of his career to the topic of trust. David routinely kicks off workshops with an exercise that goes like this. First, he asks participants to write down their definition of trust. He doesn't give any further instruction, just a Post-it Note and two minutes to write. Then he has each person read their definition out loud. Someone might say, "Trust is making yourself vulnerable." Someone else might note, "Trust is currency." Or "I know it when I feel it." If there are ten respondents, David typically receives ten different definitions. He gets a few chuckles and knowing-but-uncomfortable glances as each person realizes that, as a team, they don't have a common definition for something as fundamental as trust. Then David hands them a new Post-it Note and asks them to write down their definition of reliability, which is one of the Four Factors of Trust. Same drill, two minutes. This time person after person says the same thing: "Doing what you say you are going to do." People struggle to define trust, but they are really good at defining the core components of trust, like reliability.

As our team set out to build a new, better way to measure trust—one that leaders like ourselves could act on—we knew we needed to understand the underlying factors that drive trust. And after 500-plus hours of intensive research, a thorough study of hundreds of pages of business and academic literature on trust, and countless regression analyses, we broke trust down into four components, what we call the Four Factors: humanity, transparency, capability, and reliability. It's much easier to answer the question "Does the organization demonstrate empathy and kindness towards me?" than it is to articulate the nagging feeling that something doesn't seem quite right.

The Four Factors of Trust

We have said that trust is the promise of a meaningful, mutually beneficial relationship between an organization and its stakeholders. And, at the individual level, we adopt Harvard professor and noted trust researcher Sandra Sucher's definition that trust is our willingness to be vulnerable to the actions of others because we believe they have good intentions and will behave well toward us. We believe the question for leaders who want to build trust is: What drives people's willingness to make themselves vulnerable?

At its core, trust is built when organizations make good promises, and when they deliver on those promises. We call these, respectively, intent and competence.[7] We demonstrate intent through being **transparent** and **human**. We demonstrate competence by being **capable** and **reliable**. These are the Four Factors of Trust.

In our research, the Four Factors describe nearly all of the variation we see in stated trust scores—79 percent—which means they are decisive in a decision to trust.[8]

The Four Factors are also *highly* descriptive of human behavior. On average, customers are **2.5 times more likely to perform positive behaviors**, such as defending or promoting the brand, choosing the brand, purchasing more, and spending more, when they rate the Four Factors highly. Predicting behavior to this degree is significant because it enables people to understand how to lead with the kind of behaviors that build trust and elevate experience. We can also quantify the impact of that behavior change (See Figure 1.1.) For example, across all of the industries we studied, **when an organization is able to move a customer's humanity score from neutral to high, the customer is nearly twice as likely to defend the brand against criticism, 1.7 times more likely to promote the brand on social media, and 2.6 times more likely to spend more with the brand versus the competition.**

Customers are more likely to purchase and be loyal when the brand demonstrates high humanity

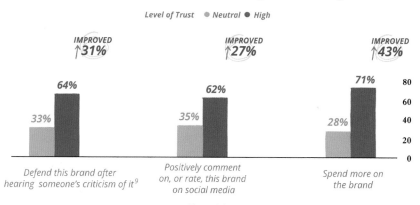

Level of Trust   ● Neutral ● High

IMPROVED ↑**31%**   IMPROVED ↑**27%**   IMPROVED ↑**43%**

64%	62%	71%
33%	35%	28%

Defend this brand after hearing someone's criticism of it[9] | Positively comment on, or rate, this brand on social media | Spend more on the brand

Figure 1.1

And while the relative importance of the factors may differ among industries (more on that in the chapters to come), the Four Factors themselves remain consistent across industries and types of stakeholders—customers, workforce, and partners. We can say with confidence that the Four Factors are the primary drivers of trust.

Humanity means an individual or an organization demonstrates empathy and kindness toward their customers and other stakeholders, treating everyone fairly.

Most customers and workers surveyed universally agreed on humanity's importance to building trust, regardless of demographic or industry.

In the decades of trust research that we have built upon, many have argued that, in order to be trusted, organizations must be benevolent, with a disposition to do good. Benevolence can also mean "generously giving," which seems not quite descriptive of the full range of business activities (corporate philanthropy notwithstanding). It's especially tricky to relate benevolence to the revenue and profit goals of business. We chose humanity because, by definition, humanity is the quality of valuing humans, marked by compassion, empathy, and consideration. Brands scoring high in humanity value people (and for some brands, extension of human needs like their environment) beyond the transactional relationship of trading money for products or services.

In our research, humanity is especially important in driving consumer behavior in the healthcare and the travel and hospitality industries—two industries that center on in-person interactions with frontline workers. We see this illustrated in the contrast between trust scores of nurses and doctors. Nurses are the most trusted profession and have been for years.[10] Doctors are also trusted, but they score fourteen points lower than nurses.[11] The difference is due to their different roles and behaviors in a typical healthcare system or hospital. Think back to when you were younger, going to see the pediatrician (or perhaps, your child's most recent visit to the doctor). Nurses are taught to be transparent and open, to feel and exhibit compassion for patients, not only in terms of medical treatment but also patients' physical and emotional comfort. They spend twice as much time in patients' rooms. From patients' perspectives, nurses supply about 87 percent of care time, doctors closer to 12 percent.[12]

Even the most compassionate and friendly doctor is in an environment that counts three nurses for every physician. These doctors simply have less time to spend building relationships and empathizing with their patients—or giving out stickers to pediatric patients—based on sheer volume of appointments in a day.

Humanity influences customer behavior more in healthcare and in travel and hospitality

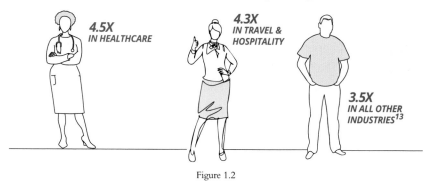

4.5X
IN HEALTHCARE

4.3X
IN TRAVEL &
HOSPITALITY

3.5X
IN ALL OTHER
INDUSTRIES[13]

Figure 1.2

What is the benefit of humanity? (See Figures 1.2 and 1.3.) When an organization exhibits a high degree of humanity, a **customer is 2.8 times more likely to stick with that brand through a mistake, and a worker is one and a half times more likely to defend their employer after hearing someone's criticism.**

High humanity scores mean customers and workers are more likely to exhibit positive behaviors

2.8X
CUSTOMERS
*are 2.8x more likely to
stick with the brand
through a mistake*

1.5X
WORKERS
*are 1.5x more likely to
defend their employer after
hearing someone's criticism*

Figure 1.3

Transparency means an individual or an organization openly shares information, motives, and choices in plain language.

The key to transparency for an organization is to reveal information relevant to the customer's decision whether to engage (not, for example, to reveal confidential information). This is not the same as the eighty-page software user agreement that only a lawyer could love. Transparency means giving people the right information at the right time through the right channels. David Kirby calls this "relevant transparency" and gives us the example of a farm-to-table restaurant whose animals are "humanely raised and processed"—a commonly understood term—while sparing diners the transparent but unappetizing details of humane slaughter. Transparency is an important driver in most of the customer behaviors we tested. Typically, where there are much more complex or complicated services and products, a customer will rely more heavily on transparency. For example, transparency is highly influential in insurance and banking, where complex financial instruments and arrangements might lead consumers to mistrust organizations. Laying out information and intentions clearly and truthfully increases customer confidence.

What is the benefit of transparency? (See Figure 1.4.) When an organization exhibits a high degree of transparency, **a customer is 1.6 times more likely to promote the brand on social media, and a**

High transparency scores mean customers and workers are more likely to exhibit positive behaviors

1.6X
CUSTOMERS
are 1.6x more likely to promote the brand on social media

1.8X
WORKERS
are 1.8x more likely to positively review their employer on a public website

Figure 1.4

worker is 1.8 times more likely to positively review an employer on a public website, such as Glassdoor or Fishbowl.

Capability means an individual or an organization delivers quality products, experiences, and services.

This factor is about the core abilities of an organization—whether it has the means to meet the expectations of its customers, workforce, or other stakeholders. For example, an auto company must be capable of manufacturing cars that meet its promises of safety, speed, comfort, and price—among others. Capability is the top driver of loyalty across all sectors we studied, but arguably capability is table stakes. If you don't have a product or service that meets a target need, there is no market. For example, you're not going to get into a vehicle you think will crash, and you're not going to go to a restaurant if you think you'll get food poisoning. Delivering against capability is a baseline requirement.

What is the benefit of demonstrating capability as an organization? (See Figure 1.5.) When an organization exhibits a high degree of capability, a **customer is 2.8 times more likely to choose the brand over competitors, and a worker is half as likely to look for a new job.**

High capability scores mean customers are more likely to exhibit positive behaviors, and workers are less likely to exhibit negative ones

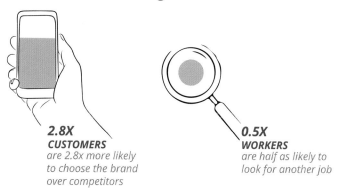

2.8X
CUSTOMERS
*are 2.8x more likely
to choose the brand
over competitors*

0.5X
WORKERS
*are half as likely to
look for another job*

Figure 1.5

Reliability means an individual or an organization consistently and dependably delivers upon promises made, time after time.

Organizations that are capable but not reliable have trouble getting consumers to trust them. The delivery company FedEx built a brand on its ironclad guarantee to deliver packages "absolutely, positively" on time. Reliability is especially important for consumer product companies, where customers have an abundance of choice.

What is the benefit of reliability? (See Figure 1.6.) When an organization exhibits a high degree of reliability, a **customer is nearly four times more likely to spend more on the brand (compared to a competitor's similar product or service), and a worker is one and a half times more likely to recommend their employer to a friend, family member, or colleague.**

High reliability scores mean customers and workers are more likely to exhibit positive behaviors

3.8X
CUSTOMERS
are 3.8x more likely to spend more on the brand (compared to a similar product or service)

1.5X
WORKERS
are 1.5x more likely to recommend their employer to a friend, family member, or colleague

Figure 1.6

The HX TrustID Is Born

Breaking trust down into the Four Factors makes it possible for us to start to build a new way to measure trust to help companies elevate the human experience (HX). We call it the HX TrustID, pronounced HX Trust "ID" (we also like the double meaning of "trust-ed," get it? Are you trusted?)

When we set out to create this new metric, we identified three key objectives. We wanted the metric to be **simple**, **meaningful**, and **actionable**. Learning from the success of other measures, we knew simplicity would be key to adoption. It had to be easy to understand and for leaders to implement in their organizations. The metric also had to be meaningful. For us, this means it had to be tied to outcomes—both behavioral and financial. Finally, it had to be actionable. Once leaders recognized the simplicity and importance of the Four Factors, we wanted them to know how to act quickly.

We'll get into the details of how we made the metric meaningful and actionable in a bit, but first let's start with making it simple. As is often the case, building something that is simple but powerful is not, as it turns out, simple. In fact, it took us nearly two years to develop and prove out the HX TrustID measurement system. And, knowing that trust evolves quickly, we plan to continue to test and evolve our model in the months and years ahead. (See Figure 1.7 for a visual timeline.)

With simplicity as an objective, we designed our trust measurement to have four questions to yield a composite trust score for each audience (for example, customer or worker). As you read the questions below, we encourage you to think of a brand you love, use regularly, and refer often to friends. Consider how you would answer these questions, from strongly agree, to neutral, to strongly disagree. (If you are up for it, you could also read the questions again with a brand you dislike in mind.)

The steps we took

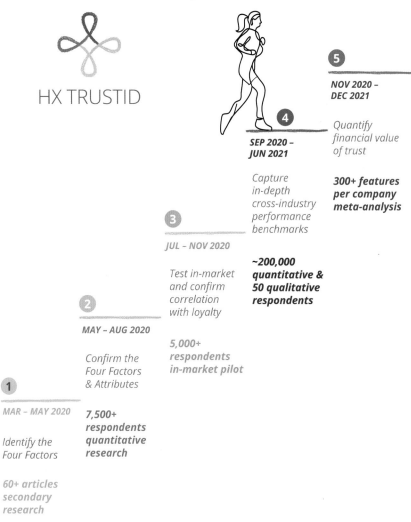

Figure 1.7

Customer HX TrustID Questions

- **Humanity:** [Brand] demonstrates empathy and kindness towards me, and treats everyone fairly.

- **Transparency:** [Brand] openly shares all information, motives, and choices in straightforward and plain language.

- **Capability:** [Brand] creates quality products, services, and/or experiences.
- **Reliability:** [Brand] consistently and dependably delivers on its promises.

And now do the same for your current or most recent employer. How would you answer these questions?

Workforce HX TrustID Questions

- **Humanity:** My employer demonstrates empathy and kindness towards me.
- **Transparency:** My employer uses straightforward and plain language to share information, motives, and decisions that matter to me.
- **Capability:** My employer creates a good work experience for me and provides the resources I need to do my job well.
- **Reliability:** My employer consistently and dependably delivers upon commitments it makes to me.

Then, to get to an organization's customer or worker overall HX TrustID, we subtract the percentage of "disagree" responses from the percentage of "agree" responses for each factor.[14] This effectively subtracts the biggest critics from the biggest superfans to get to a "net" percentage of customers or workers who trust an organization. Note that this also removes the "neutrals"—respondents who neither agree nor disagree for each statement. Our research demonstrates that neutrality, or indifference, tends to blur the results of what is happening for an organization, making it more difficult to take action. By removing "neutral noise," we can more clearly see how high and low trust drive behavior.[15]

For each dataset—customer or worker—we then take the average across the Four Factors to get to a composite number. This is the HX TrustID for the organization.[16] (Note that we weigh each factor equally because our research shows that the most trusted brands score well across all Four Factors.[17] We'll discuss this more in Chapter 4.) In the example shown in Figure 1.8, the customer HX TrustID for Brand A is 25 percent. In this case there were sixty respondents who "agreed," thirty-five who "disagreed," and twenty-five who were "neutral." In simple terms, a net twenty-five out of one hundred consumers believe that the company should be trusted. We can then compare that to other HX TrustID composite scores for organizations in the same industry. In this example, twenty-five is one point below the industry average and twenty-five points behind the industry leader.

We can evaluate HX TrustID scores for a brand relative to competitors

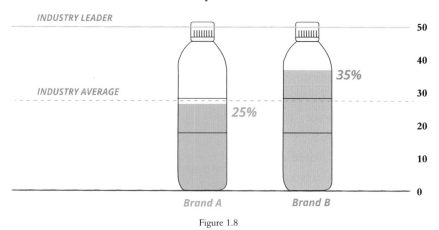

Figure 1.8

At this point, you might be wondering how such a simple set of questions is powerful enough to measure, predict, and act to build trust. Is there sufficient analytical rigor behind them? Here are the steps we took to build and test our measure—to make it not only simple but meaningful, and actionable.

Step 1: We started by conducting a meta-analysis of research from a variety of sources in the business world as well as in the academic world. With the goal of simplicity in mind, we started with the hypothesis that both competence and intent were critical to building trust. This is how we narrowed down to the Four Factors: capability and reliability to represent competence; humanity and transparency to represent intent.[18] We also identified potential variables underneath these categories to be tested further in quantitative research. This would allow us to understand what actions organizations can take to build trust for each factor.

Outcome: We identified the Four Factors

Step 2: To ensure our metric was *meaningful*, we set out to understand the relationship between trust sentiment and human behavior. We launched our first quantitative study with 3,000 customers and 4,500 workers.[19] We ran a series of multi-linear regressions to determine the degree to which each target behavior (for example, purchase or usage) correlated to overall sentiment of trust between customers and brands and between workers and their employers.[20] We kept it simple, and our statistical results were even better than we expected. As we noted above, the Four Factors described 79 percent of the variability we saw in stated trust.[21] We also noted the ability of each of the Four Factors to predict behavior (refer back to Figures 1.3–1.6)—the measure is highly meaningful.

Finally, we focused on making it *actionable*. With a variety of nuanced competence and intent variables, we ran another set of multi-linear regressions, this time to determine the degree to which different attributes contributed to each of the Four Factors. For example, if responses to the Four Factor question reveal that an organization is low on humanity (that is, empathy and kindness), we can now go one step further to see what is driving that low humanity score (for example, the brand fails to quickly resolve issues with safety, security, and satisfaction top of mind). These are the trust-building actions that will most improve humanity, and we tested a wide range to understand the drivers of each factor. We call these attributes. (You can find a full list of worker and customer attributes in Appendix A.)

Outcome: We confirmed the primary drivers of trust—the Four Factors—as well as the top four attributes that influence the scores of each of the Four Factors (for a total of sixteen attributes or trust-building actions).

Step 3: At this point, we felt confident in our new measure statistically, but we wanted to ensure that it worked just as well in the "real world." Specifically, we wanted to ensure that the questions were easy to use, to confirm the relationship between trust and loyalty, and to check the efficacy of our measure. To do this we partnered with a leading global airline that regularly surveys customers post-flight to understand passengers' likelihood to recommend based on their experience. The airline added the Four Factors question alongside their existing questions. The simplicity of the measure made this easy to do and it took little to no time investment to get approximately 5,000 responses. Our analysis from this effort confirmed efficacy (we saw a strong correlation between target behaviors such as likelihood to recommend and trust), ease of use, as well as a linear relationship with loyalty (in other words, as trust increases, so does loyalty and vice versa). The Chief Customer Officer was highly complementary of the work, stating, "For years we've been measuring likelihood to recommend, but I think the HX TrustID score, at a time like this, is far more relevant."

Outcome: We found that the HX TrustID was relatively easy to use in market, while proving out the correlation with customer behavior and with loyalty specifically.

Step 4: We had proven the viability of the HX TrustID both statistically and in the "real world." Now it was time to further refine the attributes underlying each factor and to understand key nuances across important categories, such as industry, demographics, and worker type, to name a few. To do that, we collected almost 200,000 customer trust scores and behavioral data for nearly 500 brands across over 10 industries.[22] To gather longitudinal data, we conducted qualitative research with fifty workers and conducted two additional worker studies twelve months apart, totaling 11,000 respondents.[23] We tested multiple definitions for each of the Four Factors. We then moved forward with those factors that are the most highly predictive of behaviors, and therefore the most meaningful. This is why we landed on slightly different definitions for customers and workers, as you read above. And we evaluated the relationship between customer trust and worker trust (more on this in Chapter 7). We also continued to make the Four Factors more actionable by testing which attributes or trust-building actions matter more, depending on the context—for example, the industry, and for customer versus workforce trust (more on this in Chapter 8). At the same time, we began using the HX TrustID with our own teams in our organization and working with clients not only to continue evolving and confirming our measurement platform, but to understand how to intervene to build trust. We spoke with more than fifty C-suite teams and conducted six pilots in market. We also set out to evolve our measurement systems to move from measurement to prediction, and we worked closely with *The Wall Street Journal* to test those results. We'll explore that in depth in Chapter 3.

Outcome: We built an in-depth understanding of trust at the brand level and by industry. We also created performance benchmarks to help leaders understand the relative performance for their organizations. We continued to vet the HX TrustID using more and more data, underscoring the significance of the measure.

Step 5: Next, it was time to take "make it meaningful" one step further, proving that the Four Factors influence not just human behaviors, but also organizational performance. Companies live or die based on their ability to generate profitable growth. And we knew that building trust would only be valued as meaningful if we could demonstrate the connection to financial performance. This time we focused on the following question: **What were the differences in outcomes between those organizations with higher versus lower customer HX TrustID scores?** To do this we launched a new study, one that took over a year to complete, where we used our benchmarking dataset[24] and added publicly available financial performance data at a brand level.[25] After careful evaluation, we selected total shareholder return for publicly traded organizations in our dataset as our proxy for the kind of outcomes that organizational leaders care about.

As we expected, organizations with high HX TrustID scores outperform their peers, *by a wide margin*. Specifically, organizations with a high customer HX TrustID score outperform their peers by up to four times in terms of total market value.[26] In addition, our model shows that when organizations across industries move their composite customer HX TrustID score by one point, say from a 40 to a 41, they amplify their **expected shareholder return by 4 percent**. In the financial services sector, shareholder return grows by 22 percent![27] Furthermore, these expected returns only grow as trust grows. If a company moves their score from 60 to 61, their expected shareholder return increases by 6 percent. Now we were really excited, and we hope you are too. Our research and analysis demonstrated that our new measures were predictive of trust for both customers and workers *and* correlated with meaningful financial outcomes.

Outcome: We can demonstrate that trust, as measured by HX TrustID, is a powerful driver of financial value for organizations.

Organizations with a high customer HX TrustID score outperform their peers by up to

4x **in terms of total market value.**

At this point, we felt confident that we had a metric that was simple, meaningful, and actionable. But now we had new questions: Could knowing your trust score help a leader *actually* build trust? And how was our measurement system for trust different from other measures already in wide use like Net Promoter Score? In the next chapter, we will share some of the biggest challenges we wrestled with in building a new measurement system for trust.

CHAPTER 2
Wrestling with Trust

In this chapter:

- The trust deficit
- Trust challenges

Tここ here are so many things about trust that we find hard. That's coming from us—and we literally wrote a book on trust! For starters, trust has been on the decline for decades. In this chapter, we'll share some of the things that we have wrestled with when it comes to understanding trust, measuring it, and building it. By definition, trust is as human and messy as the very humans who earn it or lose it. Today there is a gaping chasm of societal trust, what we call a "trust deficit" (defined as when there is more distrust than trust between two or more people). Measuring and building trust to climb out of that chasm feels daunting.

The Trust Deficit

Americans' trust in institutions has been declining for years. The survey firm Gallup found that confidence in all fourteen core institutions tracked has declined since it started studying the question in 1973. These include organized religion, organized labor, Congress, the presidency, the Supreme Court, big business, small business, public schools, the medical system, banks, and the criminal justice system.[28] A large majority of respondents believed this decline in confidence made it harder to solve societal problems.[29]

As you're reading this, we'd be willing to bet that you can think of dozens of examples from your own life where you have lost trust with people and institutions (we certainly can). Let's take teachers as an example. For both of us, teaching is in the family.

Amelia's mom was her sixth-grade math and science teacher. There were many nights when Amelia saw her mom grading papers and building lesson plans. Amelia would even go to school with her mom on weekends to create mosaics and bulletin boards for her classroom.

Ashley's sister Lindsey is a high school biology and genetics teacher who spends many extracurricular hours (and her own money) developing innovative lessons to facilitate learning. For example, Lindsey developed a lab experiment for her classroom to bring genetics to life. She purchased axolotl eggs (these are Mexican salamanders with gills outside of their body), aquariums, and equipment. She provided the materials to groups of lab students, tasking each group to track the development of the axolotls from egg to juvenile. After watching the axolotls grow, the students identified the genetic characteristics that the salamanders inherited from their parents.

This type of teaching is an extraordinary investment of personal time, thought, and energy outside of traditional school hours. And perhaps this isn't the norm (we believe that Ashley's sister and Amelia's mom are exceptional). However, we do know that teachers as a whole work more hours than they are paid. Many teachers already spend significant time during their out-of-school hours planning lessons and grading papers, working an average of 275 days per year, even though salaries are calibrated to be part time. By way of reference, the typical full-time worker works 261 days per year.[30]

According to Gallup, teachers are the third most trusted profession, right behind doctors and nurses.[31] Yet teachers are often not trusted to work a minimum number of hours by their administrators. Many schools monitor when teachers come to school, regardless of whether or not they have a class. Schools often require in-person planning days despite being aware of teachers' year-round extracurricular efforts. In some cases, teachers have to sign out just to get a coffee. If that is how we treat our trusted teachers—by underpaying them and closely monitoring their movements—what does that mean for the rest of us who don't work in one of the top trusted professions?

It means that we have a trust deficit—a corrosive and enduring lack of belief that people will show up reliably, perform capably, be transparent when they get it wrong, and be humane and empathetic. And importantly, this trust deficit has real-world consequences. Economists Paul Zak and Stephen Knack (yes, they really are "Zak and Knack") found that a 15 percent rise in a nation's belief that "most people can be trusted" adds a full percentage point to economic growth every year. In places with a legacy of mistrust—even modern examples like East versus West Germany—the higher-trust regions do better economically because people don't have to think twice before buying, hiring, or collaborating.[32] If you apply this math to today's U.S. economy, you find that a 15 percent rise in belief that most people can be trusted would add $208 billion to annual GDP.[33]

A 15% rise in belief that most people can be trusted in the U.S. would add $208 billion to annual GDP.

Trust Challenges

When we started to design a system for measuring customer and worker trust, we encountered no shortage of challenges. We'll tackle several here:

- Expectations matter.
- Trust is fragmented.

- Trust is difficult to measure.
- Trust is hard to build and easy to lose.

Rather than getting discouraged by these trust challenges, we tried to tackle each one in turn, transparently acknowledging what we could and could not control about the very nature of trust.

Expectations Matter

There is a particular episode in the hit 1990s television show *Friends* called "The One Where Ross and Rachel Take a Break." In the episode, Rachel suggests she and Ross pause their long-term relationship. Ross quickly has a fling, which he believes is okay because the relationship is on pause. Rachel becomes furious and hurt, feeling Ross had broken the "rules of relationships." Ross thinks Rachel changed the rules of the game. Who broke the trust? Each one points to the other, as is so often the case in breaches of trust. When we look more closely, we learn that their unspoken expectations led to a breakdown in trust because expectations matter when building trust.[34]

Just like Ross and Rachel, people in real life enter relationships with different expectations—relationships with other individuals and relationships with organizations. Expectations act as a baseline for trust, and different people have different "set points" that must be met.

Airlines are a good example of this. When you look deeper at the customer base of frequent versus infrequent flyers, you see that people who fly more have a higher trust level than occasional flyers, regardless of their brand affiliation. In Figure 2.1, frequent flyers have composite customer HX TrustID scores more than double infrequent travelers. Why? Because they know what to expect. Frequent flyers understand that flights can be delayed, weather can be bad, turbulence happens, and so forth. They don't necessarily differentiate among brands based on these problems. But infrequent flyers might take a single bad experience (uncomfortable air turbulence, or missing a connecting flight) and feel let down, losing trust based on the mismatch between expectations and experience. Since frequent flyers are an airline's most important customers, you see the companies focusing heavily on the experience they provide, independent of uncontrollable factors. This creates a set of expectations more robust than relying on routes and price alone (the primary drivers of choice in the industry, historically speaking).[35] The degrees to which different classes in a cabin afford greater or less comfort and convenience similarly set expectations that differentiate brands.

Frequent and moderate flyers have higher trust scores than occasional flyers, regardless of their airline loyalty affiliation

Level of Trust   FREQUENT   MODERATE   INFREQUENT

Figure 2.1

Trust is also highly personal. Few people have exactly the same criteria for trusting an organization or a brand, and everyone experiences trust subjectively, just like Ross and Rachel. For example, two people might purchase the same pair of running shoes that promise "comfort and durability" and have dramatically different expectations of what those words mean. If one is a daily runner, "durability" might mean the shoes wear out after three months. The other customer wears the shoes to a job in a big-box store and only focuses on how they feel after eight hours standing. Both might end up trusting the brand, or each might be disappointed in some way. Unless a brand accounts for both the experience and expectations of its customers, it is impossible to build trust with each individual who shops its products.

Trust Is Fragmented

Trust is a series of distinct experiences—made up over hundreds or even thousands of interactions—which makes it hard to control and impossible to establish "once and for all." Let's take an ordinary daily activity we love, like ordering a coffee. The first time you place an order for an Americano it's made right away and comes steaming hot. Mmm. You needed that caffeine. A good experience. The next time, you had to wait in line for fifteen minutes, and when you finally placed your order, the barista spelled your name incorrectly, causing confusion and more delay. A bad experience. A third time you show up at the cafe and find it closed due to inclement weather. Another bad experience, this time impacted by external factors. And perhaps that same day, you read an article arguing that coffee production hurts the planet. Another bad experience out of the control of that local coffee bar. Each of these occasions has the potential either to earn or erode trust.

Organizations can only do so much to control the environment they inhabit, but they can do a lot in response to circumstances. For example, if we go back to our passengers on that turbulent flight, airlines can't control the weather (shockingly), and flights often experience delays as a result. However, airlines *can* control the flow of information. Airlines can offer reasonable updates on departure timing, help for customers who need to rebook flights, and complimentary services, like snacks or water. Similarly, coffee shops can't control for inclement weather, but they can post opening times on the web for customers to find easily, and they can talk about what they are doing to mitigate the impact of growing coffee on our environment. These gestures demonstrate transparency and humanity, and as a result they improve trust.

Organizations have to consider how complex and interconnected every experience is, as they go about earning customers' and workers' trust. Like we described with the coffee shop, there is no expectation that a single small business can offset environmental harms to which its products might contribute. But acknowledging these environmental considerations can humanize the brand, boosting transparency and making it easier for a customer to forgive a misspelled name or a closure due to weather.

Trust Is Difficult to Measure

Trust is rife with potential bias traps, and can be hard to measure for three primary reasons:

Unconscious decision-making.

As humans, we rely heavily on patterns to make sense of our environments. That's the reason adults don't have to relearn to ride a bicycle every time, or remap the morning route to work every day. In fact, 95 percent of cognition is unconscious, suggesting people often don't understand their own trust experiences clearly.[36] That is, we make decisions below the level of conscious thought to trust this person and this organization, and not those ones. While unconscious decision-making is great for humans, as it frees up our mental capacity for other tasks, it can make it harder for behavioral scientists to accurately measure the decisions that we make subconsciously.

What we say versus what we do.

Humans are poor predictors of future behaviors, and we find it really hard to give a quantitative rating to an esoteric concept like trust. Margaret Mead, the trailblazing anthropologist, is famously quoted as saying, "What people say, what people do, and what they say they do are entirely different things."[37] Have you ever told someone you only eat fruit for snacks, when in reality you demolish cookies regularly in the afternoon? We like to think of this as the "afternoon snack bias." This unreliability has, for example, plagued political pollsters in recent election cycles.[38]

Survey bias.

In surveys, self-selection and self-censoring are well known. Certain people are much more likely than others to respond to surveys—for example, people who have had an exceptionally good or bad experience with a product. Well-educated, affluent people are more likely to respond. As a result, their beliefs may be overrepresented.[39] In addition, people are influenced by what they recently heard about a brand, by their last experience, by a particularly intense interaction, or even by how they feel on the day they're asked. Even a person's level of stress on the day they're asked survey questions can skew results and generate bias. Lastly, factors like confirmation bias and image management (telling a pollster what we think they want to hear, or what we want to believe but actually don't) come into play.[40] These forms of survey bias have been problematic for other experiential measures. It's also the reason we focus on *predicting* trust rather than surveying trust, another concept we'll tackle later.

To surmount these obstacles, we looked at actual human behaviors, not what they did unconsciously, thought they would do, or thought we wanted to hear from them. More on this in Chapter 3.

Trust Is Hard to Build and Easy to Lose

We have found that trust is hard to build for many reasons, not least of which includes:

Words and actions need to match *and* be human.
   Trust is about what you say *and* what you do: making good promises and keeping them. People don't trust other people or organizations that say one thing and do another. Building trust demands more than truthfulness. People want your communications to show that you understand them, know their desires and beliefs, and respect them. To build a positive, trusted relationship, your actions and words must be aligned, and they must address what the other person cares about. Otherwise, the relationship is transactional, not trusting. We know from experience that we can't just tell our teams we value well-being, encouraging them to disconnect from work; we have to demonstrate that we are willing to do the same. For example, Ashley shares with her teams that she is unavailable from 5 to 6 p.m., which allows her to focus on her family during dinner while demonstrating to teams that they can also prioritize what matters to them, like a morning run or walking their kids to school.

It is hard to build something that can be lost rapidly.

Sometimes the reason trust is lost is obvious (the individual or the brand made false claims). Other times the reasons are more subtle. Either way, it is hard to build something carefully brick by brick when it can crumble easily. The "New Coke" product launch illustrated this in the 1980s. As context, the flagship brand Coca-Cola was losing share to competition, driven by waning consumer preference and awareness. In an effort to revitalize the market, The Coca-Cola company reformulated Coca-Cola based on a large-scale taste preference test. The new brand launched on April 23, 1985. By June the company was receiving roughly four times the number of phone complaints. Multiple protest groups cropped up, and people even began hoarding the original formula (up to 900 bottles!) in their basements. In July, The Coca-Cola company announced the return of the original formula, making the front page of nearly every newspaper in the U.S.[41] New Coke's formula might have been liked by consumers in blind taste tests, but the company did not give enough weight to customers' emotional attachment to the brand and, as a result, had to scramble to appease consumers and rebuild trust. The Coca-Cola company was left with over $30 million in unwanted New Coke concentrate (equivalent to roughly $80 million today).[42] Today, however, Coca-Cola remains the world's most valuable soft drink brand globally, indicating a successful push to rebuild trust.

When we think about this phenomenon—how hard it is to build something that is so easy to lose—the image of Sisyphus comes to mind. In Greek mythology, Zeus punished Sisyphus by forcing him to push a boulder up a hill only to have it roll back down, for all eternity. We recognize that building trust can feel similarly futile at times, hence the trust deficit. We feel it too.

But then we think about the fact that we have a choice: The choice to build trust consciously, or not. And we have a choice about how we go about it. When facing these choices, we choose to do the hard work of building trust. We will choose it over and over again, despite getting it wrong in very human ways, because we would rather be a part of relationships that are trusting, both with individuals and with organizations, than not. *And* we choose to use new tools to help us build trust more effectively rather than blindly pushing the same rock up the hill.

In the next chapter, we'll detail how organizations can measure and predict trust scores using the HX TrustID, and how the Four Factors can help organizations know what actions to take, as they take on the near-Sisyphean task of building trust.

CHAPTER 3
The Path to Loyalty

In this chapter:

- The relationship between loyalty and trust
- Example: *The Wall Street Journal*

G rowing up just south of Cleveland, Ohio, Ashley was raised as a sports fan, ushering for the local baseball team, now called the Guardians, and cheering on Bernie Kosar and the Browns, who mostly lost, every Sunday. In 1995, the team's owner, Art Modell, petitioned to move the Browns out of Cleveland. The "Dawg Pound" fans, including Ashley, were at first shocked, and then furious at what they considered to be the "theft" of their team. Even Pittsburgh Steeler fans, Cleveland's most fervent rival and "football enemy," protested. Congress held hearings. In the resulting legal battle, Cleveland won the right to keep the name and team colors, and Modell won his bid to move the team for the 1996 season. Fans like Ashley lost trust in the team's owner, and as a result, loyalty to the team suffered for decades.

When the Brown's owner "stole her team," Ashley learned painfully about the relationship between loyalty and trust. If you break trust, you lose loyalty. And conversely, if you build trust, you build the path to loyalty. Her uncle and fellow Browns fan, Fred Reichheld, published his first book, *The Loyalty Effect*, shortly after the Cleveland Browns moved. At the time of the book launch, Ashley remembers her dad (Fred's older brother) proposing to Fred that he should market the book specifically to Browns fans. Fred ended up including a small orange sticker for Cleveland bookstores that said: "Art Modell will hate this book." In 2006, Fred published *The Ultimate Question*, where he introduced the Net Promoter Score (NPS), which identifies a customer's or worker's "willingness to recommend." Amelia likes to tease Ashley about whether extended family dinners were "evaluated" using NPS, as in, "What is your willingness to recommend these mashed potatoes to a family member?" Today NPS is *the* industry standard for loyalty. Two-thirds of Fortune 500 companies use NPS to measure the loyalty of their customers. Most of the remaining one-third use a similar metric.[43] And many Fortune 500 executives have some portion of their compensation package tied to NPS scores. They are literally paid, or not, based on NPS results.

The Relationship between Loyalty and Trust

To be clear, we strongly believe in the value of loyalty. Fred created NPS not only as a measurement system, but also as a philosophy that calls upon organizations to love their customers. Our goal is to elevate the human experience, which means loving all of your humans. And we believe trust is a prerequisite to elevating experience and achieving loyalty. As we set out to build a measure of trust, we were grateful to stand on Fred's shoulders.

> **We believe trust is a prerequisite to elevating experience and achieving loyalty.**

Here are some of the things we love most about the NPS system. First, the NPS metric itself is brilliant in its simplicity. And largely because of its simplicity, it is very easy to understand and use. Second, NPS is open source. Anyone who wants to deploy the questions can do so. Third, while NPS was originally set out as metric, Fred evolved it into a management system to help companies measure, learn, and act on results. You'll see this logic mirrored in our own experience engine, discussed in Chapter 9.

One challenge with open-source innovation and widespread popularity, however, is that it creates opportunities for misuse and misguided practices. Fred catalogues and cautions against these types of practices in his "Net Promoter 3.0" HBR article. There, he warns, "Unfortunately, self-reported scores and misinterpretations of the NPS framework have sown confusion and diminished its credibility. Inexperienced practitioners abused it by doing things like linking Net Promoter Scores to bonuses for frontline employees, which made them care more about their scores than about learning to better serve customers." We have seen this in real life. For example, Ashley often tells the story of buying her latest family car and being asked by the sales rep to fill out the NPS survey with only the highest scores—all tens—because it would directly impact his compensation. Ashley was torn, and ultimately chose not to submit the survey. (Incidentally, Fred had the very same experience and similarly chose not to respond.)

We set out to build a measurement system that is complementary to NPS and learns from both the good (twenty years of success) and the bad (misuses or abuses of the system). We designed HX TrustID to be simple to use. We made the questions available to anyone who wants to use them. As we discussed in Chapter 1, we focused on creating something that was immediately actionable and tied directly to behavior and to financial outcomes. We also worked to limit the potential for survey bias and manipulation. While we initially use survey instruments to ask customers and workers their perspectives on four questions, we are able to take this a step further step to predict actions based on *actual* behaviors, not what customers and workers say their future selves will be doing. In that way, we no longer need to keep issuing surveys to a small sample to continue to get results (though we do need to survey occasionally to refresh and retrain the models). On a good day, most organizations get maybe 5–10 percent of their customer base to fill out a survey. Building a predictive model based off that 5–10 percent (1–2 times a year) means we can predict trust scores for an *entire* customer population, not just the small percentage who answered the survey. Moreover, our algorithm takes matters out of the hands of salespeople looking to skew the numbers.

We also wanted to demonstrate that trust is a vital step on the path to loyalty. Our analysis shows that trust and loyalty, as measured by NPS, share a linear relationship (see Figure 3.1A). As trust increases, so does NPS. As trust decreases, NPS declines. We can be confident that there is a strong relationship between NPS and the HX TrustID.[44]

HX TrustID and NPS have a linear relationship

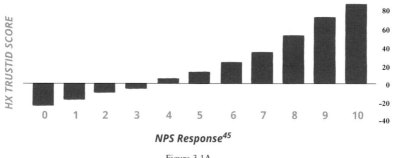

Figure 3.1A

Four Factors ● Humanity ● Transparency ● Capability ● Reliability

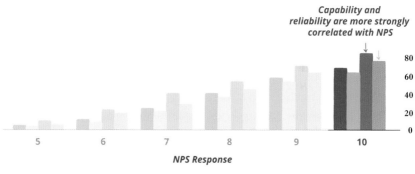

Figure 3.1B

Looking closer, our analysis revealed that capability and reliability are both significantly correlated with NPS. Humanity and transparency are also strongly related, but the correlation is somewhat weaker (see Figure 3.1B).[46] This is an important finding. As we know from Chapter 1, humanity and transparency drive critical behaviors, such as the willingness to forgive mistakes as well as vocal defense on social media. This means that the HX TrustID adds important insights that can help leaders manage to get even stronger loyalty results.

Here is an illustrative example. Figure 3.2 shows two airline customers with the same likelihood to recommend scores (the first NPS question). Passenger A sees the airline as capable and reliable but sees room for improvement in humanity. In particular this passenger is concerned about the environment and wants to see improvement in sustainability efforts (which we can see based on the attribute scores). Passenger B has the same likelihood to recommend score, but rates

Two people can look identical with NPS, but HX TrustID illuminates their unique needs

Four Factors ● Humanity ● Transparency ● Capability ● Reliability

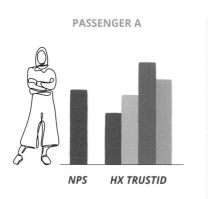
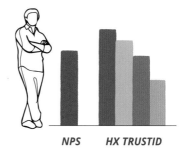

PASSENGER A

PASSENGER B

NPS   HX TRUSTID

NPS   HX TRUSTID

Intervention message for low humanity
Demonstrate care for the planet by sharing the airline's carbon footprint offset

Intervention message for low reliability
Apologize for recent delay and explain the airline's effort to ensure on-time flights

Figure 3.2

reliability significantly below benchmark. We know based on flight data that the passenger sat on the tarmac for two hours during their last flight due to a mechanical issue. While both flyers share the same willingness to recommend, the actions needed to build trust and loyalty are different. Passenger A would benefit from understanding how the airline is working to offset carbon footprint. Passenger B needs to receive a heartfelt apology and reassurance that on-time flights are a top priority.

At this point, we knew that trust and loyalty were directly correlated; building trust leads to increased loyalty. We also knew that the Four Factors that make up the HX TrustID could add valuable nuance and insight to help explain the *why* behind building loyalty. And we knew that HX TrustID is linked to financial outcomes. Next, we wanted to bring trust to life with a real-world example in an industry where trust matters.

Example: *The Wall Street Journal*

Here's a real-world example of how the HX TrustID works:

From the moment we first met Almar Latour, CEO of Dow Jones and publisher of *The Wall Street Journal* (WSJ), he underscored that trust is central to the *Journal's* purpose. He described trust both as an ethos that drives company culture *and* a critical commercial driver, saying, "The motto we use is 'truth to good ends.' It runs through the company—how we work and how we operate—from the newsroom all the way up. This has contributed to the strongest business performance for *The Wall Street Journal* and Dow Jones since News Corp acquired the company fifteen years ago. Trust is both central to who we are *and* to our future growth."

In a letter to readers, he stated: "Our goal is to be the world's most trusted source of news. We stick to facts, we admit to and correct mistakes we make, and we don't blindside the subjects of our coverage. We underpin our findings with data."

Latour and WSJ recognize that trust among readers is not guaranteed; it is something that must be earned, especially in today's atmosphere of ignition and change. By adhering to the highest standards, WSJ has established a reputation of trust over its 133-year history. The company is focused on both protecting that hard-earned trust and on building it further.

The *Journal* had been measuring trust for many years, but prior measurement tools didn't provide a mechanism to understand the *why* behind customer trust levels. Without the underlying *why*, it was hard to determine what actions WSJ could take to build further trust in the brand. The ability to separate trust into its parts created the opportunity to act that Almar and the WSJ team sought. "Trust is really complex. It means different things to different people. We use the word easily, but behind it there is a lot of nuance. Even for a brand like WSJ, which is incredibly trusted for the quality of its reporting and commitment to truth, thinking about trust in factors—capability, reliability, humanity, and transparency—begins to highlight where there are opportunities to work more effectively."

The HX TrustID helped WSJ understand what was behind their measures and how they could zero in to build trust in the brand. It was all about making trust actionable, understanding the *why* and *how* behind trust.

Here is how we worked with WSJ to **measure**, **predict**, and **act** on trust:

- We issued the four-question HX TrustID survey to approximately 16,000 current, former, and prospective customers to measure current trust levels across the Four Factors of Trust: humanity, transparency, capability, and reliability, identifying areas of trust strength as well as opportunities to bolster trust.

- We combined the HX TrustID survey (feelings about the Four Factors in the brand) with the client's customer behavioral data—for example, what customers read and how frequently they visited the company's website. Evaluating thousands of potential behavioral variables, we created a dynamic measure of trust, adapting our proprietary algorithms to predict a customer's trust scores and measure its movement over time as the customer changed his or her behavior. This meant that by surveying a very small subset of the company's customers, we could predict individualized trust scores across millions of current and potential customers.

- We then worked with WSJ to launch a series of "intervention pilots," testing which actions would increase trust scores. We designed interventions as scientific experiments, comparing how trust scores changed with each intervention relative to an untouched control group with similar trust scores. We then scaled the solutions that worked in the pilot for all customers with similar trust scores.

As a trusted brand, WSJ was already working hard to build and keep trust, so this pilot wasn't about creating more trustworthy actions. Instead it was about equipping the WSJ team with the insights to know which messages and campaigns would be most impactful for each individual. This allowed WSJ to demonstrate to customers: "We've taken the time to understand who you are and what matters to you, and because of that, we want to share this specific information with you."

Here are two examples of trust-based interventions:

- To increase transparency, WSJ ran a series of digital campaigns to remind readers about the breadth of services included with membership, such as crossword puzzles, podcasts, and the ability to share interesting content with their friends and family, who could read it without having to pay for the article.

- To increase humanity, WSJ focused on ensuring target readers felt included, promoting existing content to make sure that readers themselves were reflected in the breadth of coverage. For some, this meant sharing a recent special report on climate change, while for others this included sharing a column by a current family and technology columnist.

As a result, trust among customers grew. The HX TrustID algorithm was three times more effective at targeting individuals with lower trust scores (the customers at the highest risk of churning). We saw a notable impact on trust as well as other important measures, including:

- 33 percent growth in trust scores as predicted by our model
- 14 percent increase in website traffic (versus a control group)
- 5 percent decrease in predicted subscriber churn (a critical metric in subscription media)

Why does building trust in this way matter to the bottom line? News media companies make money primarily in two ways: subscriptions and advertising revenue. It is more efficient to keep a current customer than to win a new one, so retaining subscribers benefits the bottom line. On the advertising front, boosting web and app engagement increases direct ad revenue as well as brand value.

The pilot showed that we were able to create a dynamic measure of trust based on behavior and that we could predict and measure changes to trust scores dynamically. This allowed us to see real-time impact. We only had to survey once to be able to predict trust, change behaviors, and drive outcomes that mattered to WSJ and its customers.

In the chapters that follow, we will show how trusted organizations in different sectors choose where to direct resources among actions based on these factors. For now, we'll note that the **Trust Winners— organizations with exceptional trust scores—outperform on all Four Factors.**

Fred argues that the only winning purpose is to love your customers. We believe trust should play a vital role in ensuring customers feel loved. Fred's research found that only 10 percent of business leaders believe that making their customers' lives better stands as their company's primary purpose.[47] To us, that is a huge disconnect. It means that only a small fraction of today's companies is worthy of their customers' trust.

Ashley is often asked if extended Reichheld family gatherings include debates over the importance of trust versus loyalty. She believes that trust is not *more* important than loyalty, but rather that trust is the most important path to loyalty. When Ashley introduced the idea of working on a new measure of trust to Fred, he said: "I hope that trust, love, and loyalty stand as enduring elements of the Reichheld family legacy. I've spent my career writing about loyalty and love. I'm glad that you're writing about trust."

CHAPTER 4

The Most Trusted Organizations

In this chapter:
- Trust and performance
- The most trusted
  - Humanity Leaders
  - Competence Leaders
  - Trust Winners

We were pumped our pilot with *The Wall Street Journal* proved that an organization could convert our trust measurement from prediction to action and ultimately to meaningful outcomes. But now we were curious about new questions: What brands are the most trusted? And what can we learn from them?

Trust and Performance

The most trusted brands in our research have one thing in common: **Trust Winners get all Four Factors right**. They excel in both intent (humanity and transparency) and competence (capability and reliability).

In fact, Trust Winners have an average HX TrustID score two times that of the average organization in our dataset.

Figure 4.1 shows how high trust scores result from both high competence and high intent scores—a linear correlation that you would expect. Looking a little closer, you can see that the spread between intent and competence is larger for the most trusted brands than it is for the least trusted. This means that highly trusted brands have greater variability in their Four Factors, suggesting that there are multiple paths to earning trust and becoming one of the most trusted brands. One organization might gain trust by being incredibly competent (such as a luxury auto brand) with somewhat less humanity. Another excelling in humanity (such as a healthcare organization) might have slightly lower reliability scores (long times in the waiting room), but their humanity strengths boost their overall trust score.

The most trusted brands excel in both competence and intent

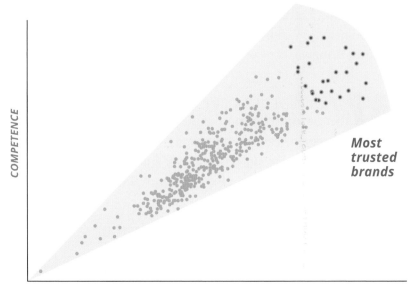

Figure 4.1

Conversely, note the lack of variability in the least trusted brands as represented by the lower left in Figure 4.1. People experience these brands as being low on all Four Factors. This might happen because the brands really are neither competent nor well intentioned, or because egregious violations of trust drag all the scores down.

What we don't see in the data are brands that are big outliers—for example, rated very high on competence and very low on intent. **Put simply: you can't fail the test of trust in one factor and expect strength in the others to make you trusted.**

The Most Trusted

When we analyze who is the most trusted and why (from the top right of Figure 4.1 on the previous page), we find three clusters of the highest trusted brands in Figure 4.2.

The *most* trusted brands fall into three clusters

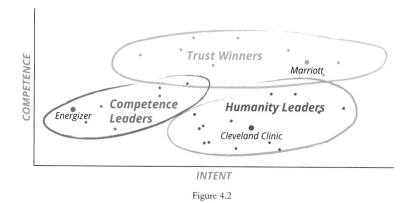

Figure 4.2

- **Humanity Leaders:** The Humanity Leaders cluster of brands are exceptional at demonstrating humanity to their customers. Humanity Leaders have humanity scores roughly two times that of the average organization (see the lower right cluster in teal in Figure 4.2).

- **Competence Leaders:** The next cluster are exceptional at delivering on competence through a combination of capability and reliability.

Competence Leaders have capability and reliability scores almost two times that of the average organization (see the lower left cluster in blue in Figure 4.2).

- **Trust Winners:** Finally, the most highly trusted brands deliver excellence in both competence (capability and reliability) and intent (humanity and transparency). These companies have the highest composite trust scores in our dataset (see top right cluster in orange in Figure 4.2).

When we chart the most trusted organizations, we find leaders in humanity, leaders in competence (capability and reliability), and leaders overall that also excel in transparency. Interestingly, transparency alone doesn't make a brand trusted, but we found that it is often the "missing element" that vaults brands to the top of the trust scale. The patterns that emerge tell an important story around customer expectations and experience.

Humanity Leaders

Getting customers to trust you begins with recognizing and treating them as human beings. The most human brands are the ones that embrace the principles of human-centered design with an extra dose of empathy for customers, the workforce, and partners. And we can learn a lot about what it means to deliver humanity from the organizations in our Humanity Leaders cluster, which includes organizations across industries—spanning healthcare, technology, and travel and hospitality.

Cleveland Clinic, a century-old healthcare company, is a great example of the Humanity Leaders cluster. It has a humanity score that is double the average. In a highly regulated industry with a strong focus on safety, humanity is what differentiates the patient experience delivered by Cleveland Clinic. When they enter a hospital, patients expect to be treated professionally in a safe environment. How long they wait, how their questions are answered, and how comfortable they are when they are feeling distinctly uncomfortable are the moments where a Humanity Leader like Cleveland Clinic sets itself apart.

In addition, Cleveland Clinic boasts a patient-centric model, designed around the actual needs of patients in the community, rather than physicians' specialties. Instead of a large stand-alone hospital, Cleveland Clinic has a tiered network of clinics that cater to the communities they serve. Former president Dr. Delos M. Cosgrove observed, as an example of designing for communities, "a suburb with an aging population may need a diabetes center, rather than a new maternity ward, while another suburb may need the exact opposite."[48]

Key actions to take that increase a sense of humanity include:

- Putting human safety and satisfaction top of mind. For example, weighing strategic decisions with a greater emphasis on human needs versus cost containment.

- Providing empathetic and relevant communications in the right channels, at the right times. During the pandemic, many medical organizations improved their text- and app-based communications with patients around routine visits, including safety protocols.

- Highlighting human-centered initiatives internally and externally and focusing communications on the human outcomes (for example, better health, lower out-of-pocket costs, or manageable routines for parents of children with chronic conditions).

- Demonstrating that you care about the individual, not just profit, or the needs of the organization. This manifests in every interaction with customers, workers, and partners.

Competence Leaders

Separate from those who cultivated trust through humanity, we observed brands that built trust through repeated demonstrations of competence. These brands built their reputations by consistently delivering on what matters most to customers and workers time and again. We know that competence is built by organizations with high degrees of capability and reliability. What brand embodies competence more than Energizer and its tireless bunny?

Energizer, the battery brand owned by Saint Louis-based Energizer Holdings, is an innovative brand with many historic firsts. They produced the first dry cell battery and the first watch battery. Energizer Holdings was the first to remove mercury from alkaline and hearing aid batteries. They were the first to create child-resistant packaging, and the first to create AA batteries made from recycled material. Their Ultimate Lithium battery set a Guinness World Record in 2018 for the longest-lasting AA and AAA batteries, both of which can retain power for twenty years.[49]

Energizer's innovation obviously requires competence in chemistry and manufacturing. And yet Energizer's strategy focuses on brand perceptions, product performance, price, retail execution, and customer service. All those qualities require a diverse set of competencies. Marketing must set the right expectations and make the brand appealing in comparison to other brands and private-label competitors (the bunny helps). Supply chain teams must ensure consistently strong production and on-time delivery to retail stores. Customer service includes strong systems integration, as well as a good dose of humanity. Beyond innovation, great competence scores are built on consistency and reliability. Customers expect this kind of consistency from each successive generation of a product, which must always improve performance without sacrificing the reliability of its predecessors. New products like rechargeable batteries must uphold the quality of the brand while addressing new customer wishes (such as fewer batteries in landfills). Organizations can learn a lot from the iconic Energizer bunny, which demonstrates that it cares enough to deliver on its promises and just keep going . . . and going . . . and going . . .

Strategies for building capability include:

- Aligning quality control measures across the entire supply and delivery chains to ensure consistently high standards of product/service quality.

- Engaging customers in two-way conversations. Make it easy for them to interact with you, ask questions, and resolve issues over the channels that are most convenient for them. A number of brands have built robust consumer responses on social media, for example. When Delta Air Lines customers complain about a problem on Delta's Twitter feed, they receive a response directly from Delta customer service, followed up by a private, direct-message thread. This can help the individual consumer, and sends a broader message to that person's followers that the brand is caring and responsive.

- Investing in tools, training, and infrastructure that enable agility in response to evolving customer needs. Many organizations demonstrated this in the pandemic. For example, distiller Beam Suntory pivoted to producing hand sanitizer in a matter of weeks—a harder switch than you might think—by reassigning everyone, from facilities maintenance to risk management, to the project.

Strategies for building reliability include:

- Meeting customers where they are—via digital channels and in-store—in the Moments that Matter, with products and services that they value. Use data tools to focus communications so that they are relevant to the individual.

- Investing in digital interactions that run smoothly, direct the consumer easily to the right information, and resolve issues to the consumer's satisfaction. (Consider your own experience of an effective online help system versus a confusing maze of information.)

- Resolving issues quickly. If one channel, such as a customer-support function on the web, isn't working for someone, offer fast off-ramps to other methods. As expensive as human helplines can be, they build trust when they solve an important customer issue.

Trust Winners

Some brands build trust by focusing on being more human, and we see them represented in the Humanity Leaders cluster. Some brands build trust by focusing on competence, and we see them represented in the

Competence Leaders cluster. But the brands that figure out how to deliver on all Four Factors of Trust, and transparency in particular, distinguish themselves to become our Trust Winners cluster.

Transparency makes you vulnerable (and that's a good thing).

In this top cluster, we find a large group of hospitality companies, including hotel conglomerates. Marriott International, a flagship brand with a long-standing reputation for top service and facilities, is one of the Trust Winners. When a doorkeeper leads you into a beautiful lobby with knowledgeable front desk staff and expert concierge service awaiting, your expectations are high—and met. And yet garnering consumer trust doesn't require luxury service. Instead, it's about recognizing and treating people as humans. Courtyard by Marriott is a lower-priced brand in our Trust Winners cluster that ranks particularly high in humanity. At Courtyard, customers don't expect a fancy suite, but they know they'll get a nice room, the staff will always be friendly and helpful, and their experience will be reliably good value. But the thing that particularly distinguishes Trust Winners like Marriott is their ability to deliver on transparency; Marriott's transparency score is 66 percent higher than the average.

Transparency makes you vulnerable (and that's a good thing). When a brand exposes itself by sharing information that is often withheld in an industry, it signals trust in the consumer to make a fair comparison with competitors. Consumers appreciate this trusting vulnerability and reward it with a greater level of trust in the brand. In the consumer's mind, this brand tells me everything with nothing to hide, and that's why I trust them. For example, when searching on Marriott.com to make a booking, you can check a box to display prices with taxes and resort fees included. That might seem like a small detail (and frankly we would like to see this become the default view), but given that competitors don't readily supply this information, this option represents a commitment to transparency. In other words, even people who are not currently customers of a given Trust Winner's brand *still* view these brands as highly transparent. This is especially true when comparing potential customers from the Trust Winners cluster against potential customers for all brands.

Trust Winners score almost 80 percent higher than the average brand on the "secret sauce" of transparency. When you are transparent, even non-customers will take note. This may be especially true when delivering bad news to the public.

In 2020, when Marriott International had to confront the reality that COVID-19 would wreak havoc on its business, President and CEO Arne Sorenson sent a video message to all the company's associates clearly laying out the situation—and he didn't sugarcoat it either.

"Here are the facts: COVID-19 is having a more severe and sudden financial impact on our business than 9/11 and the 2009 financial crisis combined," said Sorenson. "In most markets our business is already running 75 percent below normal levels." Before listing drastic cuts in the business, Sorenson announced he would not take a salary in 2020, and the executive team would take a 50 percent cut in pay. His voice trembling, he said, "There is simply nothing worse than telling highly valued associates—people who are the very heart of this organization—their roles are being impacted by events completely outside of their control."[50]

And in an extraordinary sign of personal vulnerability, Sorenson admitted his team was anxious about him appearing "in my new, bald look." He was undergoing treatment for pancreatic cancer as the crisis began (Sorenson died at age sixty-two less than a year later). It takes strong, empathetic leadership to give tough messages in plain language (we'll talk about how this type of transparent leadership builds trust in Chapter 10).

Key actions to take that increase a sense of transparency include:

- Ensuring that marketing and communications are clear, accurate, and honest. Be transparent in crisis communications. In workforce communications, admit what you don't know as well as what you know.
- Being upfront about how you make and spend money from interactions of all kinds.
- Communicating how and why personal data is used in plain and easy-to-understand language, making that information easy to find on websites and in retail locations.

- Making sure you're sharing the information that is *relevant* in a consumable way. Be clear and upfront about fees and costs of products, services, and experiences, especially add-ons and tiered product lines. For example, offer a visual checkbox of features between economy and premium versions of a product.

The brands in the Trust Winners cluster in our research take a bold approach to competency and intent. They know that doing well in each of the Four Factors burnishes the overall brand, and, in certain industries, exceptional performance in humanity and transparency increases consumers' trust in capability and reliability.

We believe that leaders of all kinds of organizations can learn a lot from the most highly trusted brands across each of these three clusters (ourselves included—more on that in Chapter 9). Next, we were curious, what could we learn from the least trusted organizations?

CHAPTER 5

The Least Trusted Organizations

In this chapter:
- The trust gap: business leaders versus customers
- The least trusted
  - Distrusted
  - Ambivalent Neutrals

As we saw with brands like Cleveland Clinic, Energizer, and Marriott, patterns in the data told us interesting things about what the most trusted brands have in common. We were equally curious (and a little afraid) to learn what the *least* trusted organizations shared.

The Trust Gap: Business Leaders versus Customers

We know that people can be overconfident when it comes to gauging how much others trust them (something we are not exempt from). The same is true of organizations. In 2021, we worked with Twilio, a cloud communications platform, to launch a study of trust with customers.

79%

of business leaders believe customers trust their brand, yet just. . .

52%

of people say they trust the brands they purchased in 2021.

We surveyed 1,000 consumers and 500 leaders of organizations in the consumer industry.[51] We wanted to know how much customers trusted certain brands, and how much leaders of those brands believed their customers trusted them. Here is what we learned: in overall trust scores, 79 percent of business leaders believe customers have *somewhat* or *very high* trust in their organization's brand. Yet just 52 percent of people feel *somewhat* or *very high* trust for the brands they purchased or used in 2021. That's a gap of 27 percentage points![52]

Even the *most trusted brands* have room for improvement. For example, a net of 33 customers out of 100 said they believed the brands they trust *most* are transparent—that those brands openly share all information, motives, and choices in straightforward and plain language. It was implied that 67 percent did not believe that the companies they trust most were transparent. As we discussed in Chapter 1, when we first explored the Four Factors, more transparency isn't always better. Think back to our farm-to-table menu being written by a chef and read by a hungry customer. The diner wants to know the farm uses humane practices for its meat, but he or she doesn't want to know what goes into humane slaughter. Likewise, the general counsel at your organization might want to share the most explicit version of terms and conditions with new customers. In both cases, the chef and the lawyer overlook the importance of curating relevant information for their humans in clear, easy-to-understand language. Similarly, a net of 48 out of 100 respondents said their *most-trusted* brands consistently deliver on their promises. Oof. That is less than half of the time!

The trust perception gap was significant across all Four Factors of Trust (see Figure 5.1). Interestingly, the biggest gap was in humanity, where 80 percent of leaders thought they rated highly in humanity, when only 35 percent of consumers said the same for a trust gap of 45 percentage points.

B2C leaders overestimate performance on all Four Factors

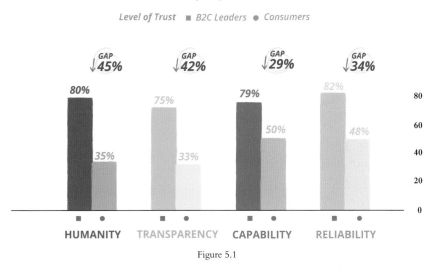

Figure 5.1

These factors are embedded in everything your brand does, whether intentionally or not. Customers may question a brand's humanity ("Do you even care about me?"), or transparency ("Why weren't you upfront about shipping costs?"). They may lose trust in a brand's capability ("This was the worst experience I've had"), or reliability ("The second time I called them was nothing like the first"). How can the perceptions of an organization's leaders be so distant from the customers' reality? The trouble often arises when organizations focus on a point in the total customer experience that is critical to sustaining the business, such as a purchase, but the organization doesn't pay attention to the total customer experience. Another reason for this perception gap is that organizations aren't measuring trust throughout the experience at the moments that really matter, which means they lack the insight needed to make changes that could build trust.

For example, 96 percent of consumers trust a brand more when it's easy to do business with that brand, but only 35 percent of consumers say it is very easy to do business with the brands they trust *most*. Even when organizations work to make it easy to do business with them, they often focus on the wrong approaches. When asked to identify the most important characteristics that make it easy to do business with their brand, executives only correctly identified one out of the top four that matter most to consumers and underestimated the importance of top characteristics by an average gap of 21 percentage points (see Figure 5.2).

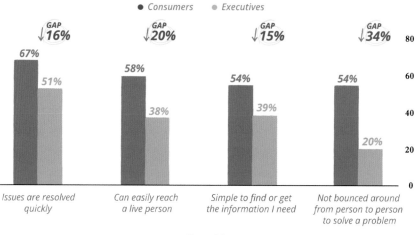

Business leaders underestimate the top four characteristics that consumers say make it easy to do business with a brand

Figure 5.2

This trust gap between organizational leaders and their customers spans every part of the organization: supply chain and channel partners, product development and merchandising, IT and communications infrastructure, web design and customer contact center, finance and commerce technology. Each impacts the trust fostered—or fractured—with customers.

Our research also found that when trust is damaged, brand leaders are especially misaligned with consumer preferences regarding how to rebuild trust. Business leaders say the solutions are "to provide outstanding customer service" and "communicate proactively about the problem and the resolution," which demonstrates *intent* to build trust through humanity and transparency without necessarily *doing* anything specific about it. Customers in our study indicated that what they wanted most were specific, real-world demonstrations of competence through reliability and capability. Customers want refunds, offers for replacements or exchanges, and an admission of error with an apology, not just demonstrations of humanity.

The good news is that when the right actions are taken, consumers can forgive mistakes, whether those mistakes are as simple as delayed shipping, or as significant as nonfunctional products. On average, consumers will accept three mistakes from a brand before losing trust, provided that the mistakes are resolved to their satisfaction.[53]

The Least Trusted

In the category of the least trusted, we see two distinct clusters emerge. First, the brands with the lowest composite trust scores are Distrusted. The average trust score for this cluster is negative 1, meaning for every person that trusts the brand, there are just as many (and even slightly more) who do not. The other cluster we call Ambivalent Neutrals. These brands score in the bottom third of our dataset. What really makes them stand out in contrast to the Distrusted, however, is how un-divisive they are. They have the lowest standard deviations[54] in our dataset, driven by a high number of neutral ratings (neither agree nor disagree). Ambivalent Neutral brands have 24 percent more neutral ratings on average. Both clusters face the threat that another, more trusted, brand will come along and disrupt or displace them. As trust becomes a more prominent differentiator, the brands with the highest HX TrustID scores will both capture more loyal customers and attract the most valuable workforce.

Distrusted

Distrusted brands have the lowest HX TrustID scores in our dataset and they are often brands that people use even if they don't particularly trust them. Our research found that the spectrum of low trust brands includes a variety of brand categories from fast food restaurants to banks to technology companies. Such variety reinforces the lesson that building trust isn't bound by industry or customer segments, but by how the brand fulfills—or doesn't—all Four Factors of Trust.

Social polarization also plays a role in low trust scores. Consider media networks, some of our lowest scoring brands overall. These networks are anchored in sharing specific views along the political spectrum. They engender a loyal following from people who share their viewpoint and strong skepticism from those who don't.

The most distrusted organizations are those that appear inauthentic. These organizations are particularly vulnerable to criticism based on saying one thing while doing another or denying something they know to be true. For decades, tobacco companies promoted smoking cigarettes, despite knowledge that this damaged smokers' health.[55] Insider revelations in the 1990s about this long-running inauthenticity from tobacco companies hastened regulation and laws against smoking in public buildings and transportation. Because the tobacco companies were disingenuous, the public lost trust, making way for the government to step in.

Organizations and products that are not trusted but widely used set up a tricky dynamic with their customers. Social media and online search brands illustrate the tensions inherent between their business models and their public image. Many sporting leagues also fit into the Distrusted cluster. According to our research, larger sports organizations, representing the most popular and well-resourced teams, are less trusted than their lesser-known counterparts. Some of this might be due to the broad media coverage that the most popular sports organizations are subjected to, and the resulting high-profile scandals when trust is violated. A special challenge in measuring trust in sports is how emotionally charged fans can be. Individual trust is heavily related to a person's team loyalty, and how his or her team is performing at any one point in time.

But we also found that smaller, more trusted organizations tend to be more engaged, human, and transparent on issues that matter to their audience. This is authenticity—when an organization says it exists for love of the sport, the players, and the fans, and then actually behaves that way even when it's not easy. A favorite example from our study is the Women's National Basketball Association (WNBA).

WNBA fans have a passion for the players, their favorite team, *and* for the league as a whole. Tapping into this, the WNBA focuses on sharing its players' stories. For example, in the middle of the pandemic, many sports leagues emphasized the importance of people getting vaccinated. While many sports leagues used their platforms to promote vaccination, the WNBA also worked very closely with the Players Association. WNBA Commissioner Cathy Engelbert knew that vaccine-reluctant individuals were more apt to listen to and trust their teammates than a governing body that vaccinations were safe, effective, and good for the community. The Players Association (WNBPA) worked diligently to share accurate information and counter vaccine myths. In a few months, the WNBA achieved 99 percent player vaccination rates, faster than any other league.[56] WNBA players such as Elizabeth Williams then extended this effort to fans, holding "E Talks with Docs" on her Instagram Live show. Additionally, the union hosted virtual panels comprised of Black and Brown women in medical fields. The panels were designed to help players get comfortable with getting shots themselves and share their newfound knowledge with their fans, especially Black and Brown women, and to encourage fans to seek reliable information about the vaccine.[57]

WNBA teams regularly engage with issues "outside" their sport that are important to many women and girls in general, and to Black women in particular. For example, the Connecticut Sun basketball team supports a "Change Can't Wait" initiative focused on marginalized groups in Black and Brown communities. This initiative touches on issues like police reform, health equity, civic engagement, and community advocacy.

When we asked Commissioner Engelbert about these efforts, she told us, "We report frequently to the players and listen closely to their input," meaning that the WNBA must work alongside players to achieve common goals. The WNBA experiences fewer public disagreements over salary, for example, than other women's leagues (not to mention men's leagues).

A league that tells fans that the players matter *and then acts that way in a crisis* earns high scores across all Four Factors of Trust. The WNBA's league office leadership treats players as thought partners in the league's decisions and actions, which can be difficult when trying to balance the needs of players versus owners. Larger sports leagues and other organizations in the Distrusted cluster can learn a lot from the WNBA, an organization that has managed to buck the trend of its industry peers.

Ambivalent Neutrals

Ambivalent Neutrals are brands with the smallest differences between high and low scores across all Four Factors of Trust, driven largely by neutral ratings. They don't inspire great amounts of trust, and yet they don't evoke mass distrust. Customers are simply ambivalent about their services.

While the Distrusted cluster encompassed brands from many industries, *all* of the Ambivalent Neutrals were in the same industry: financial services. Are you surprised? People choose these brands out of necessity: they need a bank account of some kind; they have to buy home insurance and title insurance when purchasing a house; they're required to buy state-mandated car insurance. Their emotional engagement in the brand tends to be low unless something goes wrong. The irony of course is that we don't trust the very institutions that we give our life savings to!

Generations of consumers have grown up hearing, "You have to save for retirement because Social Security isn't enough." In spite of well publicized trust violations in the last twenty years, the need to engage with financial institutions on some level has barely changed for most consumers. Negative trust incidents like learning that a bank pressured people into buying mortgages they couldn't afford, or data breaches at credit rating services, might drive confused and disgruntled customers to another institution. But once they get there, their experience tends to be similar. Absent a crisis, Ambivalent Neutrals might cruise along on customer inertia, but hardly distinguish themselves.

Ambivalent Neutrals who have not invested in building trust in each of the Four Factors expose themselves to competition by similar brands who are putting more thought and resources into their offerings. For example, financial services startups are sprouting up with a variety of services, including more privacy, greater ease of use, greater transparency in fee structure, and more "human," hassle-free interactions.

In Figure 5.3, we see that financial services brands have very little differences in their aggregate HX TrustID scores.

Many financial services companies have a high concentration of neutral trust scores

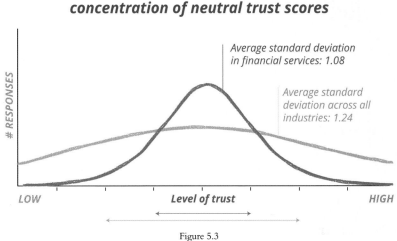

Figure 5.3

One of the very few financial services brands that distinguishes itself is Edward Jones, a financial services company with nearly 19,000 financial advisors across the U.S. and Canada.[58] You will not find Edward Jones in the Ambivalent Neutral cluster, because it has set itself apart from its industry peers.

Edward Jones has built its business on being a client-centered brand. They score highly on humanity and transparency. And their personalized approach strengthens Edward Jones's total capability: Edward Jones has a capability score that's more than 30 percent higher than the financial services industry average. This result is driven in part by the face-to-face meetings between clients and financial advisors. These advisors are trained by Edward Jones, live in the communities they serve, and come from diverse backgrounds. To deliver on transparency, Edward Jones presents fees, account choices, and other costs upfront.

When we spoke with Edward Jones's Chief Experience and Marketing Officer, Tim Rea, he emphasized that unity across Edward Jones's associates is key to delivering on the trust promise. "If you're human-centered, it's about everyone playing a role in building trust," he told us. Because they are embedded in communities, Edward Jones branch teams understand the clients' environment, culture, and desire for a trusted human to help them navigate their financial lives. Edward Jones has created effective tools, like a discovery trade-off exercise, which helps uncover what a client truly values, digital ways to let new clients share how they'd like to work with a financial advisor, and retirement, insurance, and general investment calculators that become part of the conversation with a real live person. Throughout the experience, Edward Jones emphasizes the role of customers' human qualities, such as risk tolerance, communications preferences, family profile, and long-term goals.

"Clients want to feel understood, informed, in control, and secure," says Kit Sundararaman, Principal, Client Experience and Insights at Edward Jones. "For us, that means delivering hyper-personalized experience through 'smart consistency.'"[59] Even as a client's needs and investment cycles change, Edward Jones can deliver a reliable experience. Distinguishing itself from the financial services organizations in the Ambivalent Neutrals cluster, Edward Jones succeeds in a generally low-trust environment by delivering exceptionally well on humanity and transparency.

Having learned which companies are distrusted and why, we turned our attention to the demographics of trust. Are there individuals who are more trusting than others and, if so, what drives that trust? We'll discuss this in depth in Chapter 6.

CHAPTER 6

The Demographics of Trust

In this chapter:

- Lived experience drives trust, and identity shapes experience
- Breaking down the demographics of trust
  - The most/least trusting customers
  - The most/least trusting workers
- It's not just who you are, but what you've experienced

In the prior chapters, we shared which types of organizations are the most and least trusted. In this chapter we'll discuss which *people* are most and least trusting. We were curious what made individuals more likely to trust. Was it where they live? Their gender identity? Or other dimensions of their personal lived experiences? Here is the punchline: Our lived experience, or the accumulated knowledge gained about the world through our first-hand experiences and how we interpret current and historical events, drives trust. Personal identity must be viewed in the context of that lived experience.

Lived Experience Drives Trust, and Identity Shapes Experience

Identity is both how you define who you are and how others define you. Identity is based on what makes you the same as others (shared identity) as well as what makes you different or unique. Amelia and Ashley share an identity as White women of European descent, as wives and mothers, as professionals, and as residents of Massachusetts. Amelia identifies as a heterosexual, cisgender, Catholic woman born in England. She is also a damn good dancer. Ashley identifies as lesbian, cisgender, and a citizen of the world. She is an impassioned fan of the U.S. Women's National Soccer Team.

There are many different types of identity such as cultural identity, professional identity, ethnic and national identity, religious identity, gender identity, and disability identity.[60] Identity is formed on many levels and is driven by things that are immutable (such as race or disability), as well as things that we choose (such as political affiliation, religious beliefs, and club membership, among others). As an illustration of chosen identity, think about all the zealous sports fans you know. Identity is a strong influence in how we think and act. Take, for example, one particularly ardent soccer fan from Australia. He convinced his wife to name their new daughter Lanesra, and it wasn't until she turned two that he finally revealed to his wife that "Lanesra" is "Arsenal" spelled backwards. (Arsenal is a soccer club in London, and we are not-so-secretly delighted with that example tying together Amelia's identity as a Brit with Ashley's identity as a fan of "football.")

We each can think of lived experiences, linked to our identity, that have shaped how we engage with and trust people and organizations in our lives. Even with a loving and stable family, growing up as a gay woman in 1990s Ohio was not easy for Ashley. There were virtually no role models in school or on television. The internet barely existed. The words "lesbian," "gay," and "queer" were words children tossed around to tease and insult each other. Ashley was smart enough to know that being *this kind of different* wasn't tolerated. She learned quickly to hide that part of her identity.

Ashley's experience as an adult underscored this message. For most of their twenty-year marriage, Ashley and her wife, Marijke, were unable to live legally in the U.S. They also had to undertake a lengthy process requiring intrusive background checks to have Marijke legally adopt *her own children*. Ashley would tell you that she felt exiled from her home country because of her identity as a married gay woman and vulnerable in states that rejected Marijke as a parent. Her experience has had a lasting impact on who, what, and how she trusts. Ashley still gets anxious going through immigration, wary about whether or not her partner, Marijke, will be called into the back room for further questioning, which has happened on several occasions upon entering the U.S.

Ashley knows how it feels to be treated as less than equal. However, she is quick to point out that her gender and sexuality are not what shape whether or not she trusts. Rather it is *her experiences* based on her gender and sexuality that shape her trust.

Breaking down the Demographics of Trust

To understand which people are more or less likely to trust, we used a decision tree model to find out which demographics matter most and for which of the Four Factors.[61] We asked our data scientists: Out of all the elements that make up people's identities and experience, what is the *relative* importance of each one? Which variables contributed most to an individual's likelihood to trust brands or employers, *in order*?

We created the decision tree using more than twenty variables[62] to understand how much each individual variable contributed to the classification of a person's trust level.[63] We performed two separate analyses: one for workers, and one for customers. We tested a range of demographics, including those we named "core" identity variables (ethnicity, gender identity, sexuality) and those we named "experience" variables (for example, living situation, job level, education, and geography).

As we began our research, we hypothesized that core identity variables (ethnicity, sexual orientation, and gender) would be clear predictors of trust over time. The data, however, simply didn't prove this out. We even questioned our research methods, then double- and triple-checked the data and analysis. The findings were clear: Ethnicity, gender, and sexuality were not the most accurate predictors of trust.

Instead, we found that experience variables, such as age or job level, matter more than core identity variables in understanding trust, statistically speaking. For workers and customers alike, ethnicity, gender identity, and sexuality were ruled out by the decision tree.[64] Instead *experience* variables, which directly influence agency and expectations, were more likely to help us understand trust.[65]

Agency and expectations are powerful influencers of how we experience trust. Agency is the ability to exert power. On an individual level, it means having the ability to make informed choices, take action, and accomplish goals. As a customer, having agency might mean that you have the option to switch brands easily, or to feel confident you can find the information you need without having to rely on someone else. For workers, agency could mean having the power to change jobs, to do a job well, or to make decisions about how or when to work (for example, flexible hours or remote work). In the workplace, agency also comes from being able to influence the decisions of others—the typical rewards of advancement. Thinking back to Ashley's story, not being able to choose where to live with her partner and having to take extra steps to claim parental rights made Ashley feel like she had limited agency around those choices.

People also trust based on how closely the experience of a brand matches their expectations. We discussed the dynamics of expectations in Chapter 2 (with the Rachel and Ross story from *Friends*). Expectations—especially mismatched or unspoken ones—impact trust between workers and employers, and between customers and brands. When expectations are not met, whether through misunderstanding or experience, trust is eroded. For Ashley, not knowing what to expect each time she and her partner entered the country left a residual anxiety that undermines her trust in the system. Expectations are interconnected with agency. When people are able to change their situations to match expectations, they trust more.

However, as Ashley's story illustrates, your identity—including how you are viewed by society—influences your lived experience, including your relative power in society or agency, how you are treated, and how you perceive the world. And, because we are each treated differently, how we experience trust will also be different.

The Most/Least Trusting Customers

When we measured the relationship between customer demographics and how likely they were to trust, we found that the variables most correlated with trust were identical for all Four Factors; in descending order: parenthood, geography, education level, and age. (See Figure 6.1.)

- *Parenthood:* Parents are more likely to trust brands.
- *Geography:* Urban customers trust more than suburban ones, who trust more than rural customers.
- *Education level:* More educated customers are more likely to trust.
- *Age:* Millennials trust the most, followed by Gen Z, Gen X, Baby Boomers, and the Silent Generation.[66]

The Four Factors have the same top four customer demographics in common

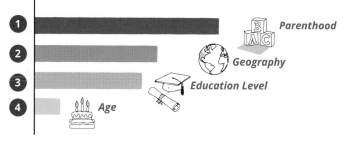

Figure 6.1

As we noted, the top customer variables are those that strongly influence an individual's *agency* and *expectations*. For example, people with more education tend to earn significantly more money, and more money means more options and greater agency.[67] People who are older tend to have a broader and deeper set of experiences, which leads to more informed expectations. And while identity variables such as ethnicity, sexuality, and gender are not as predictive of trust statistically, they remain a critical component of how you *experience* the top four variables listed above (for example, parenthood or education). For additional data and descriptions of the customer demographic variables, see Appendix B.

The Most/Least Trusting Workers

The top variables associated with trust levels for workers were consistent (but not identical) across all Four Factors. (See Figure 6.2.)

The most significant variables we found were:

- *Job level:* The more senior you are, the more trusting you are.
- *Flexible working schedule:* Those who have flexibility are more trusting, possibly from a sense of greater agency to influence their work experience.
- *Organization type:* Those who work for privately owned (versus publicly traded companies or the government) are likely to be more trusting.

The Four Factors have three top workforce demographics in common

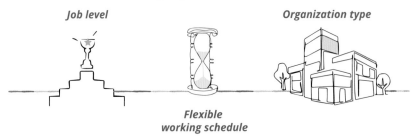

Job level   Organization type

Flexible
working schedule

Figure 6.2

Just like with customers, the most important variables for workers are the experience variables that influence agency and expectations. Take job level, for example. The higher workers move up in job level, the more likely they are to trust their employer. In our research, lower-level staff are only about 70 percent as trusting as executives. The closer workers are to "the top," the more they understand organizational strategy, and the more involved they are in the decision-making process. Seniority gives a worker important positional power. Therefore, when a worker is more senior, he or she has greater agency than those lower in the hierarchy. In addition, understanding the inner workings of an organization gives a worker more informed expectations, as well as greater positional power to get expectations met.

It's worth nothing that employers overestimate their workforce's trust level by almost 40 percent.[68] This is a workforce trust gap that mirrors how business leaders' overestimate customer trust (as discussed in Chapter 5). When executives assume everyone in the workforce trusts the organization as much as they do, they are often mistaken, and probably miss opportunities to improve engagement, retention, and performance.

Some workforce demographics are very important for one or two factors

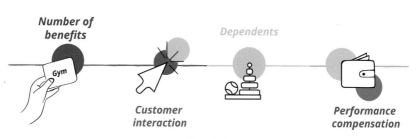

Figure 6.3

We also found some interesting nuances in the variables that influence workforce trust. (See Figure 6.3.) Some variables were very important for one or two factors, but not all four:

- *Number of benefits:* Workers with more benefits are more likely to view their employer as capable (for example, more health insurance like vision/dental, life insurance, disability, retirement/flex savings, paid time off, and/or medical leave, among others).

- *Customer interaction:* Workers who interact with customers weekly or daily are more likely to view their employer as high in humanity and transparency.

- *Dependents:* Workers who have a dependent in their household (for example, child or senior) are more likely to view their employer as reliable.

- *Performance compensation:* Workers whose compensation included performance bonuses (such as bonus pay or stock options) are more likely to view their employer as transparent and capable. Transparency includes the sharing of financial performance, and capability is implied in the organization's success.

You might be asking yourself, "Why are customer trust profiles more consistent than those of workers?" Work demands a great deal of our attention; the average American spends seven to eight hours working each day.[69] Most people don't spend even a fraction of that amount of time interacting with the brands they buy from. As a result, the relationship with their employer is much more nuanced, with many more inputs informing trust. We see that nuance reflected in the variation across the Four Factors for workers. For additional data and description of the workforce variables, see Appendix C.

It's Not Just Who You Are, but What You've Experienced

While our decision tree analysis didn't isolate core identity demographics in the top five, we can still observe two important trends:

- In general, women trust less than men.
- Times of perceived personal threat to identity (may) make identity matter more.

Women Trust Less than Men

On average across industries, women customers trust brands 88 percent as much as male customers. (See Figure 6.4.) A lack of trust is even more pronounced for nonbinary or transgender customers, whose trust scores in the Four Factors are dramatically lower than those of both women and men. People who identify as

As customers, women trust brands

88%

as much as men.

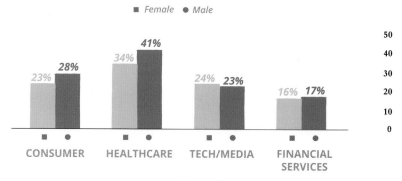

As customers, women typically trust less than men, especially in consumer and healthcare

■ *Female* ● *Male*

Figure 6.4[70]

nonbinary trust about 36 percent as much as women. Given nonbinary respondents' challenges in a system traditionally designed against them,[71] this result is not surprising. It highlights how those who do not fit into a traditional system have less agency to get their needs met.

Many organizations have a long history of designing for men and then altering these products for women (or not altering them at all), rather than being designed for—and by—women. This is summed up nicely by the phrase "shrink it and pink it," which describes how companies would take a product designed for men, make it smaller, color it pink, and sell it to women, often at a higher price.[72] Have you ever wondered why the same collared button-down shirt costs up to twice as much more to dry clean if it is called a woman's blouse rather than a man's shirt?[73] Or why women's shampoo is often 50 percent more expensive, even when the only product difference is scent?[74] We have.

Let's also talk about the historical discrimination against women customers specifically in the automobile industry, where women are asked to pay more than men for identical services and items, including auto insurance, cars themselves, and auto repair.[75] Even worse, women drivers are 73 percent more likely to be severely injured in a crash than male drivers, because safety standards are set by testing how well a car protects a man of average size and weight during simulated crash conditions (for the same reason, children and heavier adults are also more likely to be injured).[76] Therefore, we were not surprised to find that, in our dataset, women trust automobile brands 79 percent as much as men.

However, there are also great examples of companies that understand identity, and create products and services specifically tailored to the needs and experiences of their customers. One of our favorite examples in the automobile industry is Subaru, which chose to target niche groups (for example, teachers and outdoorsy types) in an effort to avoid head-to-head competition with the major players.[77] In the mid-'90s, Subaru created a carefully designed marketing campaign to appeal to gay women (this is especially notable because, at the time, more than half of the U.S. considered being gay to be morally wrong).[78] Subaru began with research revealing a pattern of high Subaru ownership by single women heads of households. When marketers spoke to these customers, they discovered many were lesbian and felt Subaru fit their active, low-key, often outdoorsy lifestyle. Subaru ran with the discovery in a progressive and daring (for the time) embrace of LGBTQ issues. They extended benefits to same-sex partners of Subaru workers at a time when the Defense of Marriage Act was American law. They advertised with clever double-meaning slogans tying together their rugged outdoors image and gay identity. Example taglines: "Get Out. And Stay Out." and "It's Not a Choice. It's the Way We're Built."[79] As a result of the focus on targeted groups like this one, Subaru's tepid sales turned into steady growth, and the parent company (previously Fuji Heavy Industries) rebranded the entire company under the Subaru brand.[80] Subaru's success continues today. The 2020 J.D. Power Brand Loyalty Study placed Subaru as number one in brand loyalty among all mainstream automakers, marking two years in a row of beating out the other (much larger) competitors.[81]

Women also trust less than men in the workplace. Overall, female workers trust 87 percent as much as male workers.[82] Not surprisingly, differences are especially apparent when intersected with the experience variables that influence trust. For example, the trust gap between male and female workers increases 60 percent when a flexible working schedule is not provided by employers. Given the roles women typically play, this makes sense. In addition to bearing children, women also bear the majority of household and family responsibilities.[83] Typical job schedules were designed long ago around male workers, and this continues to impact trust today.

Female workers trust

87%

as much as male workers.

There is also a dramatic divergence in performance-based variable compensation between men and women. Despite performance pay used as a mechanism to motivate all workers, male workers have notably higher trust levels when an employer offers performance-based incentives. The trust gap between male and female workers is 500 percent bigger when performance incentives are provided by an employer. We know that building trust leads to loyalty both as a customer and as a worker. We found it fascinating that the incentives that typically motivate men are likely to erode trust with women. Why? Women may not trust that their contributions will be viewed at the same performance level as those of men. Historically women are undercompensated relative to men, and are paid, on average, $.83 on the dollar to what a man makes performing the same work.[84] It's also well known that many performance-based compensation structures may inadvertently reinforce bias.[85] Further, we hypothesize that the different responses to performance-based compensation might stem from the cultural expectation that higher performance equates to working more hours, which many female workers, especially mothers, might not be able to meet. Is it surprising, then, that women might feel less likely to trust in a compensation system that values them less?

The trust gap between male and female workers is

500% bigger

when performance incentives are provided by an employer.

Times of Perceived Threat to Identity (May) Make Identity Matter More

We conducted our first workforce trust study in May 2020, at the beginning of the pandemic and during the national reckoning over systemic racism that erupted over the killing of George Floyd. The data confirmed our initial hypotheses that women and ethnically diverse people trust their employers less than men and people who identify as White. However, our next customer study, which ran October 2020 through May 2021, did not show a clear pattern of difference between ethnic diversity and trust. We were stumped. Why, we wondered, did ethnicity seem to be a greater factor in predicting trust for workers than for customers? As we launched our next rounds of workforce research in October 2020 and October 2021, we made sure to test the following: Do ethnically diverse workers consistently trust less than their colleagues who self-identify as White? At first, the results surprised us. Just like with customers, the trust gaps based on ethnic identity we originally saw in the workforce evened out over time. Put another way, there was no clear pattern or statistically significant difference in people's likelihood to trust their employers based on their ethnic identity alone. (See Figure 6.5.)

In the workforce, the trust gap based on ethnic identity has shrunk over time

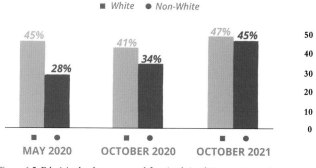

Figure 6.5: Ethnicity has been grouped for visual simplicity; see Appendix C.9 for a more detailed breakdown by ethnic identity

We had hypothesized that differences in ethnicity would be clear predictors of trust over time. Here is our revised hypothesis: Just identifying as Black or Asian doesn't make a person more or less likely to trust an employer. As we have said before, core identity variables like ethnicity are not the most significant factor in predicting one's likelihood to trust. Even when we looked at differing levels of seniority, we saw no statistically significant trend of a particular ethnic identity group—White or otherwise—consistently trusting more than another. However, we believe that the *lived experiences* of ethnic minorities, which mirrored increased personal threat and crisis in May 2020, led to lower levels of self-reported trust in our study. We believe that this hypothesis could be helpful to leaders in organizations to help raise their awareness of the importance of external circumstances impacting the lived experience of their customers and workers.

A final word on demographics. We believe it is a mistake to ignore the relationship between identity and trust and an even bigger mistake to take trust for granted. As leaders we know that building trust leads to the kinds of outcomes that matter to employers both for their workers and for their customers. And we find ourselves constantly asking whether "this action" matters more than "that action" in terms of our likelihood to build trust with the people we work with. Every day leaders are making conscious choices that either build or erode trust. Here is what we are taking away and hope you do too: We should pay attention not just to different identities to build trust but, more importantly, to the lived experiences of people with different identities and the impact to their agency and expectations. We need to pay attention to the fact that experiences of perceived personal threat to identity make people trust less. We need to pay attention to the fact that women trust less than men. More junior people in an organization trust less than more senior people in that same organization. People who do not have agency over a flexible work schedule trust less. As leaders, we must pay attention to all of these "trust flags," because, when these flags are present, we might not only lose trust, but also lose some of our most valuable customers and workers.

In the next chapter we share the stories of two companies we admire that have demonstrated how to build trust with their workers, with their customers, *and* with each other as partners.

CHAPTER 7

The Trust Ecosystem

In this chapter:

- To build trust, start with your workforce
- Delta Air Lines: A virtuous circle
- American Express: The three Cs
- You're in this with partners (and partners are people too)

We are dating ourselves, but remember the iconic Reese's Peanut Butter Cup commercials from the mid-'80s, telling us that chocolate and peanut butter were "two great tastes that taste great together"? As Amelia likes to say, she is passionate about all things that elevate the human experience, including high-quality dark chocolate, which does go great with peanut butter. We started researching other iconic pairings, like Ben and Jerry, Holmes and Watson, and the one-time "supercouple" Brad Pitt and Angelina Jolie, who made tabloid headlines as Brangelina. (As an aside, we once gave a talk on the human experience and trust and were referred to afterwards as "Ashmelia.") Joking aside, we do think there is something special about iconic pairs and their ability to build trust, not only with each other but also with others, which is worth paying attention to. In this chapter, we will talk about the virtuous circle of how investing in building trust with workers also builds trust with customers. We will also share the stories of Delta Air Lines and American Express, an iconic pair in the travel industry. Both have invested to build trust with their respective workforces, their customers, and with each other as partners.

To Build Trust, Start with Your Workforce

The idea that building trust with workers builds trust with customers and leads to business outcomes is not new. There are about as many different ways to measure customer experience and workforce experience as there are types of customers and workers. There are, however, two reasons we devote a chapter to this "not new" idea. First, we think it's important to have a single measure of trust that is used for all of your humans—customers, workers, and partners. In our research, the Four Factors are consistently the primary drivers of trust and behavior, regardless of the "role" someone is playing as a worker or customer. Second, if it were easy to build trust with workers and customers to deliver on financial outcomes, every organization would have figured it out by now. The fact that it is hard to do implies that we all still need help identifying which actions to take.

Here is what you need to know about the iconic pairing of workers and customers (see Figure 7.1):

- The more workers trust their employer, the more motivated they are to work.
- Building worker trust improves customer satisfaction by two times.
- Building customer trust improves market capitalization by up to four times.

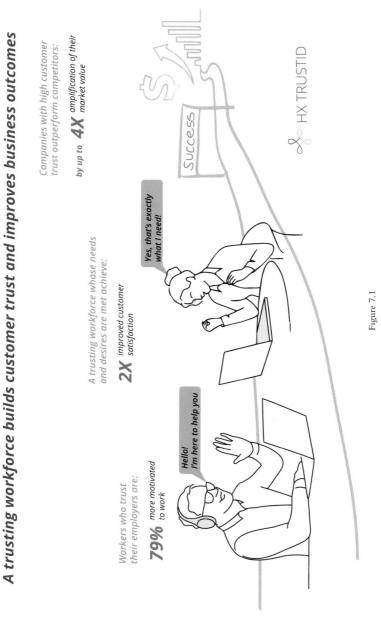

Figure 7.1

The More Workers Trust Their Employer, the More Motivated They Are to Work

Our research shows that workers who trust their employers are 79 percent more likely to feel motivated at work than workers who do not trust. They also show 41 percent less absenteeism[86] and dramatically lower turnover.[87]

Building Worker Trust Improves Customer Satisfaction by Two Times

When an employer understands workers' needs and desires and designs a human experience around their values, they are

1.6X **more likely to achieve customer outcomes and deliver** **2X** **the customer satisfaction.**

Organizations can function better at fulfilling their mission when the workforce trusts the organization, which leads to a direct, positive impact on customer trust. When an employer understands workers' needs and desires and designs a human experience around their values, they are 1.6 times more likely to achieve customer outcomes and deliver two times the customer satisfaction.[88] In addition, customers watch to see how workers are treated and use this as a guidepost for their own trust/purchasing behaviors; 82 percent of customers say that measures to ensure safety and well-being of a companies' workforce "must be in place" or would "make them more likely" to visit.[89] When customers believe that an organization takes care of their workers, our research shows that they are 2.4 times more likely to agree the brand is human.

Building Customer Trust Improves Market Capitalization by Four Times

Companies with highly engaged workers outperform their competitors by 147 percent[90] and enjoy 25 percent greater profitability.[91] This is especially true when organizations reward workers based on the company's financial success. When highly trusted companies raise stock-based compensation (for workers), they see up to four times amplification of their market cap.[92]

To provide examples of how leading organizations are building trust with customers starting with their workers, we sat down with executives from Delta Air Lines and American Express.

Delta Air Lines: A Virtuous Circle

When Ed Bastian was young, his dream job was to become a professional baseball player. He was the oldest of nine kids and hadn't flown on an airplane until the age of twenty-five. As of 2022, Bastian is the CEO of Delta Air Lines, and he is somewhat of a celebrity among his 75,000 employees. His team tells us that wherever he goes, he gets stopped by Delta people who want a picture or simply to say thank you. We wanted to learn more about Bastian's trust philosophy, which is known as "the virtuous circle." (See Figure 7.2.) "We talk a lot about the virtuous circle here at Delta. The more we take care of our employees, the better job they do for our customers, who in turn reward our shareholders with repeated business, which enables us to support our community and invest back in our employees. And that circle continues to spin faster and better and stronger as you move forward."

At the center of this virtuous circle is the concept of trust. Bastian says, "You don't necessarily deserve trust—you earn it. Trust is something people develop over time—through experience, relationship, the keeping of your word, and the commitments that you make—and continue to drive this business forward. . . . Trust is a core, critical ingredient of our brand."

One of our favorite examples of building trust is how Delta engaged with employees and demonstrated commitment to them during the pandemic. To put these efforts into context, it's important to note that Delta saw 95 percent of its revenue disappear virtually overnight, as

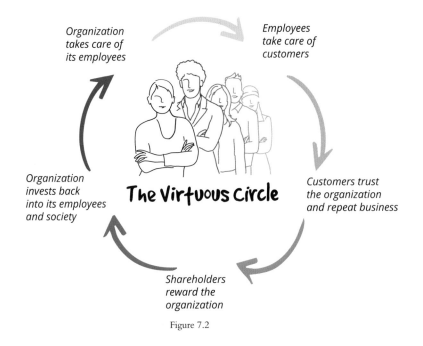

Organization take care of its employees

Employees take care of customers

Organization invests back into its employees and society

The Virtuous Circle

Customers trust the organization and repeat business

Shareholders reward the organization

Figure 7.2

travel demand plummeted. As an essential service, Delta had to keep flying, even with planes mostly empty, which meant that costs were still high while revenue was low. Delta responded to the crisis with a series of company-wide moves that demonstrated humanity and transparency, sustaining trust among both their workforce and their customers.

First, Bastian made a commitment from the beginning not to fire or furlough a single employee. Longtime industry observers thought he was crazy—the airline industry has a history of furloughing tens of thousands of people for much smaller issues and cycles in the past. Instead, Bastian made leave optional for workers, who could choose to continue working or to take voluntary unpaid leave with full benefits. This put the decision in the hands of the workers, giving them agency, a direct signal that workers' priorities were also Delta's priorities. More than 40,000 of Delta's more than 75,000-person workforce went on voluntary leave. Bastian says: "We were able to save over 50 percent in our total cost in the business without having to involuntarily furlough or lay off any of our people. They've all done it through voluntary means. We had half our people take voluntary leaves of absence all through the summer (2020), months on end."[93]

Delta employees did more than volunteer for unpaid leave. Congress received 175,000 letters from Delta employees supporting passage of the 2020 CARES Act, a nearly $2 trillion emergency bill that included $32 billion in payroll support to aviation workers.[94] At the same time, Delta invested significantly in the safety of their people, spending more than $500 million on testing, masks, access to vaccines, and pay protection for employees sick with COVID-19. Delta also appointed their first Chief Health Officer, a permanent position that ensures an ongoing commitment to well-being.

Second, Bastian builds trust by setting *expectations* transparently. Delta blocked middle seats for customers and clearly let them know what to expect when traveling again. At first, blocking middle seats was easy because they didn't have many people traveling. But as people started to come back to travel, Delta kept that commitment "until people felt confident in the return to travel," in other words, until they knew what to expect, and that Delta would deliver capably and reliably to keep them safe. Those seats remained blocked for almost fourteen months, much longer than any other airline.

Bastian brings his reasoning back to the "virtuous circle," making it clear that blocking the middle seats was important for both customers and Delta people. "The reason I did that was about trust, it was about confidence. It was safe to sit in the middle seat, but we knew people weren't comfortable sitting in a crowded plane during a pandemic and all the uncertainty attached to it. I did this very importantly, maybe as importantly, for our own employees. Our employees run those cabins all day long. That's their work environment—our crew, people at our airports, at our gates dealing with our customers. Employees didn't want to be on a crowded plane any more than our customers did. That was a message to our employees about the confidence and trust they can place in their management—that we've got their backs and we are working through it."

We asked Bastian a simple question: Was it all worth it? Unsurprisingly, he shared with pride that "our people became part of the story." Bastian recognizes that these initiatives to protect jobs were, at the time, also about protecting Delta's financial solvency. Perhaps more surprisingly, these investments in trust also paid dividends financially. Delta was the only U.S. airline to be profitable in the second half of 2021.[95]

Bastian says, "People were not just flying us, but they were also paying a higher price and investing in us because they had confidence in us. We actually wound up doing better financially, even though that wasn't our intent, because we didn't dilute our brand equity." Notably, Delta also won every major airline award in 2021 including J.D. Power No. 1 Airline in North America, JUST Capital and Forbes No. 1 Transportation Company, and Business Travel News No. 1 Airline. Additionally, Delta was recognized as one of TIME's 100 Most Influential Companies of 2021 and jumped to number 18 on Fortune's Most Admired Companies list in 2022. Glassdoor, which gathers voluntary and anonymous feedback from workers, placed Delta in the top ten of the 100 best companies to work for over the last six years.[96] As of this writing, Delta is also ranked as the number one U.S. airline by *The Wall Street Journal* and numerous other media outlets.[97]

Delta demonstrated how creating a culture of trust for workers, investing in the Four Factors of Trust, results in customers trusting the organization more. Because of these moves, Bastian says, "The trust that we have with our customers and our employees is even better."

American Express: The Three Cs

We also sat down with another client, Elizabeth Rutledge, who is the CMO of American Express (Amex). Elizabeth is a thirty-plus-year Amex veteran. She is also a mom, wife, and daughter as well as a long-time animal lover. In another life, Rutledge might have been a veterinarian (but we're grateful she's stayed focused on elevating experience for humans!). Rutledge shared the importance of the "Three Cs" at Amex—customer, colleagues (workforce), and community, emphasizing that to build trust with customers, it's important to build trust with colleagues and communities as well. Rutledge tells us, "Small businesses are vital to the success of our economy. When their communities thrive, we all thrive."

Approximately 60 percent of small businesses are owned by women or people of color.[98] Women-owned businesses have grown 21 percent in the past five years, as all businesses taken together grew by 5 percent. Businesses owned by women of color have grown by 43 percent.[99] But small businesses took a big hit in the 2020 recession and needed help to get back on track. Rutledge tells us, "Our brand has long stood for supporting small businesses, particularly in times of need. So at the start of the pandemic, we created the Stand for Small coalition in partnership with more than 100 larger companies. It was all about getting these organizations the tools they needed in the moment, including advice on how to manage remote workers, access to digital marketing tools, and support on how to manage cash flow. We were able to launch this initiative in just fourteen days because of our shared trust in each other and our mutual mission for supporting small businesses."

Additionally, Amex has specific initiatives to serve minority-owned small businesses. For example, Amex expanded the U.S. Black Chambers, Inc. ByBlack program with the first national certification program exclusively for Black ownership designation. First created as a directory of Black-owned business, the no-cost digital platform unlocks more ways to reach customers and secure contracts for Black-owned businesses across the country. ByBlack provides businesses an approved accreditation and enables both consumers and large corporations to easily find and use U.S.-based diverse suppliers. In addition, the program provides access to grant making and funding programs, local community chambers of commerce, networking opportunities, and more. This initiative is part of American Express's broader efforts to support diverse businesses and represents meaningful investment in humanity.

To build trust, Amex relies on its workforce, all of whom are called "colleagues." Rutledge says, "I firmly believe that trust starts with our colleagues . . . building that culture of trust. If we get that right, everything flows from there. I can't emphasize enough how important this is to the whole model of trust."

For example, when the pandemic hit, Amex's first priority was to ensure their colleagues felt secure in their jobs and had the flexibility and resources they needed to stay safe and healthy. Within a two-week period, Amex moved to a full-time work-from-home arrangement in virtually all locations around the world. During this period Amex completely transformed their global customer service and travel operations from brick-and-mortar call centers to virtual, home-based servicing. Amex also committed to no COVID-19-related layoffs throughout 2020.

If this sounds similar to how Delta builds trust, then it shouldn't surprise you to learn that Delta and American Express are valued partners, and that they demonstrate what it means to build trust, not only with workers and customers but also with each other as partners.

You're in This with Partners (and Partners Are People Too)

Most organizations have partners who play a critical role in delivering experience and building trust with workers and customers alike. In fact, some industries are predominantly delivered by partners—car dealerships, fast food restaurants, hotels, some financial services, and other franchises are counted on to create a trusted experience. Establishing trust with partners is just as important as it is with the workforce and customers. We approach partner trust the same way we think about customer and worker trust, because, after all, partners are people too!

Elizabeth Rutledge and Ed Bastian told us about how their trusted partnership creates additional value for their customers and their workforces. The companies have nurtured a sixty-four-year partnership—twenty-five years of which included a co-branded credit card.[100] Notably, both companies started in the travel business, and both see trust as a critical component of their partnership, though it took focus and effort to build mutual trust. Bastian remembers, "Trust sat at the core of the challenges in the early years of the relationship. We share a customer.

Amex customer, Delta customer. Whose customer are they? There was a lot of time and work spent discussing, analyzing, and evaluating what we were doing individually in the relationship. About five years ago we really flipped a switch on this and said, 'These aren't your customers, these aren't my customers, these are *our* customers. We both have to go all in to ensure that our customers see us as one.' We have created a partnership where the focus is on growing the pie, rather than spending a lot of time figuring out who gets what size slice of the pie." Rutledge says, "We have twenty-five years of history and common values, including trust, security, and service. It's a true partnership focused on increasing value for our customers and for both of our companies by bringing the best assets of both of our brands." Bastian says what makes it work is investing in the *relationships* (of the partnership), not just the business. Both companies have a human-centric focus, which allows them to work together to create value and build trust with both workers and their shared customers.

Rutledge says, "You also have to do this with a company and brand with whom you share the same values. Our focus on service and the quality of the care we take with customers is aligned closely with Delta." She goes on to say, "I think of partners as family. They are extensions of Amex and we need to operate with that intention in mind. The only way that will happen is if you treat them like family. It takes a lot of work, but trust gives you the power to be pioneers, to innovate."

> ### Trust gives you the power to be pioneers, to innovate."
>
> *– Elizabeth Rutledge, CMO of American Express*

The Amex-Delta partnership extends to their workforces. Bastian told us, "You invest in each other in relationships, not just in the business, and the creativity and the inspiration grows. We are now swapping people in each other's teams, and I love it. Sometimes you can't tell if you're a Delta person or an Amex person. You have a singular focus—to take care of your customers." "It's been a wonderful relationship," says Rutledge. "They are more than business partners."

Customers and workers have many choices when it comes to credit cards and other financial services. Same with air travel. Combining two iconic brands in a trusted partnership that embraces both workforces and shared customers empowers Amex and Delta to build customer trust and loyalty. And the business results for both firms have been outstanding. For example, Delta expects annual revenue from the co-branded card to reach nearly $7 billion in 2024.[101]

Building trust with your workforce drives better results across the board, from increasing trust with customers to better financial performance. To be a trusted organization, you must start by building trust with your workforce. You should empower agency within that workforce. And you should set and understand expectations for customers, workforce, and partners. These findings are powerful, but we also expected this to be the case, given the twenty-five-year history of the link between workers and customers. In the next chapter, we'll share more about what really did surprise us, as well as what we are still curious to learn more about.

To be a trusted organization, you must start by building trust with your workforce.

CHAPTER 8

This Is Just the Beginning

In this chapter:
- Trust will evolve (but it will always be important)
- Some of the insights surprised us
- The next horizons in trust

There is a lot we still want to learn about the nature of trust, and we'll talk about some of what we'd like to explore later in this chapter. We are reasonably confident, however, about two things. First, we expect the landscape of trust to evolve as humans and organizations evolve. Second, we are confident that the importance of trust will endure, and that the Four Factors will remain the primary drivers of trust.

Trust Will Evolve (But It Will Always Be Important)

Trust is human. From the moment we are born we start learning who and what to trust. We form near immediate bonds with our caretakers.

Evolutionarily, we learn pretty fast which berry we can trust to nourish us, not poison us. To err is also human, and it's because we are human that trust will constantly evolve. Our society is built upon our ability to conduct cooperative social exchanges, which are themselves under-pinned by trust, or a lack of it. This means that changing experiences will continue to shape how much and why people trust, or don't.

Because who and what we trust is constantly shifting, we'll continue to monitor and refine our understanding of the Four Factors as drivers of trust. We expect our growing sets of data and insights to deepen our own understanding of how the Four Factors operate in the world, and how they interact under differing circumstances. We look forward to working with other leaders of organizations, small and large, to consider the requirements for all their stakeholders, external and internal.

Trust is human. From the moment we are born we start learning who and what to trust.

We have studied the Four Factors across a range of contexts, from different industries to different types of organizations, and different types of people, as well. Our research suggests that the Four Factors will remain an accurate measurement of a human's trust. One reason for our confidence is that, as we expanded domains—for example from B2C to B2B—the Four Factors proved to be even *more* predictive of behaviors. Another reason for this confidence is that many researchers have come to similar conclusions about the components of trust. As you study various trust frameworks, you'll find a lot of similarity in what is proposed. Why?

Making good promises (humanity, transparency) and keeping them (capability, reliability) are the core of how people trust.

We do, however, expect the relative importance of the Four Factors to evolve over time, as what's important to us as a society shifts, and new customer/workforce expectations are set by pioneering organizations. We also expect the attributes that drive the Four Factors to evolve. As organizations get better at building and maintaining trust with their humans, their expectations and requirements will continue to shift.

The cable television industry of twenty years ago is a great example of how we might expect an organization's focus on trust to evolve. At that time, competition at a local level was largely nonexistent. You could have cable with company A, or you could choose not to have cable at all (there was often just one vendor). As a result, cable company revenues weren't dependent on having strong customer trust, and it showed in terms of how customers were treated and how customers rated their satisfaction. Did you ever take the day off of work to wait at home for cable repair (low reliability), only to have the company cancel hours after the intended window (low humanity and transparency)? We did, on more than one occasion, but having internet was simply too important (capability), and we stayed customers in spite of the terrible treatment.

Fast forward to today. Streaming services and other alternatives have forced cable companies to double down on a great consumer experience that builds trust. Whereas a customer might have waited for hours for a cable technician to show up to remedy yet another internet connection outage, now many companies provide a credit if the technician is late, recognizing the value of the customer's time (stronger humanity). Cable companies have also upgraded their technical abilities, so that even a phone representative can fix many problems long-distance (stronger capability and reliability). Why is that? Competition. Freed from cable monopolies, customers are turning to a full menu of alternatives.

Monopolies (and arguably some of these may be psychological monopolies rather than trust monopolies)[102] might not have to worry about trust for the moment, though we would argue that this is a big gamble. A singular market event or a start-up competitor could rapidly erode this advantage. Organizations of all kinds should all be deeply concerned about their trust levels across all Four Factors.

Some of the Insights Surprised Us

One of the best parts of conducting research is being surprised, and this happened to us on a number of occasions. We found that some deeply held orthodoxies didn't stand up to the test. We also saw interesting differences in customers versus workers, and we saw interesting differences by industry.

The most exciting surprises in large studies like ours are when data-based findings turn orthodoxies on their heads. Industries and companies develop internally held habits and rules that widely shape conventional wisdom over time. We call these orthodoxies. When we work with clients on human-centered design and applied innovation, this is very often one of the first activities we do with them. We help them identify orthodoxies (such as "That's just how we do things around here," or "That's just how it's always been done in our industry"), and then we work with them to imagine what might happen if we flipped that orthodoxy.

Flipping orthodoxies can unlock value that was previously hidden, and business history is full of this type of innovation. For example, Starbucks flipped the orthodoxy that "coffee is a commodity," designing its business on the idea that "coffee is an experience." Airbnb flipped the orthodoxy that "people won't share their homes with strangers" by creating a platform for ordinary homeowners to become mini-hoteliers. Uber and Lyft created a similar business with car owners, turning personal cars into a revenue source.

We set out to test the following "trust" orthodoxies:

- Well-known brands are the most trusted.
- Trust winners are trusted by all.
- Humanity and transparency trump capability.
- Trust looks the same across industries.

Orthodoxy 1: Well-Known Brands Are the Most Trusted

We began with the hypothesis that iconic brands would be more, well, *iconic*. You find names of such brands in annual high-level surveys.[103] It made sense that long-dominant, large brands with the most customers would also be the most trusted. To the contrary, we found that many household name-brands fell below benchmark trust scores in many industries. (See Figure 8.1.) This was one of the first orthodoxies we flipped: You don't need to be well-known to be trusted.

Iconic brands are well below industry leaders and some are even below the industry average

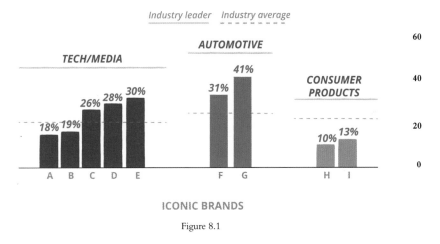

Figure 8.1

As we went deeper, we discovered a surprising flaw in previous high-level surveys. Asking simply, "Do you trust X brand?" doesn't get at the details of the relationship people have with it (recall from Chapter 2 that trust is fragmented and hard to measure). When asked about the Four Factors, people show not only *that* they trust but *why* they trust. Big brands that are well known and "iconic" invest millions of dollars in marketing and branding. However, marketing alone is not sufficient to sustain high trust. Just having a warm and empathetic—or incredibly funny—Superbowl commercial might keep you in the conversation on social media, but it won't necessarily make customers actually trust you, or buy your product.

Orthodoxy 2: Trust Winners Are Trusted by All

We tested the orthodoxy that to be a top tier Trust Winner, you have to be trusted by everyone. We expected our Trust Winners to have small gaps between existing and aware customers. The data told us otherwise. We found that there is more than one path to the top.

Disney Cruises is an example of a Trust Winner (discussed in Chapter 4) with a large gap between existing versus aware customers.[104] The gap between existing customers' trust scores versus aware customers is 44 points, which is about 85 percent larger than the average gap between existing and aware. By way of comparison, Marriott, another Trust Winner, has only an 8 percent gap. (See Figure 8.2.) In the case of Disney Cruises, we attribute this to what we call the superfan effect.

Disney Cruise—like Marriott—is a Trust Winner, despite having a large gap between existing and aware customers

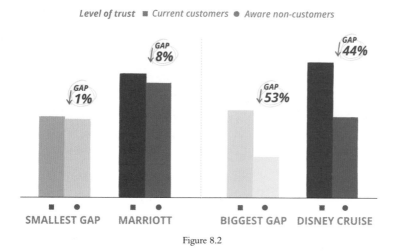

Figure 8.2

First, people who really like cruises see them more as a lifestyle than a vacation (during the pandemic, we wrote an article called "Cruisers Gonna Cruise," describing how avid cruisers were eagerly planning for the next available trip).[105] Second, the Disney brand is highly trusted.

Disney scores a little above average on trust scores of aware respondents, and the population that actively doesn't trust Disney Cruise is 22 percent less than the average. Moreover, Disney's superfans are so enamored with the brand, and rate its trustworthiness so highly, they pull up the high end of the trust score, creating the noted gap. In our dataset of nearly 500 brands, Disney Cruises has the third-highest trust score among existing customers! Disney's excellence in its businesses, including theme parks, films, television, and other entertainment, earns consistently high ratings. People who like cruises and trust Disney become superfans.

Disney Cruises has a unique value proposition. It has the smallest fleet of ships compared to major competitors, and customers pay a premium for the "Disney experience" of high touch, personalization, and custom experiences. It is the attention to detail, masterful entertainment, and the "magic" that is its signature brand statement. The magic happens with intense attention to detail. For every externally visible experience, there many more things working behind the scenes to make it happen, including training and technology, among others (capability). Disney ran a program in which stateroom hosts took an hour off in their eight-hour shift to engage and talk with guests directly, often recalling their names later (humanity). Cast members (Disney doesn't use the words "worker" or "employee"[106]) are there with guests every step of the way to answer questions and provide information (transparency), which is helpful when docking in unfamiliar ports. Underlying every customer experience is the consistency of the brand (reliability). From Disney tunes piped into hallways, to Disney-themed evening shows, to the promise of meeting your favorite Disney princess, Disney Cruises are designed for the diehard Disney lover. It is a brand focused solely on creating and serving superfans.[107]

Orthodoxy 3: Humanity and Transparency Trump Capability

We believe that elevating human experience is fundamental to winning in business. As a result, we expected humanity and transparency to be just as (or maybe even more) predictive of behavior than capability and reliability. This was reinforced in our first round of research where we asked customers to rank the importance of each factor. Consumers stated that humanity and transparency matter more in terms of driving their purchase and loyalty. Recall from Chapter 2, though, that what people say is often different from what they do. As we watched what consumers *actually* did, both humanity and transparency were shown to be overstated in comparison to the capability and reliability.

We like to think as consumers that we vote with our wallets and support more human brands, but at the end of the day, many of us still put much of our spending towards brands that are highly capable and reliable above all else. The Four Factors have the greatest influence on purchasing behavior in the auto sector, led by capability—which makes sense given the infrequency and high cost of an auto purchase. And convenience is still really important. Who *doesn't* buy what they need online from major retailers when they need it quickly? How many people have *actually* cancelled their social media accounts? Who *doesn't* weigh a low-price item against an expensive purpose-driven one?

This is how we came to understand capability and reliability as table stakes. They are required to compete. Companies with a huge footprint in the marketplace, underpinned by strong capability and reliability, have an advantage that is really hard to overcome. Recall from Chapter 4 that some brands build trust by focusing on being more human in addition to being reliable and capable (the Humanity Leaders cluster). But to be a Trust Winner, you must deliver on all Four Factors. And we continue to believe that humanity and transparency will set the most trusted companies apart and be more predictive of purchasing behaviors over time.

Orthodoxy 4: Trust Looks the Same Across Industries

At first, we thought that the attributes that drive trust might look the same across industries because the people are the same whether they are showing up at a bank or at a doctor's office. Nope. It turns out that there are significant differences in trust with both customers and workers across industries. We drilled down on each factor to understand where leaders for different organizations can most readily increase trust.

For example, we found the following differences in humanity for *workers* in different industries:

- Feeling engaged by your company's culture is more important in tech and retail. This makes sense as a lot of "superfan" brands exist in retail, and a lot of tech companies put great effort and resources into developing a distinctive culture.

- Having an employer who considers the good of society and the environment is more important in healthcare. There, organizations are literally caring for society's health. Notably, some of these data were gathered as healthcare workers were on the pandemic's front lines.

- Employers having a purpose you believe in is more important in banking. Consumer banks market themselves as an important pillar of local communities that serve as trusted guardians of customers' financial well-being (a message that became substantially more important after the 2008 mortgage crisis). A sense of purpose among workers drives these messages.

- Feeling comfortable sharing new ideas at work is more important in travel and hospitality. This may be born from necessity. There is a vast array of stakeholders who are responsible for delivering on and improving customer experience such as, field agents, branch managers, and franchise owners in hotel, car rental, and restaurant businesses. The volume and diversity of front-line workers requires greater inclusion to improve the customer experience.

Humanity operates somewhat differently for *customers* in those same industries. In short, context matters. What's important to a human depends on multiple factors, such as the role the human is in (customer versus worker), the industry, the company culture, and the brand promise, among others. Understanding differences at this level of granularity helps organizations direct their resources to have the most impact.

- Belief that a brand or organization values the good of society and the environment is more important in tech. Tech companies are some of the largest publicly traded companies in existence these days. Their products permeate society and drive social change. Nearly two-thirds of consumers expect CEOs to do more to make progress on social issues.[108] Given their scale and omnipresence, it makes sense that many consumers put these expectations on tech companies.

- Fast and friendly customer support is more important in banking and healthcare. This attribute of humanity makes sense for these industries, because there are often complex customer issues to be solved here around payments or insurance, for example.

- Believing that a brand or organization values and respects everyone regardless of background, identity, or beliefs is more important in travel and hospitality, and retail. These are both experience-driven sectors with a lot of in-person interaction between a diverse population of customers and workers. Customers want to feel valued and respected, regardless of their background or identity.

The Next Horizons in Trust

For as much as we now know about what it takes to build trust, we are aware that there is so much more to learn. In particular, we are curious about how trust is built in cultures outside the United States, and how building trust varies for different stakeholder groups.

We have yet to conduct research on the differences on how trust is built and lost across cultures. Our studies are based on data from businesses and organizations within the United States. We have both lived and worked in many countries (more than fifty between the two of us) and our experience is that culture and trust are inextricably intertwined.

In Japan, Ashley had to learn that nonverbal cues can be more important than the words used in a meeting (surprising for the American who is used to speaking her mind). For example, prolonged silence during a meeting could be a social buffer to indicate disagreement (sometimes accompanied by the sound made when you suck air in between your teeth) or it could be positive, indicating "I like what you're saying and I'm thinking about it." This is also a culture where researchers traditionally need to use longer Likert-type scales (for example, 1–9 instead of

1–7) because Japanese respondents do not traditionally choose the end-points of these scales. This could have significant implications for both how transparency is valued, and what it means. In Japan, it can be impolite to share one's thoughts with American-style candor. Note that this is the complete opposite of the Dutch, who believe that anything that can be said should be said, and directly. This is considered transparent, not rude (more on this in Chapter 9).

Amelia spent almost two years working in the Middle East, where she learned that no real business happens until many cups of tea have been poured. She learned a lot about the fact that trust comes only after relationships have been built. As we research trust globally, this might imply that we can expect to see trust grow at varying rates.

Cultures even think of cleanliness differently. During Ashley's first weeks living in Australia, she was baffled by some of the signs in women's bathrooms, which were pictures advising people not to stand on a toilet seat. Why did Australians feel the need to point this out? As it turns out, China is one of the largest sources of permanent immigrants in Australia.[109] In China, sharing a toilet seat with a stranger is considered unsanitary, and many of the public toilets are squatting toilets (actually holes in the ground where you squat over the hole), which are considered more sanitary. While this probably won't make it into our trust measurement platform, it does illustrate how cultural values shift norms, which need to be accounted for in measuring trust.

In addition to understanding cultural differences, we would also like to spend more time understanding how trust is built with different stakeholder groups.

Government

There is limited trust in government,[110] and the Biden administration has signaled a commitment to improving experience and building trust.[111] Still, the U.S. government in some ways is more constrained than ever, and has different responsibilities, all of which require a deeper look. For example, in our original government benchmarking study, there was a stark difference between trust in the federal government versus trust in major government agencies, like the Departments of Veterans Affairs, Health and Human Services, and the Treasury. In terms of trust, the sum of the parts (individual agencies) was 57 percent better than the score of the whole (the federal government). As the government and government agencies continue to build trust with Americans, we hypothesize that integrity will become a critical attribute of humanity.

NGOs and Nontraditional Business Models (Co-ops, B-Corps, and Trade Organizations)

Although we worked with the Center for Women and Enterprise (see Chapter 10), we'd like to continue to further our thinking on how the Four Factors can be applied to NGOs and other nontraditional business models, all of which have different priorities, purposes, needs, and stakeholders.

Investors, Shareholders, and Boards

We'd like to spend time understanding in more detail trust from a shareholder perspective, and how companies might improve trust with investors, shareholders, and board members by using the Four Factors.

Regulators

No matter what type of organization, everyone has to follow the law. Maintaining trust with regulators is a critical part of virtually any business or organization. It remains to be seen how trust in regulation itself appears in a study. For example, it might be similar to the federal government. People often say they don't like regulation, but they count on OSHA, the SEC, and other agencies, whose mission it is to protect the public.

Taking a page out of Adam Grant's book *Think Again*, we remain open minded about what future research on the Four Factors will reveal in diverse cultures and with different stakeholders. Now we want to turn our attention to the practical actions that you as a leader can take to build trust with the humans you call customers and workers.

The "How-to" of Trust ———————————

n Part I, we defined trust and demonstrated the importance of measuring, predicting, and acting to build trust. We shared with you the Four Factors that drive trust and how they come together in an HX TrustID score for customers and workers. We also introduced the clusters of the most and least trusted organizations, as well as how building trust varies for customers and for members of the workforce. We hope we have given you a broad understanding of how organizations win and lose trust, as well as a compelling set of reasons to invest in earning trust.

In Part II, we will turn to the practical actions leaders can take to build trust. Everything an organization or an individual does can contribute to either growing or eroding trust. Trust us—this is a good thing. We'll start in Chapter 9 by sharing a pragmatic approach for using the HX TrustID to build better human experiences, and we'll let you in on how we've been doing this in our own organization. We'll also share how we've grown and evolved our own leadership philosophies based on what we've learned about trust.

In Chapters 10-15 we'll explore six organizational areas that are typically associated with executing against and protecting the organization's growth agenda (see Figure P2.1.) Don't get us wrong, this is not to say that other functions aren't important. To the contrary, all functions are required for building trust. To state some obvious examples: legal departments must follow regulations (and the law); financial accounts need to add up; and risk functions must ensure compliance. These functions are table stakes to organizations staying in business, and indeed, building trust. For the purpose of this book, we will focus largely on the areas that must earn trust to drive growth.

In Part I, we demonstrated that we have both a deep curiosity for, and some hard-earned expertise in, the topics of trust and the human experience. However, there are critical business issues that fall outside our wheelhouse. That is why we are very grateful to have had the opportunity to collaborate with functional experts whom we admire both inside and outside our organization. We hope you enjoy learning from them as much as we did about what it takes to build the kind of trust that drives measurable results.

Building trust requires an enterprise-wide approach

Executive Leadership

Set strategy & lead by example

Cybersecurity

Safeguard against threats

Sustainability & Equity

Steward brand's collective consciousness

HX TRUSTID

Operations & Technology

Deliver the brand's promise

Marketing & Experience

Communicate and guide the brand's promise

Talent & Human Capital

Foster top talent experience

Figure P2.1

Once you finish Chapter 9, you might choose to skip around between the organizational chapters, starting with your own specialty. You can also learn about the challenges and strategies of adjacent specialties. We have written each chapter to read independently, though we do recommend you read them all. Building trust across an organization is an interdependent, holistic journey. The more you know about your colleagues' trust challenges, the better you will be able to take that journey together.

CHAPTER 9

How to Build Trust

In this chapter:

- How you can build trust as an individual
- How we are building trust with our teams
- Getting your organization started on a trust journey

Think about the last time you just knew that trust had been broken, either with your customers or with your workforce. Now think about what you did through trial and error (just like we used to do) to rebuild trust. In this chapter, we aim to make trust-building less of a guessing game.

We hope you will begin to measure trust using the HX TrustID, and, more importantly, we hope you will take the time to invest in trust-building actions both internally and externally. Our aim is to empower you to do this over time, improving trust scores and reporting progress to ensure accountability. We'll share the steps we have used and refined for more than a decade to build trust outcomes with our teams and our customers. But we will start with how you as a leader can build trust as an individual.

115

How You Can Build Trust as an Individual

Whatever your specialty or level of leadership, there are ways to get a trust movement underway—to conceive a trust ambition, design and pilot a practice, and change the way you're working. Even if you can't get a large trust practice going, at least you can make trust part of your own leadership philosophy and how you show up every day. We approach this ourselves in ways that are consistent with our workstyles and temperament. While we built the HX TrustID measurement system to help organizations build trust, we recognize that organizations are collections of humans. With this in mind, we can—and have—applied the HX TrustID to individuals, starting with ourselves.

For example, Ashley's leadership ambition is to build trust and earn loyalty—and she wants to leave people with more energy than she takes. She is driven and curious. She knows that relationships are built on empathy, vulnerability, and understanding. Ashley relies on the Four Factors to guide her choices, to deliver significant growth for clients, and to earn followership with her colleagues. Here is an excerpt from Ashley's leadership philosophy:

- Be Human: I strive to cultivate an inclusive practice. I strive to demonstrate empathy, kindness, and vulnerability. I will value and respect people as individuals regardless of background, identity, or beliefs.

- Be Transparent: I aim to be like the Dutch. Transparency is so intrinsic to Dutch culture that there is a word for it—*bespreekbaarheid*—which roughly means that everything can and should be talked about.

- Be Capable: I endeavor to create long-term solutions and improvements that work through collaboration and innovation. Progress happens when we are courageous, skillful, and look to change things for the better.

- Be Reliable: I will take ownership and action to deliver consistently and dependably on the promises I make.

To hold herself accountable, Ashley makes her leadership philosophy public to her teammates. (See Figure 9.1.) She seeks feedback from her leaders, her peers, and her direct reports to understand what she is doing well and where she has opportunity to grow. For example, humanity for Ashley has meant intentionally slowing down (did we mention that Ashley moves and speaks quickly?) to make sure everyone is on the same page. In working with Amelia, it's meant sharing out loud how both might feel about the latest round of late-night edits.

Ashley's leadership philosophy

BE HUMAN
I strive to cultivate an inclusive practice. I strive to demonstrate empathy, kindness, and vulnerability. I will value and respect people as individuals regardless of background, identity, or beliefs.

BE TRANSPARENT
I aim to be like the Dutch. Transparency is so intrinsic to Dutch culture that there is a word for it—*bespreekbaarheid*—which roughly means that everything can and should be talked about.

BUILD TRUST
EARN LOYALTY

BE CAPABLE
I endeavor to create long-term solutions and improvements that work through collaboration and innovation. Progress happens when we are courageous, skillful, and look to change things for the better.

BE RELIABLE
I will take ownership and action to deliver consistently and dependably on the promises I make.

Figure 9.1

Amelia is passionate about elevating the human experience, and she believes that leaders need to find ways to humanize themselves. As a leader responsible for making the "tough calls," it can be challenging to share a more human side. To show up as more human with her practice, Amelia created "Joy Day." Starting in the earliest darkest days of the pandemic in 2020, Amelia sends an email to her entire practice every Wednesday titled "Happy Joy Day," in which she shares anything at work, in her family, or in the world that brought her joy that week. (See Figure 9.2.) The team replies with their own joyful news. It can be as simple as a picture of a puppy romping around, as profound as welcoming a new child into the world, or as impactful as recognizing a team member's great work. Some weeks she has to dig deep to find joy. Other weeks there is an abundance of joy. But in this way, Amelia puts humanity front and center every week. That is why her leadership philosophy is "People grow and become their best selves when you believe in them and love them."

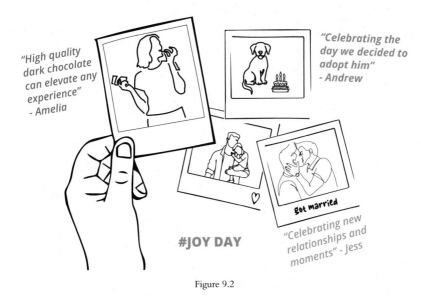

Figure 9.2

As you consider your own leadership style and the journey to earning trust, we'll remind you that we started working together with a trust deficit. But our mutual dedication to building trust in organizations to elevate the human experience drove us to be accountable for building our own trusted relationship.

How We Are Building Trust with Our Teams

Would you be willing to use software from a company that doesn't use their own product? Or would you want to fly on an airline whose CEO regularly takes private jets? Using your own product is a testament to how valuable you think it is. At Deloitte, we are working not only to measure ourselves using the HX TrustID, but to invest in earning even higher trust with our clients and workforce by analyzing the data so that we can continue on our own trust journey. While there are other metaphors to describe this approach, we like to think of it as "drinking our own champagne." Cheers!

Investing in building trust is not new for Deloitte. What is new is taking a scientific approach to measuring and building trust through pilots. We use the HX TrustID to measure how much our global priority accounts trust us. Trust scores are shared with account leaders. They are also used to inform new client offerings and programs that can help to build trust. Our methodology is being used to inform our new go-to-market strategy, including the experience we aim to create for our clients. We have also begun using our measurement platform to understand areas of strength and opportunities to build trust for our own workforce. Here is an example of what we have been doing with our workers.

First, we started with our talent trust ambition. We aspire to have our workers be our most powerful brand advocates. We must earn this advocacy by delivering talent experiences that build trust. These experiences are informed by a deep understanding of our worker needs, emotions, and motivations.

Second, we set out to build a robust understanding of our people. We ran a series of AI-powered focus groups with 1,600 of our Deloitte professionals, across all of our main business functions. We also ran over twenty ethnographic interviews (unstructured, human-led interviews designed to uncover what people do and think) with individuals across the satisfaction spectrum—both public promoters of the Deloitte culture and those at risk for low engagement—to uncover talent motivations and lived experiences. As is often the case with research, these early rounds helped us revamp our annual talent experience survey, which goes out to over 150,000 of our colleagues across the organization.

What did we find? Deloitte's HX TrustID scores are highest for humanity and capability. As a large organization, Deloitte has more work to do on transparency, followed by reliability. (See Figure 9.3.) That's not an uncommon problem in a privately owned organization with a long culture of carefully guarding confidential client information. Moreover, we also feel the effects of the talent scramble (we'll talk about this more in Chapter 13). Our business is growing rapidly and we're hiring at the same pace. As such, we have an unprecedented number of people who are either in new roles or new to Deloitte. Trust takes time to build, and, with less time, we need to be more intentional about transparency and reliability to earn trust more quickly.

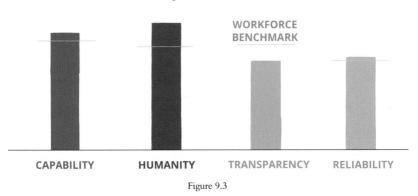

Deloitte workforce HX TrustID scores

WORKFORCE BENCHMARK

CAPABILITY   HUMANITY   TRANSPARENCY   RELIABILITY

Figure 9.3

We believe there is always more work to do on all Four Factors, but following our own advice about where we might have the biggest feasible impact, we started with transparency. Here are a few early transparency actions we are piloting:

- If we want to be more transparent, why not start with the talent data itself? The Talent Experience team created an open dialogue with leaders by developing deep insights from the annual talent survey that were action-oriented and explained those insights, in lieu of simply sharing reports on raw data. Leaders reported having a clearer understanding of focus areas and successes. The Talent team also set up the Talent Experience Network, a team of representatives from all areas of our businesses and at all career levels, to share and validate insights with the workforce, and to provide a channel for continuous input. This was the first time Deloitte had done this. As a result, Deloitte consultants have shared that this effort makes them feel heard and that their survey responses and personal experiences are not just being sent into some void. In addition to working towards greater transparency, this demonstrates humanity and empathy.

- Of course, just sharing the data isn't enough. The team is also creating solutions to close the transparency gaps. Deloitte professionals have the opportunity to be involved in tackling the solutions as a team, so more people can get engaged in creating the solutions to the trust gaps described. That last action honors our principle that, in order to be trusted, you have to demonstrate trust (more on this in Chapter 13). We are demonstrating trust by bringing our professionals into solution development.

- Lastly, Deloitte made a point of sharing, both internally and externally, our first ever transparency report on diversity, equity, and inclusion (DE&I). We'll talk more in depth about this choice and the outcomes in the next chapter, but this is an important step in promoting transparency and creating accountability for workforce DE&I objectives.

Next, we focused on our other "work to do" factor: reliability. We know that leaders' behaviors, norms, and ways of working have a direct impact on our workers' experience. Our talent research tells us that a single leader has the power to change one worker's trajectory and build long-lasting trust. At the same time, inconsistent or unreliable leadership behaviors create negative sentiment and fracture trust. In an organization of Deloitte's size and complexity, consistency can be difficult to achieve. So we set out to understand, define, measure, and provide formal learning opportunities. Deloitte established a leading-edge educational institute designed to set a consistent standard for supporting growth-oriented and inclusive professionals who can lead and thrive in the future of work, centered around building trust and elevating experience.

Our ambition is to develop holistic, human leaders who build trust through the Four Factors. As we write this, the wide-ranging work is just getting started. As we would for a client, we are starting with a multidimensional research approach. We asked ourselves, what does it mean to be a leader at Deloitte? What does a "distinctively Deloitte" leader look like? What are the leadership norms, behaviors, and ways of working that make our professionals feel an emotional sense of trust as well as a desire to continue to work with a leader who is able to tune in when she receives a message from them?

To answer these questions, the talent team will use a variety of research techniques, including ethnographic research, focus groups, pulse surveys, external research on best practices, and our existing talent research data. Then, through human equity-centered design methodologies, they will develop concepts for our leaders to shape and deliver these behaviors. Over time, they will measure the program's effect on trust scores and look for patterns that suggest new insights.

At Deloitte, establishing reliability with our workforce is a meaningful way to differentiate ourselves in today's complex, dynamic, and shifting environment. Strong trust from workers can make the organization more adaptive to the dynamic forces of the marketplace. As we become more trusted, we can quickly and positively change. A trusting workforce will create more trust with our clients.

Getting Your Organization Started on a Trust Journey

Our approach to building trusted brands is similar to how we build customer or workforce experiences. First, start with your **trust ambition**: what are you trying to achieve? **Gather data** to know where you are today and to target where you want to be in the future. Use these insights to **innovate on actions** and create small or larger moments to build trust. Prioritize your actions, and then pilot trust-building projects. And just as we shared in our own experiences above, learn as you go. Finally, **scale strategically** what's working and **measure the impact**. We call these steps an organization's *Trust Experience Engine*. (See Figure 9.4.)

Set Trust Ambition

What does it mean to be trusted in your organization? Each organization should have a well-articulated trust ambition that supports its purpose.[112] Articulating a trust ambition is important because it enables the humans in the organization to work collectively and collaboratively towards a shared future. This collective ambition should come before any individual or functional goals, helping to drive prioritization and alignment across the entire organization.

An organization's trust ambition should be aspirational, and it should be easily and succinctly explained to all stakeholders. We like to think of it as within sight, but just out of reach. Sometimes you may have to squint, but you should always be able to see it. For example, *The Wall Street Journal*'s ambition is "to be the world's most trusted source of news, data, and analysis to help people make decisions." This ambition led the *Journal* to create a framework and a set of principles that will guide future actions. Consider how the *Journal* has maintained complete independence in its news division: WSJ's clear separation between news and opinion helps ensure impartiality in its news reporting and freedom of perspective in its opinion pieces. The *Journal* also maintains separation between the newsroom and other functions to ensure integrity and build reader trust, by ensuring that journalists are not influenced by the profit-driven pressures of advertising, sales, and marketing departments. CEO Almar Latour states,

> *Each organization should have a well-articulated trust ambition that supports its purpose.*

The Trust Experience Engine

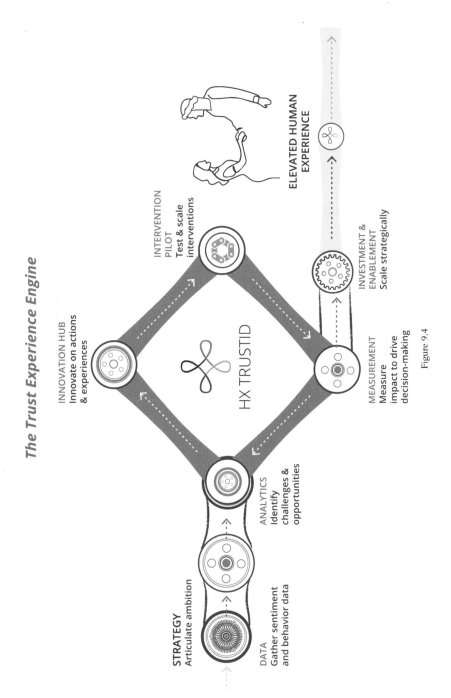

Figure 9.4

"At Dow Jones and *The Wall Street Journal*, we are responsible for earning the trust of our readers every day. We are committed to providing the tools needed to help differentiate high-quality, fact-based news and analysis from misinformation."

Like a strategy, a trust ambition will be unique to your organization. Goals like financial performance and customer loyalty are metrics, but not ambitions in and of themselves. So, how do you go about setting an ambition? There's no right or wrong answer, but one of our favorite ways to get started is to conduct what we call a "Trust Ambition Lab." We pull together a diverse group of C-suite leaders, and we spend a day together. Typically, we start with an exercise designed to challenge orthodoxies (as discussed in Chapter 8), and we agree on which organizational orthodoxies need to be "flipped" to achieve the ambition. We encourage participants to think about the "Art of the Possible," taking inspiration from other organizations to bolster aspirational ambition setting. Next, we spend time identifying uncertainties to be evaluated through research, focusing on what would need to be true to feel confident about the ambition. We then spend several hours charting the course ahead, considering a portfolio of trust building initiatives. We align on action items and general timelines to build out an initial roadmap.

Once your organization defines its trust ambition, you might consider setting very specific HX TrustID targets to underpin your ambition (if you don't yet have this data, don't worry; you can collect it in the next step). Note that the ambition itself must be shared and reinforced through measurement to ensure that all groups are outlining how their processes, systems, and capabilities work towards achieving this ambition. We'll share more on how to execute throughout this chapter and in the chapters to come.

Gather Data

Building trust starts with a deep understanding of your humans. Of course, your first step should be to gather HX TrustID scores. We also encourage investment in data and insights gathering to enable a rich, human-centric view of both trust opportunities and challenges. To that end, we encourage exploring both evaluative and generative research methods.

Evaluative research (for example, a quantitative online survey to understand usage habits) is a systematic study of an existing solution or issue. A car rental company might use quantitative research to understand how their customers choose between available providers when booking a trip. Generative research, like an ethnographic study of how customers behave on vacation, is useful for exploring human issues that don't yet have a specific solution. For instance, the same company might want to understand how vacationers who didn't choose to rent a car get around on their trip. In simplistic terms, evaluative research enables us to understand *what* people do, while generative research helps us to understand *why* people do what they do.

It is important to understand and track insights within the context of a person's journey, which starts *before* they engage with you or your organization. If we stick with the same rental car example, this journey might start as people start thinking about their next vacation. Conducting evaluative and generative research with people throughout their trip will help you to identify the *Moments that Matter*. *Moments that Matter* (MTMs) are those touchpoints along the journey that disproportionately drive value for the individual and the organization. They may be pain points (for example, long lines at the rental pickup counter can be a hassle) or joyful moments (such as receiving an unexpected upgrade to a convertible) that significantly affect the customer's relationship with your organization. You can think through potential options for improving MTMs, and we suggest prioritizing MTMs and target initiatives based on what will create the most value for the customer and for your organization. You should estimate the benefits of intervening, and then select the most effective actions that get you closest to total possible benefit without overwhelming the organization. The rule of thumb is that you want to find the 20 percent of initiatives that can get you 80 percent of the benefit (the old 80/20 rule of Pareto Analysis).

Metrics architecture

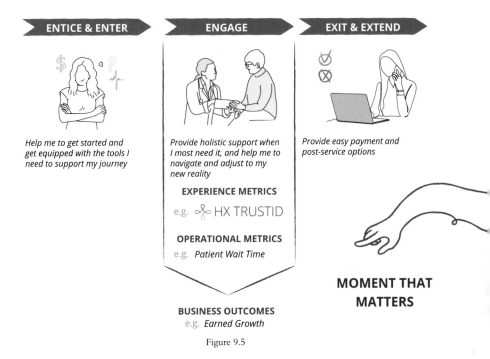

Figure 9.5

Once you identify those moments for your customers and workers, you then define the experiential and operational metrics aligned to each moment. Operational metrics are what you did (such as a car upgrade). Experiential metrics are how the person *felt* about it (perhaps surprised and delighted). Chances are good that you already measure some part of your customer and workforce experience. These metrics will help you unlock the insights that build trust. (See Figure 9.5.) Ongoing tracking here is critical in order to create a real-time view into opportunities, challenges, and outcomes.

The next steps are to innovate on potential actions you might take to build trust, prioritize what to test, and evaluate effectiveness.

Innovate on Actions

Once you have a rich picture of the MTMs, you can weigh the trade-offs of what will have the biggest potential impact relative to the level of investment required (time, capability, dollars). Start small by creating prototypes to test and run pilots, which will help you evaluate impact in a controlled setting. For our rental car example, this could take the form of piloting an automated check-in process in one or two locations where the customer can go straight to choosing from a line of vehicles. When the pilots produce the desired impact (sometimes after several rounds of modification), the new check-in process can be scaled to all relevant locations.

We always recommend running even a small project like a scientific experiment. Remember, building trust is both an art and a science. Start with a hypothesis that you want to test and then design and conduct an experiment to test that hypothesis. (In causation, the metrics move because of the pilot intervention you implemented. In correlation, the metrics move in the same direction, but may be caused by something else.) When possible, set up a control group so that you can measure the relative impact to inform whether the interventions you create are making a measurable, positive difference.

A good way to prioritize could be to start where you have a critical target audience with neutral or low trust. For example, an airline may have created strong trust with their most frequent flyers, but it may not be as trusted by those who travel less often. Upon evaluating the gap in more detail, perhaps the airline learns that the trust deficit is most severe in the New York area for parents traveling with small children. The HX TrustID might show a low level of humanity, driven by the feeling that the airline's priorities (such as keeping planes full or tiered-price ticketing) outweigh parents' concerns (such as family seating or hassle-free boarding). Knowing all of this, the airline could pilot a program for families traveling from JFK airport targeted towards meeting some of these needs. The airline could intervene with a set of families in one terminal on a handful of specific routes. Then they could compare the results with the operational, experiential, and financial metrics of the families who weren't included in the pilot to determine if the program produced the expected results. This would help to inform choices about which family programs warranted further investment.

Sometimes it's not possible or even desirable to run a scientific experiment. For example, when managing a worker trust deficit, testing a solution with some stakeholders and not others could lead to unintentional bias. In healthcare, providing medical treatment for some patient groups and not others may be unethical. The most important thing to get right, regardless of whether or not it's a controlled experiment, is to track trust scores and adjust based on outcomes.

Another challenge we would like to touch on is the notion of behavior change. We have been asked, "Is it ethical to try and influence what people do?" Well, sure. When a beverage company releases a new flavor, they want to encourage people to try it, and the company may offer a promotion (such as two for the price of one) to tempt customers into sampling the new product. Offering a coupon is more than a free drink. It is also an attempt to influence behavior. In and of itself, this is neither unethical nor unscrupulous. What we are proposing isn't a game of manipulation, and it certainly isn't about making empty promises (such as greenwashing or false advertising). Organizations win loyalty based on making and keeping good promises. The goal of trust pilots is to drive mutual advantage by making and delivering on the *right* promises. Leaders shift their behavior in order to shift the behavior of their workers and customers in a way that creates a mutual value exchange.

> *Organizations win loyalty based on making and keeping good promises.* **The goal of trust pilots is to drive mutual advantage by making and delivering on the right promises.**

Scale Strategically and Measure the Impact

Once you have established the validity of the pilot project and interventions, you can determine how far and fast you want to scale. Here we would take a lesson from successful organizational technology rollouts, which use pilot projects and use-cases to anticipate roadblocks and demonstrate value. A series of small wins can prove the value of the trust practices at a larger scale. It makes a strong argument for rolling out the practice to the whole organization.

We don't mean to imply that running and scaling these pilots is easy. There are numerous challenges that we aren't specifically addressing, such as the challenge of getting data, the cross-functional collaboration that is often required, or the need to adapt operations or supply chains. Some solutions are just harder than others and require backend technology builds. External supply chain challenges can disrupt an attempt to overcome a capability deficit. In the auto industry, if your suppliers can't deliver enough chips, you can't make enough cars, and that creates a downstream effect on customer perceptions of capability, warranted or not.

In our experience, some of the quickest wins come from observing the effects of *how* you communicate with people and what access you're giving them to information. Transparency and humanity, though they might require a change in cultural norms, are good places to look for a win. Because trust is a multifunctional practice, it's best to start scaling with internal partners. Marketing can help communicate your trust promise. Bigger projects might enlist the help of Talent, Technology, and others, as we will describe in the following chapters. It's critical that the pilot have the interest and support of the C-suite, because the executive team ultimately sets the bar for how an organization builds trust.

Over time, your commitment to building trust, either as an individual or as a brand, can drive practical action that will change your organization, your relationships, and (we hope) you for the better. In these next few chapters, we aim to kickstart your journey to building trust, where, function by function, we dive into trust challenges and principles.

CHAPTER 10
Executive Leadership

In this chapter:
- The CEO's role in building trust
- Trust challenges faced by CEOs
- Principles of trust-building for CEOs

The CEO's Role in Building Trust

We have a lot of empathy for CEOs these days. The work itself is hard, and the weight of the responsibility and public gaze can be heavy. In a world of information everywhere and any-time, CEOs are responsible not only for their own actions, but they face the potential consequences of every product recall, customer service complaint, poorly worded internal email, or badly executed advertising campaign. Anything any employee, customer, or partner says or does could make headlines and erode trust. And it all stops with the CEO, regardless of the type of organization—whether publicly traded, privately held, for profit or not-for-profit.

Not surprisingly,

96%

of surveyed CEOs rate building and maintaining trust as a high priority. And yet many organizations treat trust a bit like a fire alarm.

Not surprisingly, 96 percent of surveyed CEOs rate building and maintaining trust as a high priority.[113] And yet many organizations treat trust a bit like a fire alarm. Some leaders assume everything is fine and only become concerned when the alarm sounds. A recent study on the impact of negative trust events for large companies found that a negative trust-related event eroded market cap by up to 56 percent.[114] With this kind of consequence, CEOs cannot afford *not* to prioritize trust.

To gain insight into what it means to navigate trust in these challenging times, we sat down with two CEOs we admire from both the for-profit and not-for-profit worlds. The first is the leader of the largest professional services organization in the United States, our own Deloitte CEO, Joe Ucuzoglu. Joe is actively engaged with clients across multiple sectors and frequently speaks about building a culture of inclusivity, the future of work, the evolving nature of leadership, and the role that businesses must play in leading society. In addition to being a CEO, Joe is a husband, father, and avid sports enthusiast. He proudly displays a football, a basketball, *and* a soccer ball in his office, visible just over his shoulder in his video conference window. We also sat down with Gabrielle "Gaby" King Morse, the CEO of the not-for-profit Center for Women and Enterprise (CWE). The Center for Women and Enterprise is dedicated to helping women business owners launch and grow their businesses. Gaby has been CEO since 2019, and she is a passionate advocate for the economic empowerment of women. In addition to her role leading CWE, Gaby and her family enjoy life as "suburban farmers," taking care of ducks and chickens, and producing what Gaby assures us is the best pesto thirty miles west of Boston. To get to know Joe's and Gaby's perspectives on the role the CEO plays in building trust, we should tell you a little bit about the history of their respective organizations.

In 1845 William Welch Deloitte opened an accounting firm, Deloitte, in London. For much of its existence, Deloitte focused on accounting and auditing, as "the protectors of trust in capital markets." A few years after opening the company, William Deloitte became the first independent accountant of a public company when he took on the role for the Great Western Railway. The intent of his appointment was to "inspire general confidence" in the railroad's management at a time when its stock was faltering. Several years later in 1856, the city of London asked Deloitte to investigate fraud at the Great Northern Railway (GNR), arguably the most high-profile case of his career. GNR insisted that Deloitte's probe be conducted swiftly and cheaply, but William Deloitte held his ground, arguing that GNR could not have both, while also getting a complete and accurate audit. As a result, GNR abruptly halted the audit and fired Deloitte. In upholding a high standard of integrity, William Deloitte demonstrated that his word could be trusted—the most important thing that can be said about a professional services advisor. Trust remains the foundation of the organization's values and governance today, as well as its commitment to an equitable workplace. As Joe often says, "Our credibility is our ultimate asset. If Deloitte says something, people expect it to be right." Joe spent the large majority of his career at Deloitte because of that premise—the incredible opportunity to be a part of an organization helping clients solve their most complex problems, and the vital responsibility and privilege of upholding trust and confidence in the capital markets.

Originally founded on the principles of micro-lending to support women entrepreneurs and by extension their communities, the Center for Women and Enterprise has been "lifting up women who lift up the world" for more than twenty-five years. CWE has provided support, training, and tools to nearly 60,000 women primarily of low-income backgrounds. A third of these women are racially and ethnically diverse, and almost 20 percent are unemployed. Gaby shared that, when she started as CEO, she was excited to focus on how to unlock greater economic empowerment for women. Before joining CWE, she had been working for ten years at uAspire, a college affordability organization focused on the economic empowerment of students. Taking on the role of CEO for CWE aligned her passion for economic equity with her experience in building high-functioning leadership teams focused on social impact.

In the fall of 2021, Fortune and Deloitte surveyed more than a hundred leading CEOs, asking them how they saw their jobs. Responses ranged from "Chief Clarity officer" to "one part coach, one part philosopher, one part execution leader." Joe told us that he sees himself as a "Trust Advocate."[115] Gaby said, as the CEO, one of her most important roles has been partnering with and coaching CWE's executive management to become an effective leadership team, and "trust is a huge part of that."

Trust Challenges Faced by CEOs

We identified three critical challenges CEOs face when trying to build trust:

- The evolving role of the CEO
- Many stakeholders with conflicting priorities
- Lack of accountability for purpose

The Evolving Role of the CEO

When we started talking about trust with Joe, he reminded us that the autocratic, all-knowing CEO sitting comfortably in the corner office issuing edicts is a thing of the past. As he put it, "If it was outdated before, the pandemic put the command-and-control CEO completely behind us, opening the door to a new generation of leadership and new expectations for the role." He elaborated, "Now, it's not about having all the answers, it's about being able to synthesize tremendous amounts of complex information and make sense of it with your stakeholders to help them see around corners."

At a time when trust in almost every institution has degraded, employees look to their own CEOs for credible and transparent information, particularly in unsettling times. The 2022 Edelman Trust Barometer reveals that business is more trusted than NGOs, government, and media. "My CEO" is seen as the third most trusted source of information (as opposed to "other" CEOs which are seventh), behind scientists and co-workers.[116] As Joe put it, the CEO is expected to be a credible "source of trust as well as a source of optimism." The way a CEO does that is by "constantly re-earning trust." When things were changing rapidly, even daily, during the pandemic, Joe told us it was important to offer credible information that wasn't sugarcoated. He was aware that as CEO he was expected to have direct and transparent conversations, not always telling people what they wanted to hear, but what they needed to hear. Only then could he pivot to a voice of optimism that would not ring hollow.

Many Stakeholders with Conflicting Priorities

There have always been a diverse number of stakeholder voices—from shareholders to board members, employees, clients/customers, regulators, and local officials—that a CEO must consider. The fact that there are a lot of stakeholders is not new. What is new is that the balance of power and priorities a CEO must focus on are shifting. The CEO used to have a clear hierarchy of needs to serve, ultimately accountable to their board and shareholders to deliver on profit. Now, the CEO must build trust with competing stakeholders who don't always align on a shared goal, taking into account a much broader set of stakeholders. It was newsworthy in 2019 when the leaders of the Business Roundtable released a statement signed by 181 CEOs committed to leading their companies for the benefit of all stakeholders, not just shareholders. The statement called for companies to deliver value to customers, employees, suppliers, and communities by behaving ethically and fairly. The Roundtable's members committed themselves and their companies to transparency, diversity and inclusion, and sustainability, enabling the success of communities to create economic prosperity for all.[117] Former IBM CEO and Business Roundtable member

Ginni Rometty said at the time, "Society gives each of us a license to operate. It's a question of whether society trusts you or not."[118]

CEOs must address conflicting demands, making decisions that can be seen as ideal by some stakeholder groups, and wrong by others. This dilemma—the trade-off between cost and stability—is one example of the many faced by CEOs.

Gaby offered another example of tradeoffs that a CEO for a not-for-profit faces between a funder and the employees of CWE. "If I have a funder who wants to give money for a new program, but my staff tell me they're not sure how we'll pull this off with our current capacity, I'll go back to the funder and say, 'We love what you want to do, and it aligns with our strategic plan, but we would need more staffing capacity to make it happen.'"

She continued, "I prioritize staff well-being. Many organizations make a commitment to an unsustainable definition of dedication, which has the capacity to harm an organization and its people in the long term. People think dedication is going above and beyond all the time for your clients. What ends up happening is higher staff burnout and turnover. When we need to rely on junior or less-experienced staff, we are not as efficient, and we're not giving our clients the best. Overworking in the name of dedication is such a short-sighted view. I see it at not-for-profits all the time."

When Gaby realized a member of her staff hadn't taken vacation in the past three months, she informed her that taking vacation was not an option, it was a requirement. She reminded her team members, "We have to make sure we deliver to our clients to the best of our ability, and you burning out isn't going to help anybody. You are an example to your staff and taking care of yourself will have an important positive impact for your colleagues and for the women entrepreneurs we support."

Lack of Accountability for Purpose

Purpose[119]—the "why" in the eyes of its stakeholders—is foundational to any organization, providing the rationale for why the organization exists, what problems it solves, and the role it plays in society. CEOs often see themselves explicitly or implicitly as chief purpose officers in their organizations, whether or not they hire someone else with that title. One of the biggest challenges to leading an organization with purpose is the lack of accountability. As Joe shared, having a purpose-driven organization is only successful when leaders instill a sense of purpose "for the right reasons, not because you're trying to generate a headline," and then back those statements with action and accountability. Deloitte's 2021 research with *Fortune* found that 68 percent of CEOs surveyed planned to put more emphasis on corporate purpose as a way to attract and retain talent.[120] Yet, currently, 26 percent of leaders report their organization does not make it a priority to collect and report on purpose-related data, and 67 percent of leaders report their compensation is not tied to their organization's purpose priorities.[121] An organization's purpose is the best way to keep focused on long-term value and to navigate complex risks, making the organization more focused, resilient, and trustworthy. Nevertheless, delivering on the organization's purpose is not consistently measured, reported, or tied to compensation.

Gaby shared with us what being accountable to the organization's purpose means for CWE. "When I report to my board of directors, they want to know two things: First, how are we doing hitting our financial targets, just like investors in any company, and how are we delivering on our purpose. Delivering on our finances means nothing if the women that we support are not able to increase levels of economic empowerment." To that end, Gaby said, "It is crucial that women entrepreneurs have a seat at the table at every organizational level to share their feedback, their ideas, their challenges, and how CWE can work better on their behalf."

When we first introduced Gaby to the HX TrustID as a way of measuring how much CWE's customers and employees trust CWE to deliver on its purpose, she was enthusiastic. The interest was *not* because CWE had very high initial trust scores. Gaby and her leadership team were excited because they could start to see very clearly areas where they needed to focus on increasing trust among the women they work with every day. As Gaby said, "If we're not trusted by our most vulnerable clients, then that's where we need to focus. Only then will we have the greatest impact for all clients."

Principles of Trust-Building for CEOs

Much of the CEO's attention is focused on building and strengthening capability and reliability. Both are table stakes for driving growth and value for all stakeholders and are indispensable for earning trust in employees and customers. As a result, it's understandable that delivering those factors across the enterprise consumes a great deal of executive attention.

Our focus here is on two additional principles (beyond delivering on capability and reliability) for CEOs to help build trust:

- Set a clear trust ambition
- Serve as a role model for more "human leadership" traits

Set a Clear Trust Ambition

Building trust should be a CEO's top priority. To make that priority clear to their organizations, CEOs need to set goals around trust so that they can hold both themselves and their teams accountable. These goals are achieved through transparent measurement and reporting. Many leaders struggle with transparency because they worry misinterpretation could erode trust. Joe affirmed that the role of the CEO is to be transparent with context in ways that create accountability: "Trust does not mean providing a sense of certainty in an inherently uncertain environment. It is about being clear that you don't know everything and you're giving

> **Trust does not mean providing a sense of certainty in an inherently uncertain environment. It is about being clear that you don't know everything and you're giving the whole truth."**
>
> — *Joe Ucuzoglu, CEO of Deloitte U.S.*

the whole truth." The context matters. And accountability to and by stakeholders matters. Trust is earned when a CEO is able to help their stakeholders understand the holistic picture—good and bad—behind the data, information, or evidence they're sharing. This context can facilitate a better-informed decision-making process and help to set goals that will drive the most impact while holding leaders accountable.

As an example of delivering on a clear trust aspiration, Joe made the decision in 2021 to publish Deloitte's first ever transparency report on diversity, equity, and inclusion (DE&I). The Diversity, Equity, and Inclusion Transparency Report makes measurable commitments to increase the number of Black and Hispanic/Latinx professionals in the U.S. workforce by 50 percent. It also commits to increasing female representation in the U.S. to 45 percent by 2025. In equally significant cultural terms, it includes pledges to "Address inconsistencies in the talent experience so that Black, Hispanic/Latinx, non-binary, and LGBTQIA+ professionals feel they can be their authentic selves."[122]

Joe was aware from the outset that sharing this report represented a trade-off. On the one hand, it was a big step forward to declare transparently where the organization was with respect to its goals to foster equity and build trust. On the other hand, this kind of transparency could open up the organization to criticism or risk. As a result, there were a lot of different perspectives Joe needed to navigate about whether some of the information disclosed could be negatively received. Deloitte could say too much and say too little at the same time. The idea of "putting it all out there" made some stakeholders uneasy.

From Joe's perspective, the risk of sharing the information on DE&I transparently far outweighed the risks of saying nothing. Joe took this approach: He acknowledged where progress had happened too slowly and committed to holding himself and fellow executives accountable. "Our work is not done. Our organization must continue to acknowledge the reality of where we stand, and the progress we need to make internally and in our communities. We must be committed to a growing impact in the long term, well past fluctuations in the news cycle." He then went further, pivoting from transparency to accountability to build trust: "If you overly aggregate data, people think that you're trying to hide the uncomfortable stuff, whereas when you put it all out there you are reporting on where you are in DE&I *and* how you intend to improve, you gain credibility and build trust." This kind of transparency with specific measurable goals and timelines also allows for accountability both internally and externally, both of which lead to greater progress.

Serve as a Role Model for More "Human Leadership" Traits

We have seen again and again how important humanity is in helping organizations and leaders build trust. So the second principle is about serving as a role model for the rest of the organization as to what humble, vulnerable, authentic leadership looks, sounds, and acts like. This is a central pillar for Joe. "I am a big believer that people don't expect perfection. It's okay to be human and humans make mistakes. But your organization should be able to expect honesty and vulnerability. They want to know both what you got right and what you didn't get right. Most importantly, they want to know what you learned from it, and how you are going to do better moving forward."

Gaby shared with us a story of how she took a risk with a leadership team she managed at her previous organization that has forever changed how she leads and works with teams. "At an offsite retreat, we agreed to run an experiment and have my leadership team decide what my priorities and my goals should be for the next three months. While my team discussed, I went back to the retreat center to make dinner for all of us. They spent the next two hours creating my goals and my priorities.

❚❚ When you feel alone, you're not doing it right."
— Gaby Morse, CEO of Center for Women and Enterprise

I realized very quickly that they knew very well where I should spend my time, and when they showed me what they had created, I could see that there were things I had been focused on that I needed to let go of, delegate, or set aside to be effective."

Talk about humble leadership. What if every leader could have this experience with their team? "I like to say, 'When you feel alone, you're not doing it right,'" says Gaby. The relationship with your team has to be one of complete mutual trust in the workforce, underpinned by humanity. Gaby summed it up well: "It's a matter of trusting each other, and, at the same time, being completely trustworthy."

In the following chapters we'll turn our attention to another top priority for leaders around the globe: Sustainability and Equity.

CHAPTER 11
Sustainability and Equity

In this chapter:
- The role of sustainability and equity in building trust
- Trust challenges faced by sustainability and equity leaders
- Sustainability and equity principles for building trust

There is perhaps no issue more fundamental than the trust that each generation must have in the one that came before to create a sustainable future. Between us, we have five children and more than a dozen nieces and nephews. You better believe we are concerned about the future world they will inherit. And yet we are painfully aware that younger generations distrust that older generations will make good decisions for their future.

The concept of sustainable development was described by the 1987 Bruntland Commission Report as: "Development that meets the needs of the present without compromising the ability of future generations to meet their own needs."[123] UNESCO has built on this definition noting, "Sustainability is a paradigm for thinking about the future in which environmental, societal, and economic considerations are balanced in the pursuit of an improved quality of life."

Within this space, the acronym ESG has taken the world by storm, and in many cases has become synonymous with sustainability and equity overall. Environmental, social, and governance (ESG) refers to the three central factors of an organization's impact on society. "Environmental" describes an organization's total impact on the planet, including direct effects like pollution outputs or net-zero goals. "Social" explains how an organization treats people, both its workers and others, through actions like diversity programs, equity-centered policies, advocacy on social and political issues, and philanthropy. "Governance" concerns the internal mechanisms for compliance with laws and regulations as well as self-governance (such as anti-corruption rules and business ethics). Together, the three elements of ESG measure an organization's sustainability, equity, and overall impact across a full spectrum of social issues.[124]

To help us understand the relationship between sustainability, equity, and trust we called upon our friends and colleagues Chris Ruggeri and John Peto. Chris leads the Sustainability, Climate & Equity practice for our Risk and Financial Advisory team. Chris is also an urban gardener and often found in her backyard in Brooklyn or volunteering in a community garden as chair of Citizens Committee for New York City, a non-profit founded on the principal of improving opportunities for all New Yorkers. John leads Sustainability, Climate & Equity for our consulting practice in the U.S. We were surprised to learn that he has worked as a cattle farmer, commercial fisherman, journalist, and a recruiter—all jobs that have given him a rich perspective on people as well as the planet.

We also sought expertise from frontline experts, including Amy Weaver, the president and Chief Financial Officer for Salesforce, and Dr. Caroline Flammer, a professor of International and Public Affairs at Columbia University. Amy Weaver is responsible for balancing revenue growth with future investment and is a self-stated champion of sustainability. Weaver serves on the board of Habitat for Humanity and, as Ashley is quick to point out, is a fellow Wellesley alumna. Weaver is also a Bay Area mother of three boys and an avid traveler. Dr. Flammer is an expert in sustainable investing and the recipient of numerous awards. Her research examines how firms can enhance their long-term profitability by playing a critical role in addressing climate change, inequality, global health, and other grand challenges related to society and the natural environment. Dr. Flammer is also the chair of the academic advisory committee of the United Nations' Principles for Responsible Investment.

The Role of Sustainability and Equity in Building Trust

The practice of managing sustainability centers on the belief that purpose, including an organization's broader impact on society, and profit can and should mutually reinforce each other. That hasn't always been the case, however, and it's taken many years for this concept to fully take root. If we look back at organizations in the United States twenty years ago, most were oriented toward maximizing shareholder value. Nonprofits were fully focused on their individual missions.[125] Problems in the environment or society didn't register as corporate issues, and governance was mostly about complying with the law.

The practice of managing sustainability centers on the belief that purpose, including an organization's broader impact on society, and profit can and should mutually reinforce each other.

Fast forward to today: leaders who want their organizations to be trusted know they must address sustainability and equity concerns (as we discussed in the previous chapter, illustrated by the Business Roundtable statement). After all, can you trust a company that doesn't care about our environment, one that neglects the fundamental needs of human beings, or one that disregards the law? In a Deloitte 2022 study, 84 percent of respondents said they lose trust in consumer product organizations when their brands don't meet sustainability expectations.[126] Fifty-four percent of executives saw sustainability as the most important area for innovation in 2022. Nearly one in two consumer products companies (45 percent) are making significant investment in increasing their ESG reporting.[127] And customers are watching how organizations treat their employees. When an employer understands employees' needs and desires, and designs a human experience catered to their values, customers are 2.4 times more likely to rate them high on humanity.[128] Organizations who want to build trust must reflect on their relationship with the planet and its people. (See Figure 11.1.)

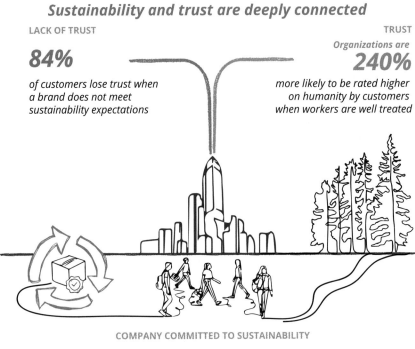

Sustainability and trust are deeply connected

LACK OF TRUST   TRUST

Organizations are

84%   **240%**

of customers lose trust when a brand does not meet sustainability expectations   *more likely to be rated higher on humanity by customers when workers are well treated*

COMPANY COMMITTED TO SUSTAINABILITY

Figure 11.1

And there are wide-ranging trust benefits that can result from a focus on sustainability. For example, stepping up your focus on sustainability will help attract the best talent, because in-demand workers want their employers to share their values, like a concern for the environment. Generation Z, who began graduating from college and entering the workforce in 2020, identify climate change and protecting the environment as their single largest concern.[129] People expect to work in a culture that respects humanity in the broadest possible terms: by treating workers fairly; by making progress on diversity, equity, and inclusion; and by disengaging with suppliers who abuse human rights, just to name a few. When top talent at leading tech firms staged walkouts to support #MeToo, they were telling companies to do better on an important equity issue. And they were demanding measurable progress.

More than half of executives indicated their sustainability efforts had a positive impact on revenue growth and overall company profitability.[130] Executives, especially CFOs, are taking notice. Salesforce CFO Amy Weaver says, "We have to focus on profit *and* sustainability performance and they don't have to be mutually exclusive. We like to take a holistic approach—we've found it's no longer enough to just develop great products and deliver profits. Integrating sustainability into our business strategy helps us ensure that we are living the values we were founded with twenty-three years ago."

The trust imperative for sustainability is even transforming some professions. For example, an attorney we know who leads the sustainability practice at a major law firm told us that, for most of his career, he saw his role as asking, "How do I keep my clients out of trouble?" This included lobbying against new health and safety regulations and defending companies against complaints of environmental harm. Now he sees his job as helping his clients "do the right thing." His point of view has undergone a nuanced but crucial shift. The new question he asks is: "How do I 'prove' my client is doing the right thing?" It does not lend itself to easy measurement, and stakeholders may have different definitions of doing the right thing. We discuss this and other challenges in the section to follow.

Trust Challenges Faced by Sustainability and Equity Leaders

One reason it's challenging to build trust with sustainability is because the way it's measured and reported through ESG is a relatively new domain. To start, ESG expertise is growing, but demand continues to outstrip supply. Broadening an organization's scope beyond profit to address the needs of multiple stakeholders is a balancing act. Finally, the world lacks global standards for measuring and reporting ESG, so comparisons between companies or industries are difficult. In this section we will discuss these three main challenges:

- Demand for ESG skills exceeds supply
- A long-term balancing act
- Missing reporting standards

Demand for ESG Skills Exceeds Supply

Many organizations are scrambling to satisfy rising public expectations around sustainability, and, as a result, the need for ESG expertise has accelerated past some organizations' ability to keep up. In fact, 70 percent of CFOs are concerned that ESG talent shortages will impede their ability to meet short-term goals.[131] A 2020 review of job descriptions by the CFO Institute found that 6 percent of investment jobs mentioned sustainability-related skills, while only 1 percent of investment professionals listed those skills in their LinkedIn profiles.[132] This challenge is especially acute in the finance industry, which has been rapidly transforming to show visible financial support for and investment in sustainability issues. For example, sustainable investments have grown rapidly over the last several years, and in 2020 totaled more than $35 trillion dollars, which represents nearly one-third of all assets under management.[133]

The talent supply shortage is due in part to how young the sustainability field is. Arizona State University lays claim to the first school of sustainability, opened in 2006. Now there are many major universities with sustainability programs that weave together sustainability, business, and engineering. Sustainability as a topic has also exploded in business schools. In 2021, the Wharton School of Business offered over fifty courses related to social impact. In September 2022, Stanford plans to launch a new school dedicated to "creating a future where humans and nature thrive in concert and in perpetuity."[134] We expect to see increasing levels of expertise in this domain, though experience can only be gained over time, which suggests that more senior and seasoned roles will remain challenging to fill.

A Long-Term Balancing Act

Twenty or thirty years ago, there was a fairly clear hierarchy of needs; organizations were ultimately accountable to their board and shareholders for delivering on shareholder value. Now, however, organizations need to consider how to drive profitable growth sustainably, while improving and protecting the environment, and building equity among all of their human stakeholders, not just their shareholders (though, shareholders care, too, as there is an increasing market for sustainability investment).

For us, this is a question of trust, which shouldn't come as a surprise. How can workers trust a company that doesn't invest in equitable social development? How will customers trust a company if it ignores its impact on the environment? How can shareholders confidently invest when trust among workers and customers is low? Increasingly, we expect to see that driving profit and a focus on sustainability are not, in fact, conflicting. John Peto told us, "Sustainability and trust are the closest of bedfellows. Transparently sharing progress against goals and keeping commitments will earn trust from stakeholders. And that trust will in turn generate loyalty from customers, partners, and workers. The opposite is also true. Failing to earn trust will generate skepticism and disbelief, making it even harder to accomplish the mission. Going further, authenticity of intent and deed matters. Everyone knows becoming fully sustainable is hard and progress will not always be smooth and perfect. Demonstrating seriousness of intent and real transparency is what sets the best apart."

There is already evidence that strong sustainability performance is linked to better financial performance, especially over the longer term.[135] And a sterling ESG record can be seen as an indicator of overall organizational health. Organizations with a high ESG rating are more resilient, tend to have stronger systems and governance, and are better at both navigating disruption and mitigating volatility. Research conducted by Bank

Organizations with a high ESG rating are more resilient, **tend to have stronger systems and governance, and are better at both navigating disruption and mitigating volatility.**

of America Merrill Lynch found that S&P companies with an ESG rating in the top quartile showed 5 percent volatility in earnings per share, while S&P companies in the bottom ESG rating quartile showed 25 percent volatility in earnings per share.[136] The same study showed that evaluating ESG ratings could have helped investors to avoid 90 percent of bankruptcies. Out of the seventeen bankruptcies in the S&P 500 from 2005 to 2015, fifteen were companies with poor environmental and social scores.[137]

Organizations who ignore sustainability also risk running afoul of the law and inviting shareholder activism. And sustainability issues can cost a lot of money. Just as deferred maintenance raises the eventual cost of fixing a road or bridge, deferred action on sustainability may require steep investment increases in the years to come. Most importantly, we know that sustainability issues can take a toll on financial performance; companies with sustainability-related issues can see a negative impact to stock prices for a year or longer.[138]

Does that mean that organizations should weigh in on all sustainability issues? According to HBS professor George Serafeim, organizations should focus on the sustainability issues that are strategically important for their business. An airline with a large carbon footprint should consider managing environmental impact. This same topic may be less relevant for a financial technology company, whose products and services don't have the same carbon impact. Serafeim writes, "The results are very consistent: firms making investments on material ESG issues outperform their peers in the future in terms of risk-adjusted stock price performance, sales growth, and profitability margin growth. In contrast, firms making investments on immaterial ESG issues have very similar performance to their peers suggesting that such investments are not value relevant on average."[139]

Of course, the challenge lies in understanding which investments are material. Many organizations don't understand the details behind what is required to decarbonize, and many still do not have the financial knowledge to support the business case for the type of investments required. This will continue to be an issue until talent supply catches up, and expertise in sustainability finance is more widely available.

We can be reasonably confident that 1) investing in sustainability is an important driver of trust for organizations, and 2) making investments in material sustainability issues of strategic importance to an organization correlates with better financial performance and lower volatility. The catch: This focus requires the ability to measure relative sustainability performance, and today a lack of standards and a lack of expertise present significant challenges to doing so effectively.

Missing Reporting Standards

To date, ESG reporting and disclosure in public markets has largely been based on an "honor system" without any type of third-party data verification or common standards consistently applied. As a result, many stakeholders remain skeptical of ESG data quality. Even the companies that have been tracking and reporting ESG data have not been doing so for very long, and it's questionable if ESG data across peer companies can really be compared apples to apples.

Dr. Flammer agrees that there is a fundamental challenge, saying, "Measurement is a big issue. In many countries, there is no mandatory disclosure requirement for nonfinancial information. That means that many companies around the world don't need to report their environmental and social performance. This lack of mandatory disclosure also comes with a lack of standardized disclosure. That is, companies may disclose this information voluntarily—but very often in a non-standardized fashion." This makes it hard for investors to compare social and environmental performance across companies, and for companies to benchmark themselves effectively against industry peers.

Measuring performance against ESG goals is also hard because many types of impact don't lend themselves to easy quantification. If racial and ethnic equity—a social and business goal—correlates with better corporate performance because of a more inclusive/motivated workforce, stakeholders will be interested in racial and ethnic equity KPIs. Unless well designed, however, those measurements are hard to track, easy to manipulate, and, therefore, difficult to quantify—which can ultimately impact trust.

We are starting to see progress in terms of standardization. At the 2021 COP26 conference in Glasgow, which is the annual UN climate change conference, the International Financial Reporting Standards Foundation trustees announced the formation of the International Sustainability Standards Board (ISSB). The ISSB will lay the foundation for consistent ESG reporting, potentially driving major progress in standardizing ESG reporting. The SEC has periodically evaluated regulation of climate change disclosures, and in March of 2021 invited public input on over a dozen questions regarding potential disclosure rules for public companies.[140]

In addition to regulatory action, we are also seeing a new industry emerge: ESG ratings. ESG ratings providers include MSCI ESG Research, Dow Jones Sustainability Index, Sustainalytics, Thomson Reuters ESG Research Date, Moody's Investors Services, and S&P Global, among others. However, each ratings provider has its own methodology, and as we write this there is not a clear market leader. How these ratings are used and by which organizations is also still evolving. For example, some financial institutions are starting to consider ESG ratings as part of their underwriting process for investment decision-making and as input into proxy voting. But it is still too early for standard industry practices to have emerged. We anticipate the industry to follow a typical adoption curve, in which a few players emerge as leaders, setting standards that are both well understood and more broadly adopted.

Sustainability and Equity Principles for Building Trust

Sustainability, equity, and trust are deeply connected. To build trust with key stakeholders, organizations must continue to invest in sustainability, equitable business practices, as well as ESG reporting. These efforts will also require a continued focus on the "G" in ESG, as well as the need to model corporate responsibility through the workforce. We'll discuss these principles:

- Commit, measure, and report transparently
- Deliver sustainability through the workforce

Commit, Measure, and Report Transparently

First, an organization must commit to sustainability and equity goals, measure progress, and be transparent about results. If only this were as simple as writing it down. The world is watching and is deeply invested in sustainability outcomes. Investors are increasingly looking at ESG data to inform their investment choices in publicly held companies. The more transparent companies are with their sustainability and equity programs, the more they will attract these investors.[141]

Salesforce is considered a leader in sustainability, delivering both growth and innovation alongside ethical and social responsibility.[142] Weaver emphasizes that measuring and reporting on sustainability is critical to accountability and trust with stakeholders: "We have the ability to drive resource allocation, transparency, and accountability for sustainability. Finance teams, in particular, can shine a spotlight on the metrics that demonstrate what is actually being achieved." When Weaver took the CFO seat, she saw the need to create a new role—EVP, ESG Finance—to ensure that ESG was front and center in the finance organization.

Workers, customers, and investors increasingly want objective data on how an organization is measuring the environmental externalities of its business—in particular the ones that impact the climate and human rights. They want data that proves their organization and their suppliers treat farmers, animals, miners, and other raw goods suppliers well. They want to know that a company's business is not somehow enabling human rights abuses or environmental damage in the developing world.

Government and regulators are considering this shift, too. Both are moving toward a more active role in ensuring environmental and social progress is being made as claimed, and as required by law. Within the next five years, 65 percent of institutional investors believe that evaluation of ESG criteria will be standard practice, and global ESG assets are projected to grow to a third of total assets under management, totaling $53 trillion in market value.[143] Organizations that get ahead of the news cycle, by identifying problems and acting substantively to fix them before being forced, will likely earn trust in the humanity and transparency domains.

While the movement toward common measurements should give you some lead time, recent regulatory evolutions suggest that the window may be closing. "Get out in front of sustainability issues with the best data you can. Leading companies are already setting a new standard for reporting," says Chris Ruggeri. "They are getting ahead of the curve to set the narrative themselves and this means they can position outcomes in a way that is accretive to their brand." Until we have recognized standards for disclosure and reporting to build trust, organizations are in control of the narrative. Those that authentically lead stakeholders on their sustainability journey burnish both brand and reputation in the process. However, those that are "greenwashing," or marketing products as sustainable when they are not, erode trust. In fact, "greenwashing" is cited by consumer product executives as the third largest reason that consumers lose trust.[144] Dr. Flammer notes, "You do see an increasing number of actors in the ESG space, and it's critical to be able to distinguish between those who are just 'greenwashing' versus those who are seriously trying to improve their social and environmental performance and walking their talk." Dr. Flammer explains, "The information asymmetry between companies and external constituencies (for example, consumers) makes it difficult for those constituencies to assess companies' actual sustainable business practices versus their claims. Companies can mitigate greenwashing concerns by adopting a voluntary ESG disclosure standard and by certifying their products and services by independent third-party certifiers."

Companies should build the technologies, processes, controls, and governance to capture data on a consistent basis and "prove" the quality of what they are reporting to stakeholders in the absence of recognized standards.

Strong internal governance measures for sustainability work enables internal decision-making and external compliance with reporting standards. This is why companies can't forget the "G" in ESG. These structures enable sustainability practitioners to measure progress against goals. Governance also helps to elevate sustainability to the same level as other domains, like financial reporting, by awarding it the same formal recognition. By having a reporting structure and titled officers, sustainability and equity earn a seat at the table in key conversations. This increases trust throughout the organization, as sustainability representatives can argue for resources and display results in the same quantitative language as the rest of the business.

Deliver Sustainability through the Workforce

Business performance isn't the only reason to get ahead on sustainability and equity. Sustainability performance will increasingly function as a competitive advantage for the workforce, serving as a critical differentiator for attracting and engaging workers. Organizations with the highest employee satisfaction scores have ESG scores 14 percent higher than the global average.[145] In a DE&I study conducted by Deloitte, 40 percent of respondents would even consider leaving their employer if they couldn't trust the employer to fulfill its DE&I commitments.[146] Millennial and Gen Z talent are especially interested in working in organizations that practice sustainability and equity, suggesting that the topic will remain critical in the future as these generations become the dominant workforce.

Workers are at the center of every sustainability question, from making choices about how to source products, to communicating sustainability efforts, to engaging with and serving customers in ways that embody an organization's sustainability strategy.

And workers are arguably the most important advocates. According to one study with CFOs, workers were the most commonly cited group

(42 percent) when asked which stakeholders were powering sustainability (versus organizational leadership at 39 percent).[147] For sustainability initiatives to be successful, workers at all levels of the organization need to be accountable for driving it forward. Delivering on sustainability means delivering through the workforce. It's important that organizations both equip workers to address sustainability issues and effectively incentivize the types of behaviors that drive long-term sustainability performance.

First, organizations should articulate clearly why this is important, both at the organization level and the individual level. What is the "so what" for the organization? For me? At its heart, sustainability is all about humanity and our shared ability to thrive, so organizations must make it relevant for their people. People are more likely to trust an organization that demonstrates empathy and kindness toward its stakeholders. For example, people who are passionate about environmental issues will likely feel heard and understood as the organization demonstrates progress on those issues. An organization earns trust by acting on those concerns because they honor those people's values. A customer living in a big city might not suffer materially if a company pollutes a faraway river, but she will likely lose trust in that company because she cares about the people and animals who rely on that water supply.

Sustainability also means making socially responsible commitments, and then meeting them. As we talked about with Joe Ucuzoglu in Chapter 10, communicating goals transparently drives accountability. For example, in 2021, Salesforce achieved net-zero emissions across its full value chain. They've also helped grow collaborative efforts like the Clean Energy Buyers Alliance, to help the entire sector advance renewable energy procurement. When asked about accountability, Weaver said, "For any executive, but particularly for a CFO, there's a growing recognition that ESG isn't just a nice to have, or something that's simply going to make employees happy—it's critical to building a strong, durable company."

Second, workforce policies offer a visible manifestation of the sustainability strategy; the workplace represents both an opportunity to enhance sustainability and equity credentials and a critical method for delivering them. Take, for instance, organizations that welcome people to bring their whole selves to work, whatever their background and beliefs. These workplaces end up cultivating social capital. Office policies that promote environmentally friendly choices, such as recycling and sourcing materials from sustainable sources, demonstrate commitment to the environment, which appeals to younger workers, who face a changing climate. And these actions reinforce the importance of sustainability choices for workers, while encouraging their active participation.

At Salesforce, every function of business is brought together to drive long-term collaboration toward sustainability goals. Weaver believes that by working together, teams can better collaborate on pressing issues such as privacy, equal pay, and climate action. She recognizes that stakeholders are demanding sustainability progress and Weaver has committed to "continue to find ways to bring all these teams together to effectively address sustainability transparently and with a high degree of accountability."

Third, companies need to provide incentives for the right behaviors. Incentives and performance systems should encourage long-term benefit—not just short-term gains. Many of these goals take real time, but that doesn't mean organizations should avoid them in the short-term. Dr. Flammer tells us that socially responsible practices are often not considered to be an integral part of corporate strategy and governance today. There are two potential reasons. The first is "myopic behavior" or a "lack of long-term orientation." The second is "a lack of private incentives to get business managers to pay attention to sustainable business practices."

Sustainability is and will remain a critical trust issue. It is central to the humanity of an organization. Communicating goals and outcomes transparently will be paramount to building trust. Leaders must demonstrate they are not just making good choices in the short-term but that, over time, they can be counted on to prioritize sustainability and equity issues reliably alongside business growth.

While sustainability has emerged as a relatively recent priority for businesses, marketing has long occupied that status. Its recent technology-based transformations, however, make marketing just as dynamic of a domain for understanding and earning trust. We'll discuss this in our next chapter.

CHAPTER 12

Marketing and Experience

In this chapter:

- The role of marketing and experience in building trust
- Trust challenges faced by marketing and experience
- Marketing and experience principles for building trust

This chapter takes us back to our roots, and we are excited to share our combined experience in the domains of marketing and experience. We both started our careers at the Monitor Group, a management strategy consulting practice which was acquired by Deloitte in 2013. Amelia joined the New York office in 1999 after finishing her master's degree in theology. Ashley joined the marketing practice in 2001, putting her behavioral science degree to work. We were each attracted to marketing and experience because at their core, they are fundamentally human domains.

Although advertising has existed since the fifteenth century, modern marketing, and a focus on differentiating products from the competition using market research to understand customer behavior, took root in the 1920s. A century later, Chief Marketing Officers (CMOs) are still

responsible for driving marketing strategy, caring for brands, and direct-
ing marketing campaigns. Chief Experience Officers (CXOs) represent
a newer leadership cadre, and are typically responsible for the customer
experience strategy, including mapping customer journeys and targeting
interventions to elevate the experience of their customers. Increasingly,
we see CXOs tasked with workforce experience as well. The number of
companies with a CXO or equivalent increased from approximately 60
percent in 2017 to nearly 90 percent in 2019.[148] While most companies
still have both a CXO and a CMO, the roles can have somewhat over-
lapping expectations. CMOs are expected to understand and contribute
to the customer experience even after customers have purchased a product or service, and CXOs equally must know how to create compelling
narratives to attract new customers.

To get additional perspectives, we sat down with Jeff Logan and
Robert "Bob" McDonald. Jeff Logan is the Group Vice President of
Patient and Market Experience at Providence Health and Services, a
large nonprofit healthcare system that spans across seven states. Logan
previously served as a lieutenant in the U.S. Navy, and his leadership
skills have been in practice for over twenty years as former Senior Vice
President of Enterprise Customer and Employee Experience at U.S.
Bank and Staff Vice President of Marketing Planning and Strategy at
Anthem. We first met Jeff Logan when we invited him to record an
episode on the topic of trust for the Deloitte Experience Channel. He
is passionate about utilizing all he has learned in financial services, insurance, and the military to transform the patient's experience in healthcare.

We also spoke to Bob McDonald, the former Secretary of Veterans Affairs (VA), about his experience building trust with veterans and
their families. Prior to joining VA, McDonald was the chairman, president, and CEO of Procter & Gamble, one of the world's leading brand
marketing organizations (you likely have a dozen P&G brands—such as
Tide, Gillette, or Crest—in your home).[149] Following a public crisis over
patient access and quality of care, and the resignation of the former Secretary, he led VA through a transformational journey to be the number
one customer service agency in the federal government. McDonald's

on-screen background is framed by an American flag from his office at VA and a painting of American flags lining a rainy city street. He bought the painting because it reminded him of *The Avenue in the Rain* by Childe Hassam, which hung in the White House Oval Office while McDonald served as Secretary. He shared that "seeing the flags and the painting constantly remind [him] of [his] responsibility."

The Role of Marketing and Experience in Building Trust

Marketing has come a long way from the days when "Mad Men" would shoot from the hip with advertising ideas using limited (or no) insights to inform campaigns. They assumed that creativity would drive sales and that placing a Super Bowl ad would drive a profitable return. They weren't asked to prove it with data, and there was no discussion of ideas like "customer experience."

Today, however, marketing and experience leaders are swimming in data and must balance art with science. Leaders are expected to be scientific about ROI and judicious with their spend. Inspired creative ideas are still vital, but they are also subject to multiple rounds of analysis and feedback. There is an ongoing proliferation of communication channels, many of which are digital. Two-way vehicles for communication are increasingly vital. And customers have changed, too. Fifty years ago, the savvy customer read *Consumer Reports*. Today, everyone has access to facts and opinions from easily accessible sources. Online, crowdsourced star ratings recommend or caution against every product, service, or brand. And people are also inundated by marketing. Customers and potential customers are targeted everywhere they go (and sometimes this can be creepy—we'll talk about that in Chapter 14).

What hasn't changed is the role of the marketer. At its core, marketing is the discipline of identifying and matching human needs with what the organization offers. This takes strong storytelling, even stronger listening and observation, and a big dose of empathy. Now add experience, and you have a multifaceted, challenging discipline that can both create and erode value through trust. And if you're trusted as a brand, you don't have to use your finite marketing dollars to convince people that your product is high quality and high value. Instead, you can communicate what your brand stands for and even trade on earned trust to take good creative risks.

Trust is essential to marketing and experience, but you knew we would say that. Is your brand delivering on what is promised? Is it a good promise (in other words, is it relevant to me, is it good for me and others)? Are you building a trusting relationship with the right customers instead of a one-time shopper? And are you establishing trust so that you can spend less time proving to people that you're trustworthy and more time communicating value?

Trust Challenges Faced by Marketing and Experience

In the simplest terms, brands build trust when they make and deliver on good promises. To make these promises a reality, marketing and experience teams have to wade through massive quantities of data, engage across multiple and constantly evolving channels and technologies, and rely on others both to communicate the promise and then to deliver the promise. We'll discuss three core challenges:

- Evolving engagement
- Effective use of data and technology
- Limited control over experience implementation

Evolving Engagement

The past decade has seen a vast proliferation of channels. Customers are spending more and more time on screens (often multiple screens at once) and ad dollars have followed. In 2021, digital advertising accounted for over 60 percent of all ad spend. In 2022 social media is expected to account for the largest share of ad dollars in digital *and* traditional media, with an expected annual growth rate of 20 percent.[150] In addition to becoming a dominant channel, social media enables brands to engage customers in a two-way dialogue, which print and TV can't do. Digital environments provide access to customers at many new touchpoints, enabling conversation in lieu of one-way advertisement.

The benefit is not without its drawbacks. For starters, the world of social media can be profoundly negative. Social media has been linked with anxiety, depression, lack of sleep, and a lack of self-esteem.[151] Cyber bullying has become a common problem, with nearly half of teens receiving intimidating, threatening, or nasty messages online.[152] And social media can propagate the rapid spread of negative information. In fact, false information or negative data is much more likely to spread quickly than the truth.[153] More than half of people now get their news from social media, where friends and family as well as the people you follow curate what you read through their choice of what to share. And because of this combination, people who get most of their news on social media are less knowledgeable about what is a fact than those who use other, more traditional news sources.[154]

Digital influencers, who have a large social media following, and creators, who create content for social media platforms, play an outsized role in the dissemination of information. This is a different game from years past in which brands contracted with just a limited set of celebrities to endorse their products or services. Now the ability to influence has moved from a single person or a handful of sponsors to a vast array of influencers and content creators. Brands and companies must learn how to engage with and work with them to drive engagement and reach other influential marketing goals. A popular figure can independently endorse, snub, or opine about a brand to millions, outside of the control or consent of the brand's marketers. Further, these influencers may or may not represent organizational values, and they aren't necessarily in formal alignment with the brands they discuss, or even aware of its messaging.

Add to this the speed by which cultural movements flourish and spread, and you get a sense of the challenge. For example, in 2013 Alicia Garza shared her sadness and words of comfort on social media in response to the death of Trayvon Martin, saying "our lives matter." Two of her friends, Patrisse Cullors and Opal Tometi, inspired by her post and looking to initiate a viral movement, created #BlackLivesMatter (BLM). The #BlackLivesMatter hashtag was used roughly forty-seven times per day in 2013. In August 2014, spurred by Michael Brown's shooting, the tag was used more than 52,000 times a day.[155] On November 24, 2014, when the court announced that a grand jury had decided not to indict Darren Wilson, the police officer who had killed Brown, the tag was used 92,784 times in the four hours following the announcement.[156] This one social media post has since become part of U.S. social fabric, with expression in film, music, and art with over forty member-led chapters globally.[157]

Reacting to the power and speed of social media, leading companies are increasingly bringing influencers and creators with a wide range of identities and lived experiences into the creative process. They are also introducing new poly-cultural research methods to better understand these lived experiences and multiple dimensions of culture by which one may source their identity and especially those elements of their identity that relate to their consumption choices and patterns. As we discussed in Chapter 6:

Identity can shape lived experience, and marketing and experience teams must consider "trust flags" when building and sharing brand narratives.

While digital channels have created opportunity, they have also created risk for brands. The always-on dialogue, the vast web of influencers and creators, and the constant barrage of conflicting information can lead to negative brand perceptions that spread quickly. To share the brand promise and create the foundation for a trusted, engaging experience, marketing and experience leaders need to manage a wide variety of stakeholders across an increasing number of channels in a space challenged by false information and negativity.

Effective Use of Data and Technology

Many leaders, bombarded with data from all sides, are trying to figure out the most powerful ways to use all the information now available through sophisticated tracking and measurement. Leaders rely on getting the right data and metrics so that they can create desired outcomes with customers and stakeholders while manifesting value for the company. And they must do all of this while also respecting the privacy of their customers (more on this in Chapter 15). More than half of CMOs report that they are challenged to find the right data and aggregate the right information to have a clear view of their customers.[158] Only 26 percent surveyed strongly believed their analytics capability was ahead of other companies in their sector.[159]

Bob McDonald underscored that even with all of the data available, sometimes organizations aren't focused on the right metrics. With refreshing candor, McDonald told us, "When I got to VA, I realized we were measuring the wrong thing." Veterans Affairs tracked wait times for appointments but didn't realize that their target metric—the number of people getting appointments within fourteen days—was irrelevant to customers. The critical factor was not time but urgency. When people need routine care, wait times aren't terribly important. When they need urgent care, they need it *now*. What mattered was that customers got the service they needed when they needed it.[160] He made veteran trust and experience the new "north star" metric for the agency and reconsidered the metrics used for each Moment that Mattered.

Another challenging data problem is illustrated by how organizations approach targeting customers. Segmentation is an important tool for any organization. Choosing to focus on some segments and not others enables leaders to be more efficient with their organizations' time, money, and resources. There are many different types of segmentation, but since the '90s, many organizations have focused on demographics to find patterns in their customers and workforce. Demographic data is relatively easy to obtain and easy to measure, which makes analysis straightforward and targeting more cost effective. However, demographics just don't tell the whole story (as we saw in Chapter 6). It's not *who you are* but *what you've experienced* in life that shapes your behavior. For example, in our data set a high-income, married white Gen X man from Arizona gave an identical trust score to a retail brand as a single, middle-income, unmarried white Gen Z woman from Massachusetts. (See Figure 12.1.) The driving factor behind their shared profile is individual experience, not demographics, which is why we structure our research design around poly-cultural research to get a broader and more nuanced understanding of lived experience and cultural dimensions.

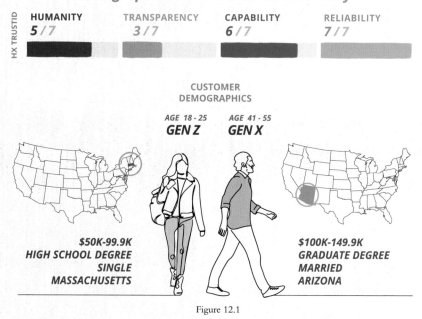

Figure 12.1

Beyond selecting the "right" metrics and the "right" segmentation, marketing and experience leaders must grapple with increasing concerns over data privacy. As we near a cookieless[161] future, in which people have increased choices about the visibility of their online footprint, marketing and experience professionals will have to expend more effort collecting data directly from customers, which will require earning their trust. These experts will need advanced analytics to understand "look-alike" customers to proxy what used to be a one-to-one relationship. CMOs from high-growth brands are deploying first-party data in more sophisticated ways, including dynamic, creative optimization to deliver personalized content and programmatic media to serve data-driven ads to users.[162]

Finally, as marketing and experience leaders navigate the latest tools, from artificial intelligence (AI) to machine learning (ML) to augmented and virtual reality (AR/VR), they will encounter ethical challenges and decisions that may feel unprecedented. Navigating these uncharted waters will require an even more advanced set of data and insights capabilities, with underpinning frameworks focused on ensuring ethical practices that do their best to be aware of and eliminate bias. For example, early AI tools in recruiting talent have demonstrated bias against women and people of color.[163] These algorithms were based on faulty training data and inputs that weren't carefully cleaned or corrected. Protecting against both malicious and accidentally harmful applications of technology is both vital and difficult.

Limited Control over Experience Implementation

Marketing controls the initial narrative of a brand to customers, but not how the narrative is *fulfilled*. Similarly, experience teams set the strategy for elevating the experience of their customers, but do not typically control all aspects of its execution. This is where trust across functions and between internal teams comes into play. The degree to which the rest of the organization fulfills these expectations, whether through product research or advertising, determines whether stakeholders ultimately trust the brand.

> *Marketing controls the initial narrative of a brand to customers, but not how the narrative is __fulfilled__.*

Consumers are extremely savvy and crave authenticity in the marketing experiences that are served to them. Secretary McDonald experienced this at VA and made improving service delivery a core focus of his first ninety days plan: "more doctors, more space, better salaries." McDonald also put himself on the line to build trust, stating, "My job was to get out, meet people, and do a lot of town hall meetings with employees, stakeholders, and media. My job was to open my heart and demonstrate my care and concern, trying to create intimacy to develop trust. In my first national press conference I gave out my cell phone number. To this day, I still get calls from veterans needing care, and I still help them." McDonald retired from VA in 2017.

McDonald didn't conflate listening with progress, however. He told us, "At the same time as you're trying to build trust, you've got to get the right leadership team in place to work on the systems, the strategy, the culture." In other words, having determined the right data to gather, he worked with his team and across functions to change VA materially and culturally so it would deliver on its promises. McDonald handpicked a team of people from private and public companies, as well as longtime civil servants, to elevate trust through large-scale projects like upgrading VA's information systems, which were thirty years old.

Marketing and Experience Principles for Building Trust

It is challenging to build trust when you can't control delivery. To do it well, you need to invest in collaboration with other functions, as well as focus on using all of the tools at your disposal, including your workforce. Technology is critical, too, though it must be used for good ends to ensure trust is built and not eroded. We will discuss these three principles to build trust:

- Collaborate to keep your promises
- Activate workers as a brand asset
- Use technology to good ends

Collaborate to Keep Your Promises

We could say this for any function, but it's especially true for marketing. CMOs and CXOs must be unifiers in the C-suite. Building trust with others is paramount to success. And yet CMOs can be some of the worst collaborators in the C-suite. Fewer than one in five CMOs reported collaborating with other C-suite members.[164] Many CMOs similarly don't recognize collaboration as an important skill, with only 25 percent prioritizing collaboration as a critical skill.[165] We think lack of collaboration is one of the reasons CMO tenure is slipping.[166]

There is a surprising crisis of confidence among CMOs. For instance, when we indexed C-suite respondents on their ability to impact strategic decision-making, the overall direction of the business, and the ability to garner support for their initiatives amongst their peers, CMOs gave themselves a harsh assessment—only 5 percent of CMOs consider themselves high performers, the lowest in the C-suite. This stands in stark contrast to the CEOs, 55 percent of whom consider themselves high performers. The average for CEOs, Chief Information Officers (CIOs), and Chief Financial Officers (CFOs) is 35 percent.[167]

Most C-suite members perceive the CMO to be performing at a level much higher than they see themselves, especially in areas such as demonstrating financial impact, customer expertise, and initiating collaborative efforts. In nearly all cases, some of the most influential players in the C-suite—CEOs, CFOs, and CIOs/Chief Technology Officers (CTOs)—believe CMOs deliver effectively on multiple fronts. For the CMO, who often assumes poor self-performance, this zoomed-out view suggests that much of the C-suite respects, and leans on, the CMO's expertise.[168] We'll touch on the importance of collaboration across all C-suite functions in the coming chapters.

Collaboration is a tall order in most organizations, where incentives, and human nature, drive leaders to protect their separate resources. Contemporary work is interdependent among all departments, and yet old bureaucratic structures and thinking stubbornly persist. However, the benefits to collaboration are substantial. For example, 50 percent of IT leaders who work closely with their firms' marketing leaders claim their companies are in a better competitive position. They are 1.3 times more likely to see substantial year-over-year growth, and 72 percent see profit margin growth of more than 5 percent.[169]

Jeff Logan of Providence Healthcare has a unique role in that he not only manages the customer experience but also controls the market operations as well. This means that he can both create and deliver on the ideal experience, earning customer trust by setting and meeting customer expectations—appointments will be kept, individual accounts in Providence's MyChart digital interface will be accurate, and billing is both correct and what patients expected. Logan tells us, "One of the things that attracted me to this role was that I could both set new customer-oriented expectations and deliver on them through our operations." Logan is using his dual responsibilities to ensure experience is elevated. "Patients and their families often come to us in their most vulnerable state, and if we contribute to their uncertainty, we might erode their trust! Even if there is an issue with the experience, if we communicate well and focus on the patient, we can still earn trust. My philosophy is that trust isn't the destination. It's all of the little steps along the way, the Moments that Matter. And when we set expectations and deliver against them for each of those little steps, we make everyone a little happier and a little more relieved."

> **My philosophy is that trust isn't the destination. It's all of the little steps along the way, the Moments that Matter."**
>
> **—Jeff Logan**
> **Group VP of Patient and Market Experience, Providence Health and Services**

Activate Workers as a Brand Asset

Despite evidence of the connection between workforce experience and customer experience, many marketers spend little or no time on internal marketing and communications. There are still plenty of CXO positions where the experience mandate is for customers alone. Today, most worker communication seems to take the form of company memos or newsletters, often drafted by HR professionals, who are not necessarily marketing and branding experts (for more on talent, see Chapter 13). There are also plenty of examples where external advertising doesn't match internal messaging, creating confusion among workers.[170]

We think this is a lost opportunity. Workers can be powerful brand advocates and trust builders, and marketing and experience functions have a critical role to play in creating an emotional connection. Marketing and experience functions can help turn the workforce into brand advocates in at least three ways. The first is by increasing workers' understanding of customers, and leaders' understanding of workers. This greater understanding will help to ensure that customer and worker perspectives are baked into the organization's strategic decision making. The second is by providing unifying messaging and experience to help workers authentically represent the brand. Brand messaging must be woven into the fabric of workforce experience and reinforce on-brand behaviors so that they become instinctive. The third is by helping to empower frontline workers to solve customer problems in real time (making sure the brand is able to keep its promises). Of course, this all requires the collaboration we discussed above.

At VA, Bob McDonald embraced this philosophy. He knew that transforming the culture for *workers* was the key to delivering better experience for *customers*. One module of his marquee Leaders Developing Leaders (LDL) program was titled "Veterans Experience," which focused on imbuing a spirit of values-based leadership and individual agency to VA employees. Prior to his arrival, a rules-based culture sometimes prevented commonsense actions. McDonald told the story of a veteran who had broken his foot and drove himself to the hospital. But upon arrival, his condition had declined such that he needed help to go from his car in the parking lot to the hospital. He called to ask a hospital employee for help and was refused, because the employee had been told "Don't abandon your post." Instead, the veteran had to wait for the fire department before he could get the help he needed (to travel about ten feet), a waste of resources and a miserable experience for the pained veteran. McDonald sought to fix this issue and focused on cascading responsibility and individual initiative through the organization. The change helped people do the right thing for patients even if the situation couldn't be found in a rule book. (McDonald was quick to point out that the employee in this situation was doing just that—following the rules.)

McDonald also presented VA workers with a new conceptual model of leadership, in which his name appeared at the bottom of an inverted pyramid, and the customers appeared at the top. The message was, "The customer is boss. That's the person you're serving." Just below the customer are the frontline workers, and just below that are the administrators. The "top" leaders are at the bottom of the pyramid because they are the ones bound in duty to serve everyone. Jumpstarting a culture of service led to more innovation at VA. McDonald was not only able to empower his people to be frontline problem solvers but also innovators who cascaded their best practices to other departments. It's a success story similar to Ed Bastian's virtuous circle (as we shared in Chapter 7). Over 24,000 leaders and 111,500 employees benefited from the LDL program.[171]

Logan shared a similar philosophy, noting that workers are critical brand ambassadors in terms of how patients *experience* the brand. To deliver on this, Logan is building a culture where caregivers know they're the most important aspect of delivering on customer experience. Thus, as the organization builds a trusted relationship with its workers, so that they have a wonderful experience, workers will in turn provide exceptional service with an empathetic mindset when and where customers need it most. Logan says, "We are doing a lot internally to create this empathetic culture of service. We train our frontline workers and caregivers to be very deliberate in how they provide this empathetic service to our customers. It's not about just hoping workers have it figured out—it's about removing barriers to delivering on a trusted experience, including training, frontline empowerment, and a mindset shift, allowing workers to provide the best service possible."

Use Technology to Good Ends

In marketing and experience, machine learning and data modeling are used to create better experiences by generating and applying customer insights at scale to customize or personalize content, messaging, and offers. The goal is to optimize spending and ROI in the process.

Starbucks is a leading example of a company that uses AI to create better experience. Personalization has always been a core part of the Starbucks philosophy, and their website proudly notes that customers have 170,000 ways to customize their Starbucks beverages. In 2019, Starbucks launched "Deep Brew," an AI platform that drives the brand's personalization engine. Deep Brew takes in data from the Starbucks app, such as when orders are made and what is ordered, and then uses predictive analytics to process the data and serve customers with personalized marketing messages. These messages might include special offers to increase the customer's average order value. Or they might be personalized to a specific store as a customer physically approaches it. Gerri Martin-Flickinger, Starbucks' Chief Technology Officer, says that Deep Brew has been a critical part of its success. She has shared future plans to expand AI outside of marketing and experience to help improve operations at the store level—for example, anticipating equipment maintenance or predicting staffing needs.[172]

Starbucks is clear though, that while AI can be used for good, like making the act of placing your daily coffee order more personal, it can also be used to bad ends. Former CEO Kevin Johnson notes the importance of using AI responsibly, stating, "Technology has done so much positive for the world, but it has contributed to some unhealthy outcomes as well. When it comes to enhancing human connection and enabling people to be present and feel a part of a community, I believe technology, if used in responsible and thoughtful ways, can also be the enabler of freeing up people to be more human and better serve society."[173]

In this chapter, we've written about the ways that marketing and experience can't focus only on the customer as they go about building trust, because that overlooks a core set of humans: the workers. That's where talent and human capital come in—and those are the functions we'll turn to in the next chapter.

CHAPTER 13

Talent and Human Capital

In this chapter:

- The role of talent in building trust
- Trust challenges faced by talent
- Principles for talent management to create trust

We've said it before (in Chapter 7) and we'll say it again: You can't build trust with your customers if you don't first build trust with your workforce. And building trust with workers takes many of the same skills and disciplines as building trust with customers. We often say that none of us woke up this morning as an "employee," just as we don't think of ourselves as "customers" when we sip our much-needed, life-giving first cup of coffee in the morning. We are simply humans.

To understand what it means to bring trust to life for the humans we call workers, we sat down with the leader of Deloitte's HR Strategy and Solutions Market Offering, Jessica Britton. Jessica has spent roughly twenty years helping her clients design and deliver elevated workforce experiences. She is a travel enthusiast, podcast junkie, and new mother of two. She likes to joke that when she isn't designing talent experiences for her "grown-up" clients, she is trying to create the best experience for her "little" clients at home.

The Role of Talent in Building Trust

Everything an organization does, it does through the workforce. And while the Chief Human Resources Officer (CHRO) is likely the person responsible for defining the workforce strategy, ultimately everyone in the organization must deliver across thousands of daily interactions, if not millions. This makes designing workforce experiences for maximum trust and maximum engagement both incredibly important and incredibly challenging.

Our perspective is that workforce experience, which we define as *the sum of a human's lived experiences and how they feel about their organization*, should be treated just like customer experience. Worker experience must be informed by human values, needs, emotions, and desires as they relate to the critical relationships each worker has with the organization. Winning organizations create a human-centric environment with this understanding in mind, and this serves as the foundation for building trust.

As we saw in Chapter 7, earning the workforce's trust is critical to earning customer trust. Tiffani Bova, Global Growth Evangelist and author of *Growth IQ: Get Smarter about the Choices That Will Make or Break Your Business,* wrote, "The fastest way to get customers to love your brand, is to get your employees to love their job."[174] The same is true about trust: Workers who trust an organization are more motivated to win trust from customers. They are **1.7 times** more likely to recommend their employer to talented friends and family, and **1.9 times** more likely to promote the brand outside the company.[175] The Chief People Experience Officer of Pfizer, Payal Sahni Becher, tells us that after its COVID-19 vaccine launched in 2021, the company's internal online store was tied up for three days as proud workers bought clothing and gear with the Pfizer logo. You can't buy that kind of attachment—but you can earn it.[176]

Trust Challenges Faced by Talent

Today's leaders are faced by several significant trust challenges. First, there is high turnover and a scramble for talent. This talent crunch is exacerbated by low worker trust, linked to lower retention and less satisfaction with salary—all of which contribute to turnover. And many organizations are operating in a hybrid model creating new trust challenges both for employers ("Are my workers actually working?") and for workers ("How can I get to know and trust an organization when I haven't spent time in person with anyone I work with?"). We'll explore each of these:

- The scramble for talent
- Low worker trust
- A new hybrid model

The Scramble for Talent

In 2021, the *Harvard Business Review* reported that 89 percent of workers said that their work-life was getting worse. 85 percent said that their well-being declined. And 56 percent said that their job demands had increased.[177] It's probably not surprising, then, that many workers are reconsidering who they want to work for. Fidelity's annual Financial Resolutions Study found that roughly four in ten workers are planning to switch jobs in 2022.[178] Another indication: by late 2021 the job postings for *recruiters* had doubled from pre-pandemic levels, meaning organizations are spending much more time and money just trying to attract workers.[179]

As we write this, there are more jobs available than there are unemployed workers. On the last day of December 2021, job openings totaled nearly 11 million, more than 4.6 million above the total unemployment level.[180] All of these factors suggest a lasting scramble for talent. Our colleague Jessica Britton told us, "No industry is immune. From healthcare to tech, no one can ignore the race to hire." This is where trust comes in. A trusting workforce is a major driver of talent retention and further encourages current workers to refer qualified candidates to their employer. We'll explore in this chapter how trust will be a significant variable in surviving the talent shortage. The most trusted companies will have the ability not just to weather this period but to come out ahead.

Low Worker Trust

While we have seen improvements in overall worker trust since we began our research in May 2020 (approximately 9 percent net improvement), our latest study, conducted in October 2021, found that less than half of all workers surveyed (47 percent) trust their employer. Given that trust drives retention and other favorable behaviors, leaders should see low workforce trust as a call to action.

Let's underscore the enormity of the problem. Even professions that are typically viewed as "lifelong" careers are facing significant turnover. Historically, education and healthcare services exhibit some of the lowest rates of turnover.[181] Yet organizations are seeing these trusted professions lose people not just to other employers but to other careers. Annually only 8 percent of teachers leave the profession.[182] Today a staggering 55 percent of teachers are considering leaving the profession.[183] In Chapter 2, we told the story of Ashley's sister Lindsey and the trust impact of monitoring when teachers enter and leave the building for something as trivial as a coffee break. When suspicion is an employer's default attitude, why would a worker trust the employer in return?

The low-trust state of workers places an even greater burden on an organization, because we already know that it is harder to rebuild trust from a position of low trust. Roderick Kramer is an experimental social psychologist and a professor at Stanford. Kramer argues that we are hardwired to trust: "In fact, in many ways, trust is our default position; we trust routinely, reflexively, and somewhat mindlessly across a broad range of social situations."[184] However, he also notes that when we have been traumatized into a low-trust perspective, we are far more likely to evaluate new evidence with skepticism, making it more difficult to regain trust.

Rather than leaning on the natural tendency to trust, humans instead look to confirm what they already believe—that distrusted organizations remain unworthy of trust (psychologists call this confirmation bias). Kramer conducted a study to demonstrate this effect and found that "individuals who were primed to expect a possible abuse of trust looked more carefully for signs of untrustworthy behavior from prospective partners. In contrast, those primed with more positive social expectations paid more attention to evidence of others' trustworthiness. Most important, individuals' subsequent decisions about how much to trust the prospective partners were swayed by those expectations."[185] Another term for this phenomenon is self-fulfilling prophecy, and it's not hard to see why.

In other words, a trusted organization will find it easier to maintain and grow trust, while a distrusted organization needs to work harder to regain trust. The low level of worker trust makes this a significant obstacle for organizations to overcome.

A New Hybrid Model

While we can't fully predict how much work will be hybrid in the future, or even how it will evolve, we can say with a reasonable level of confidence that hybrid work, a model that allows for work at different locations and at different times, is here to stay.[186] Certainly there is worker demand for this model: approximately 79 percent of workers want location flexibility and 94 percent of workers want schedule flexibility.[187]

As remote work creates new trust challenges for both employers and workers, employers who are accustomed to deciding where and when people work have to let go of some level of control. Micromanagers have to shift from observing activity to focusing on outcomes. Workers who once could separate work from home have to find a way to combine them in a way that doesn't leave them exhausted or resentful. And there is also the complexity of managing engagement differences between those workers that do come into an office versus those that are remote.

Jessica tells us, "We know hybrid is not going anywhere, but we are also starting to see the costs on a human and an organizational level."

Already we see that hybrid workers are signaling the need for better, more human engagement with their organizations. The majority of workers (91 percent) desire a hybrid or even fully remote model.[188] However, according to a 2021 Google study, hybrid work is taking a toll on connectedness: "The majority of respondents said they feel disconnected from their organization and co-workers (57 percent), that limited networking opportunities negatively impact career growth (62 percent), and that limited social interactions with co-workers has had a negative impact on their mental health (54 percent)."[189] People want flexible hybrid work arrangements even though they feel more disconnected, believe it limits their career growth, and makes them feel depressed or anxious.

The shift to hybrid work also necessitates new ways of helping workers to bond—with each other and with organizations broadly. Humans are social creatures and the (vast) majority need a personal connection in order to build trust. Leaders in organizations are facing the tension of championing hybrid models while also championing workers' need for connection, advancement, and support. Intentionally building trust through activities that demonstrate humanity, transparency, capability, and reliability are necessary to managing this tension.

Principles for Talent Management to Create Trust

Trust represents an organization's deliberate cultural commitment. Trust represents an organization's deliberate cultural commitment. Given the scramble for talent, the already low levels of worker trust, and the tensions in hybrid work, trust-building cannot be implicit. Leaders responsible for influencing the talent agenda, including but not limited to CHROs, should focus on the following four trust principles:

- Understand that workers are human first
- Extend trust to earn trust
- Demonstrate equity
- Apply learnings from customer experience to worker experience

Understand That Workers Are Human First

Leading companies understand that workers are human first and make committed efforts to understand them as individuals with individual needs. To give us a perspective from a leading CHRO, Jessica introduced us to Rhonda Morris, VP and Chief Human Resources Officer (CHRO) for Chevron Corporation, a leading, integrated energy company. Morris is responsible for shaping and driving Chevron's people and culture strategy, including leadership succession, learning and talent, diversity and inclusion, workforce planning, and total rewards. Morris is the first Black female corporate officer at Chevron and has received several distinguished honors and awards, including the National Diversity Institute's Most Influential African American. Morris is a northern California native and currently resides in Oakland, California, with her husband and daughter.

Morris shared a story about a worker who was unable to attend an after-work event. Previously, the team leader had made it clear that although in-person attendance was not technically *mandatory*, he did want all of his direct reports to be physically present. After the worker said she was not able to attend, the leader followed up to ask why. She explained that if she attended the after-work event, she would not be able to drop her kids off at daycare for the next two weeks, due to the daycare's COVID-19 policies. The team leader later shared with Morris that this was a learning moment for him—it taught him to lead with empathy and ask questions. He humbly recognized that he didn't know what each of his direct reports might have been dealing with on the home front. For future meetings, he started from a place of trust—trusting that members of his team would navigate their own personal challenges and show up in the best way possible. By giving that trust to his team, he was able to earn their trust in return (more on this in the following principle).

Morris's story also reveals the need for CHROs to recognize their workers as whole humans with both personal and professional selves. As we emphasized in Chapter 7, we are all human first. This means that we bring our values, emotions, anxieties, and triumphs with us in whatever role we play. These parts of our lives are what make us who we are, and we aren't able to separate them when we log on or walk into work. In one of our workforce focus groups, we discussed with workers how they want to be treated. A mother who is an hourly wage worker shared how important flexible working hours are to her because they make her feel that her employer understands and respects her other obligations. She said, "You're not just an employee. That's just one facet of your life. It's allowing you to be your whole self at work and being flexible with these other facets of your life."

Recognizing workers as humans who are more than their work lives also means that organizations cannot expect workers to concentrate their attention on work if they don't have their other needs met. If they can't trust that they will have good healthcare benefits, if they don't have faith that they're going to be able to afford housing, if their employer doesn't provide a safe, well-equipped workplace and a reasonable work schedule—in short, if workers don't have the basic things they need in their lives outside of work—then they won't have the mental or emotional bandwidth to do their best work. A company's responsibility to its workers extends beyond the physical or virtual workplace and outside the nine-to-five workday. When organizations provide support for learning and personal growth, families and health, downtime (including vacation and daily unplugging), and privacy, they demonstrate humanity and earn trust and loyalty. One CEO we admire ended his first in-person leadership team meeting in two years of his top five hundred leaders by saying, "One last thing. Be more human. It makes a difference."

Extend Trust to Earn Trust

In our research, we found that workers want employers to treat them with mutual care and trust. Organizations earn trust when they stand by workers during tough times for the company (a downturn), society (a pandemic), or an individual (a health or family crisis). Workers also want organizations to put safety first, ensuring a secure environment for everyone. And workers want to be seen as whole humans, with their needs addressed both within and outside of the workplace.[190]

Under the leadership of Morris, Chevron has many programs to ensure worker needs are individualized and prioritized. One such example is Chevron's Employee Assistance Program, which the company put in place over fifty years ago. The Employee Assistance Program is an internal consulting service that is designed to help workers resolve a broad range of problems, from practical, everyday issues to more complicated personal and work-related concerns. This program is available for current and retired workers and their families, and it can take the form of professional guidance or connected services, such as access to fitness programs, access to childcare, or even helping with flexible work schedules. The Employee Assistance Program is designed to recognize and aid individual needs, which emphasize a focus on the person rather than on the worker. Morris says, "If you think about our workforce, we have a range of employees with intersecting identities, lived experiences, and needs. The Employee Assistance Program is focused on listening and offering counsel and resources based on each employee's personal circumstances. This way there is support for leaders across a wide range of issues."

When workers are trusted, they are more likely to trust their employer in turn.[191] This idea is supported by research demonstrating that high expectations lead to better performance. Conversely, low expectations lead to worse performance. This concept, called the Pygmalion Effect, is named for a story from Greek mythology about a Cyprian sculptor who is so in love with one of his sculptures that he begins treating it like a real person. As a result of his infatuation, the goddess of love, Aphrodite, brings the statue Galatea to life, highlighting the concept that, if you expect something to come true, it is more likely to happen.

The Pygmalion Effect was first observed by Robert Rosenthal and Lenore Jacobson. The two researchers studied the impact of expectations on performance by observing the relationship between teachers and students. Student performance was statistically higher when teachers

Leaders in organizations need to give trust in order to get trust.

had the expectation (with IQ scores selected at random) that students would perform better.[192] In the context of trust, this underscores our belief that leaders in organizations need to give trust in order to get trust.

Yet when you look objectively at a typical organization's ways of working, it's surprising how many policies assume that workers can't be trusted. One example is an attendance points system, a program commonly used by the largest retailers in the consumer goods sector, in which employees earn points for being absent, arriving late, or leaving early (unlike earning points in our favorite loyalty programs for free stuff, these points are not positive). Workers are subject to progressive levels of discipline based on the number of points earned, in many cases ending with termination. Some of the biggest companies in the world use attendance points systems. While at face value these types of systems may seem neutral or even positive for discouraging absenteeism, they indicate distrust, and even imply that workers' needs are unimportant, sending a constant reminder that things like traffic accidents or kids' doctors' appointments don't matter to the organization. These systems may even encourage workers to come to work while sick or to put off needed health visits, which again undermines the connection an individual has with an organization.

Demonstrate Equity

High-trust organizations demonstrate in both words and actions that the well-being of workers is more important than the well-being of the organization. This emphasis on worker and organizational well-being is borne out through talent policies that balance the needs of workers with the needs of the company. By exhibiting empathy and regard for each individual, and by communicating openly about the rationale behind both easy and tough decisions, trusted organizations demonstrate humanity and transparency for their workforce over and over.

It's important to note that equity doesn't always mean equal, and in the context of talent, compensation is a great example of where this is true. In general, workers understand the concept of market value, which means that highly capable workers with scarce and in-demand skills will earn higher compensation. Different salaries are also acceptable to a trusting workforce, when the criteria are based on performance, and when there are effective measures of accountability and transparency in place.[193] However, this also means that people with equal value should be paid equally. When compensation seems based on demographics versus performance or market value, this will breed distrust.[194] Another worker from our focus group commented, "Being a woman in technology, the pay gap is huge. I was making less than my male counterparts . . . like $14,000 less than my male counterparts. I'd been there seven years, and they were just coming in." In a society where information is increasingly democratized, organizations will be expected to justify their choices, and we expect that disparities will be viewed with increasing distrust.

In this scenario, speaking plainly and transparently to the workforce is a critical driver of trust. This includes difficult conversations that many are reluctant to have. For example, if someone does not believe they're being fairly compensated, a semitransparent answer might be: "This is the industry benchmark for your position and level." A more transparent answer (and ultimately a more respectful one) might be framed differently: "Some capabilities have greater market value than others, and this is how we view your capabilities. In addition, this is how we view your contributions and your performance."

These types of conversations are difficult because people *are* being assessed. It's natural to conflate market value with personal worth to the organization, so there's a lot of emotion in such conversations. However, it is also an *honest* conversation and a *transparent* conversation, which leads to higher trust. And this trust, or lack of it, has meaningful outcomes. For example, when employers are not transparent about pay, employees are 50 percent more likely to leave their job in the next six months, according to a recent PayScale study.[195]

As discussed in Chapter 7, one of our favorite examples of both treating workers as human-first and promoting equity is how Delta engaged with workers and demonstrated commitment to them during the pandemic. It is inspiring to listen to Delta CEO Ed Bastian talk to the importance of trust, and his own beliefs in how to build it. One thing that Bastian didn't mention during our interview, however, was that, while he was making sure all of his workers were cared for, he didn't take his own salary for a full six months. Bastian prioritized workers and cared for their individual needs over his own needs. As Bastian said, "Crisis reveals character." We revisit the importance of designing for—and with—humans in Chapter 14.

Apply Learnings from Customer Experience to Worker Experience

Having spent many years thinking about how to deliver growth through exceptional experience, it's fascinating to us that organizations have been slow to take what they know from building phenomenal customer experience and apply those same principles and investment to building workforce experience.

When C-suite marketing experts create a customer experience program, they craft a strategy for how customers want to engage, and how the organization will make that happen. After in-depth study of the current customer experience (CX), they plan how the organization will innovate products and services that will elevate the experience. Marketers find more valuable ways to engage customers and do deep research to understand customer motivations and needs. Then they target new products and services toward what customers are trying to accomplish, or what problems they need to solve, or what new experiences they will find delightful. They run ethnographic research. Marketing departments observe customer behavior, because customers can't always tell you what they need. And as they develop products and services, they create physical and digital platforms that monitor the customer experience, learn from it, and iterate offerings and experiences around it. (Of course, you know all of this if you've just read Chapter 12.)

Talent management can learn from these techniques to improve workforce experience. One way to get started is to prioritize the same focus on observation. By using ethnographic research in the workplace (and on remote platforms), human resource professionals can observe workers' behavior, rather than just asking about their beliefs, which invites bias. This type of research can be incredibly valuable, because it can help to uncover both opportunities and challenges for workforce engagement. Before you worry that we are advocating for surveillance of your home office, let's bring this to life with an example.

A number of recent studies use observational research to explore gender dynamics in meetings. One study evaluated how often Supreme Court Justices interrupted each other. It turns out that the male justices interrupted the female justices roughly three times as often as they interrupted each other during oral arguments.[196] Another meta-analysis of forty-three studies showed that men were more likely than women to interrupt others, and in ways that were more intrusive. Interestingly, still another study of 5,000 people listening to men and women interjecting found that impressions of women were substantially more negative, even though the scripts and interjections were identical between genders. As a result, you may not be surprised to know that women tend to speak 40 percent less versus men (though it is widely, and wrongly, believed that women talk more than men).[197]

Observational studies such as these help to reveal what is *actually* going on. They are important tools for creating benefits and training that can address the opportunities and challenges uncovered. Given findings like the one above, what could talent management do to guarantee that female workers and management are heard? Training all workers in better communication would be a start. Continuing additional research might help to tease out the structural problems (for example, lack of seniority among women) and habitual behaviors that can be changed (such as failing to start a meeting with introductions). Once people learn that their experience is important, and they are empowered to speak up, the culture can become a virtuous circle of better behaviors, better experiences, and better performance.

In our workforce focus groups, many participants expressed frustration at the response they received from their employer when sharing their opinion. For example, workers told us they were especially frustrated when, after sharing their concerns, they were told that noth-ing could be done because "It's company policy," or "It's the way we've always done it." If this reminds you of our orthodoxy-flipping discus-sion from Chapter 8, you're not alone. This type of rhetoric implies that organizations are not doing enough to suggest to workers that they are listening, responding, and willing to change.

Listening to workers and soliciting input is another area that Chevron and Rhonda Morris are tackling head-on. When she was creating remote work guidelines, Morris solicited ideas from each of the compa-ny's twelve worker networks. They gave honest and open feedback, and the company incorporated many of their ideas into the guidelines. As a result, worker networks became advocates across the company. "They really felt empowered and part of the solution," Morris said, "because their opinions were asked, and they felt heard."

When talent management measures workforce experience, it can manage and improve the experience along the same critical path that marketing uses to create new and better products and services. Compet-ing for talent today is like competing for customers. The competition is fierce, the tools are available, and the stakes are very high. As talent remains scarce and trust remains low, leaders need to be doing more to continue to "recruit the talent they already have."

And workers *want* to trust their organizations. In general, workers gain personal satisfaction from making a positive impact on those they serve. Further, they are proud to work for an employer that performs well. In one of our focus groups, this was particularly well articulated by an incident manager at a technology company: "A lot of my self-worth comes from how well I perform my job. So I want to work for a com-pany that is good at what they do. It makes me happy. I don't want to work for a company that has an inferior product."

Delivering positive impact and earning the confidence of workers has a lot to do with the systems that underpin an organization, whether technological or operational. In the next chapter, we'll explore the ways an organization's operations and technology functions can enable or impede trust, especially through its focus on the Four Factors.

CHAPTER 14
Operations and Technology

In this chapter:

- The role of operations and technology in building trust
- Trust challenges faced by operations and technology
- Operations and technology principles for building trust

We've talked repeatedly about the importance of capability and reliability. Simply put, you don't build trust unless you have the ability to deliver on your promises. Whether you provide a service like financial planning or entertainment, or a product like a can of soup or a tablet computer, delivering what you promise consistently and on time is what it takes to build trust. And typically the functions responsible for making this happen are the operations and technology groups. To gain insight into what it means to bring trust to life in the field of operations and technology, we sat down with our fellow partner Abdi Goodarzi, who leads Deloitte's U.S. Enterprise Operations business, and Sabina Ewing, the Global CIO, Vice President of Business and Technology Services at Abbott, a global healthcare leader that operates at the nexus of healthcare and high tech and that makes devices like implanted pumps that support a failing heart.

Abdi has been in and around the operations and technology space for over twenty-five years. When he isn't advising global manufacturing operations, you might find him watching soccer with his two children, or you might see him scanning the latest car magazines—he's both an auto enthusiast and an expert on how all of the parts come together through the manufacturing process.

We met Sabina Ewing when the three of us participated on a panel about trust at the *Fortune* Most Powerful Women Summit in 2020. This event was important to us because it was the first time we shared the HX TrustID with a group that is so personally meaningful to us: senior women executives who are recognized as powerful in their respective fields. Ewing is an example of the powerful women the event attracts. Prior to joining Abbott, she served in multiple IT leadership roles at Pfizer and held management roles at Arthur Andersen Business Consulting, BearingPoint, and American Express. Ewing is passionate about learning and giving back, so much so that she took a year off early in her career to serve as a fifth-grade teacher in the South Bronx.

Information is Ewing's domain, and people trust her company—and, by extension, her—with their lives. "I'm in life sciences for a reason," says Ewing. "Consider where our devices and therapies are used, and you realize it's extraordinarily important that we deliver on quality. We build products that help people live longer and better at all ages and stages of life. And we're building them as if they're for our family members, whom we love. That's about credibility, and it's also about integrity, which is foundational to trust."

The Role of Operations and Technology in Building Trust

For those of us not in the operations or technology functions, it can be hard to wrap our heads around exactly how much goes on behind the scenes to make sure a product or service is designed, developed, built, and maintained effectively. Let's bring this to life. Most of us spend five or more hours on a smartphone every day.[198] Although you use this device all the time, you might not know that your smart-phone contains eight or more semiconductor chips that enable it to do all the incredible things you rely on and enjoy. Those chips are designed in one location, manufactured at another, warehoused some-where in groups of millions, and delivered to the final smartphone assembly plant.

That's just the chips. Consumer tech products like these can contain hundreds of similar components. In short, millions of individual actions result in the phone in your hand.

This is the kind of complex planning and management the opera-tions groups of large-scale companies do on a daily basis. Technology teams are responsible for building the systems that make it all work, another task of incredible complexity. And all of these capabilities and processes, from product design to quality control to information man-agement, must be continuously refined to align with evolving strategic choices, revenue expectations, and market demand. The operations and technology teams are what enables an organization to be *capable* of deliv-ering against the customer's needs and desires, and to do so *reliably*.

Trust Challenges Faced by Operations and Technology

Operations and technology leaders have a charter—delivering capably and reliably in the face of significant complexity—that can seem unwieldy. They need to have a mastery of the systems and platforms that work-ers and customers use to do their jobs. They need adequate experience with the ecosystem and business partners' technologies to deliver the outcomes clients and customers expect. (We talk more about the impor-tance of trust in technological networks in Chapter 15.) And they need reliable, timely information in order for everything to work smoothly. We will discuss two primary challenges that can impede these responsibilities:

- Internal trust
- Transparent communication

Internal Trust

The challenge here isn't just the complexity of the job. It's actually trust itself. Our colleague Abdi says, "These teams face competing objectives, and many have made faulty assumptions about what the other does or doesn't know, or what they can or can't do. At the end of the day this breeds distrust, which can result in unstable systems and unreliable performance." As Abdi put it, the heart of this challenge is the failure of business teams to trust and collaborate with partners in IT and operations (and vice versa). In order to collaborate effectively, business leaders must be able to describe *what* they hope to achieve, and then let IT and operations teams define *how* to make this happen. All too often, however, business leaders fall into the trap of assuming that IT won't understand the nuances and complexities of their business. Rather than taking the time to describe what they need, business leaders jump to describing how they want the technology to work; they are unlikely to fully understand the strengths and limitations of technology (after all, this isn't their expertise). In turn, this can result in expensive workarounds and customizations that drive complexity and expense.

On the other hand, technology teams may end up making decisions about technology and software without fully understanding business requirements. IT is often accused of saying no without collecting the business context behind a request or suggesting alternatives. These dynamics can lead an organization to use technology platforms that don't meet the needs of the business, resulting in low adoption and inefficient business processes.

Abdi shared an example of a company that undertook a large-scale transformation to migrate from their existing technology platform to a new system that would enable scalable business growth. The technology and business teams shared a deep mistrust for one another, leading to a lack of collaboration from the outset. Critical people were left out of early planning, which meant that many of the business requirements (in other words, the fundamental capabilities needed by the business to do their job) got lost in translation. Similarly, the business teams didn't value IT expertise about how to use the technology, leading to higher levels of required customization, driving up cost and inefficiencies. The budget ballooned by 250 percent, while the desired functionality fell short by 30–40 percent. This meant that the new solution failed to serve the needs of the business, and, as a result, the company could not decommission many of the legacy solutions it set out to replace. As Abdi told us:

> **" *I really can't overstate how important it is for technology and business teams to embrace the Four Factors of Trust.***
>
> *Take the time to listen and understand each other (humanity). Openly share both objectives and constraints (transparency). And of course, do the work effectively over and over (capability and reliability). Investing in building trust from the outset will continue to pay dividends."*

Transparent Communication

Communication and collaboration are known challenges for any function, and they are just as important for operations and technology, which rely on inputs from others to effectively deliver on business requirements. Compounding the challenge is the increasingly global nature of most organizations. It is now standard for companies to boast offices, workers, and customers in multiple cities, supply chains that source parts from dozens of countries, and shareholders from around the globe. This globalization adds undeniable value, but it presents distinct challenges, too.

Moreover, a lack of collaboration between headquarters and distant offices can lead to uneven participation in choices that impact global stakeholders. For example, if HQ doesn't involve its global stakeholders in creating strategy, they risk losing critical inputs about how a strategy might play out in local markets. Cultural misunderstandings, as we mentioned in Chapter 8, can certainly erode trust. More commonly, those who are not included in creating a solution are more detached and often less invested in its success.

To make a system that works for everyone, one designed to elevate the human experience for a diverse, far-flung workforce, the ops and tech teams must collect input from all kinds of stakeholders at the outset of the design process and throughout implementation. You might be thinking, "With all these people at the table, we're going to need a bigger table." And you're right. The complexity and time required to gather input from everyone involved can be daunting, but that's the path to building solutions that deliver what they promise reliably. And not incidentally, that's also a way to get early buy-in from critical players around the organization to build trust.

One of our favorite illustrations of this challenge is the beer game, an exercise created in the 1960s by Jay Forrester from MIT. At the time Ashley and Amelia joined the Monitor Group, all new U.S. consultants were challenged to play the beer game as part of introductory training (and before you jump to conclusions there was, unfortunately, no actual beer consumed). Both Ashley and Amelia were on losing teams. Though to be fair, all teams lose, at least to some degree.

So how do you play? The game consists of twenty-four rounds with four steps each: 1) check deliveries, 2) check orders, 3) deliver beer (although if the team didn't plan well, there may not be any beer to deliver—this is called backlog), and 4) make order decisions. There are team members representing retailers, distributors, wholesalers, and the manufacturer. Team members cannot see anything other than what is communicated to them through pieces of paper with orders or product numbers written on them. The goal is to minimize costs of the game, and players receive a one-point cost for holding excess inventory and a one-point cost for backlog orders.

How does it play out? Retailers place their order, which takes four weeks to arrive. Feeling mounting frustration from stockouts, retailers increase orders dramatically. Likewise, the wholesaler finds themselves out of stock due to the increase in retailer orders and orders larger batches from the brewery. The brewery, which takes two weeks to produce the beer, sees a large backlog of orders building up and in no time, all players are frantically trying to build inventory or to get rid of inventory in dramatic cycles (known as the bullwhip effect).

We love this exercise because it illustrates that humans are the weakest part of the supply chain. It also underscores that transparent communication is needed to deliver capably and reliably to build trust.

Operations and Technology Principles for Building Trust

As organizations get more and more complex, operations and technology need to expand their capabilities to deliver reliably, without jeopardizing the transparency of their business or the humanity of their stakeholders. In this way, the often back-office functions of ops and tech have a large role to play in establishing and scaling trust in a company, product, or service.

To build trust through operations and technology, concentrate on these principles:

- Focus on the fundamentals
- Consider humans, not just systems

Focus on the Fundamentals

Internally, delivering capabilities in operations and technology makes the difference between good and great performance. *Good* means the business platforms run smoothly, and the organization can focus on enterprise strategy, mission, and objectives. *Great* means the business platforms are nimble, adaptable, and easy to maintain. This allows the organization to focus on growth and stave off potential disruptions. To create an ecosystem that enables this future focus, the operations and technology groups must have a rock-solid foundation. Leadership has to "see over the horizon" to anticipate the point at which advanced systems, taking lots of time and money to set up, can meet long-term strategy, rather than lagging changes in enterprise direction. Just like any balancing act, this requires a lot of core strength.

Technology, in particular, plays a key role in establishing reliability, since many of the goods and services provided by organizations exist on digital platforms. As Ewing says, "The more connected we get, the more it's important for technological savvy to be a part of everything, including having cybersecurity front and center. You have to be intentional and focused on the fundamentals, and you can't go chasing after every new shiny object. It is the fundamentals that put a company on their toes and leaning forward, versus being back on their heels." (We agree with Ewing, and we'll dive into cybersecurity in the next chapter.)

Ewing's focus on delivering those fundamentals makes Abbott's operations and technology trustworthy in an evolving technical landscape. Demonstrating capability *reliably* over time builds trust and confidence that leaders in other disciplines will have the technical and business design support they need to grow their part of the business.

Consider Humans, Not Just Systems

We know that building interconnected systems for our complex, global organizations comes with many challenging decisions. As you weigh these choices, the most important thing to keep in mind is to make sure you're designing systems *for humans* (a topic you may recognize from last chapter, in our discussion of talent).

Ultimately, a good human experience (we dislike the word "users") is critical to driving the right outcomes. For the technology function especially, making products usable, intuitive, and simple is a good way to build trust. As a CIO, Ewing knows her decisions have an effect on every single person with a stake in Abbott. "We're not just the folks in the rear with the gear!" she said. "The systems that are foundational to the business are engaged one way or another by our workforce, our customers, and also with regulators around the world."

Often, your organization's technology and process super-users are just as important to a successful product or process launch as their executive managers. These workers, who operate "in-the-weeds," may have a reputation for technical or process expertise, which gives them "trust capital." Figure out who the equivalent influencers are within your organization, and you can leverage their "trust capital" for any needed technology or process changes. Likewise, it is important to identify key external stakeholders beyond the obvious; for example, business partners can be as important as customers. Today, there is not a single organization that doesn't have downstream and upstream partners in their supply chains. The success of the enterprise performance depends on every single one of them.

Once you've gotten acquainted with your humans, engage with them as early in the design process as possible. Typically, people are more likely to accept a new technology or process if they've helped shape it, since they often adjust their expectations during the process of co-creation. Ewing explains how treating one another with humanity can breed reciprocity and stronger working relationships: "It's not just honoring the humanity in others in terms of how you engage, but also offering grace in recognizing that the notion of perfection in anyone is a fallacy. Humanity also means offering yourself a little bit of grace. You still have to push, you still have high expectations, but see if that humanity pillar includes a little bit of grace. Recognize that even you are an imperfect human being."

And remember that designing for humans requires transparent communication. As the beer game so neatly illustrates, transparency formed through open lines of communication and relevant information at every stage helps to facilitate a smooth production and delivery process. Transparency requires balancing the information users and teams need to trust the technology and processes, and not overwhelming them with too much complexity. To this end, Abbott recently updated its consent forms and privacy statements to use everyday language, as opposed to legalese. Abbott is also working to build greater transparency with healthcare providers who use their products by developing a secure environment to encourage open feedback, while still protecting sensitive information. Ewing says:

" *When people think of transparent, they imagine seeing all the way through, but sometimes it's more a function of being forthcoming with the right information, such that it's relevant, digestible, and meaningful to the situation."*

What you communicate to a patient must be qualitatively different from what you communicate to a regulator's compliance team, because their transparency needs are different. Consider also that compliance data could just confuse and/or frustrate a consumer, which is not the purpose of transparency (Just like diners at a farm-to-table restaurant would rather be spared the transparent details of humane animal slaughter, as we suggested in Chapter 1.)

One area where this kind of transparency—and reliability—is increasingly important is in the realm of security, especially as it relates to technology. Look no further than the organizational charts of most every major tech company to see a "Trust and Safety" group, or some similarly named function. With that in mind, we turn to cybersecurity in the next chapter, to explore how you can build, preserve, and strengthen trust on this important dimension.

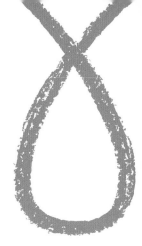

CHAPTER 15

Cybersecurity

In this chapter:

- The role of cybersecurity in building trust
- Trust challenges faced by cybersecurity
- Cybersecurity principles for building trust

The Role of Cybersecurity in Building Trust

L et's talk about data. Every time you take a photo, write an email, or even visit a website, you are producing data. Across the globe, there are 500 million tweets, over 300 billion emails, and nearly 19 billion text messages sent every day.[199] Today, the best estimates suggest that at least 2.5 exabytes of data are produced *daily*. And how big is an exabyte? An exabyte is one quintillion bytes. That's a one with eighteen zeros behind it! Let's put that into perspective. The largest physical library in the world is the Library of Congress, which holds more than 167 million items. One exabyte is equivalent to about 3,000 times the size of the Library of Congress[200]—which means that as a global society we produce enough data to fill 7,500 Libraries of Congress *every day*.

Cybersecurity teams are charged with protecting *all* of this data and keeping unauthorized users from accessing information that they shouldn't. In doing so, cybersecurity teams are also responsible for protecting identity—all the things that make you "you" online, such as usernames and your online activity: your de facto digital footprint. And, of course, cybersecurity teams must govern access to data in a manner consistent with applicable laws while doing so.

Cybersecurity teams play a critical role in fostering trust across a spectrum of stakeholder groups. Customers and workers expect their information to be secure and their privacy to be respected. Business partners and investors demand high levels of security. Regulators impose high expectations on organizations in their handling of personal data and proprietary data like intellectual property. And the stakes are high. While the literal cost of a breach (also called a "security event") or poor cyber hygiene can take the form of regulatory fines, or temporary disruption to service, the greater costs are typically those that harm longer-term brand reputation and value. Organizations impacted by these events fall 26 to 74 percent behind their industry peers in value.[201]

To articulate the challenges faced by cybersecurity, as well as the principles to consider when building trust through cyber, we enlisted help from our colleague Deb Golden, who leads Deloitte's U.S. Cyber and Strategic Risk practice, and Mike Hughes, the Chief Information and Security Officer (CISO) at REI.

We love that, in addition to being a cyber expert, Deb also raises and trains puppies with the Guide Dog Foundation and America's VetDogs, work inspired by her family's military history. Deb brings her service dogs with her to meetings and on trips to acclimate them to the world. Should you take a flight to or from Washington D.C., you might find her on that flight with her current steward, Benny.

Mike Hughes has spent over twenty years in the system engineering and information security space, leading teams at prominent companies like Target and Starbucks. Upon joining REI, he recalled, "My most vivid memory involving REI is almost twenty years old. A good friend purchased *Snowshoe Routes: Washington* and after many attempts, convinced me to rent snowshoes from REI and go snowshoeing in the Mt. Baker Forest. Two more rentals later and I was investing in backcountry snowshoes and mountaineering boots—and we spent the entire winter enjoying the outdoors. That led to years of exploring the mountains in the snow, when up until that point I had only ever experienced backcountry in the summer months."

Trust Challenges Faced by Cybersecurity

Cyber becomes more challenging and complex as a field every year. Not long ago, protecting data was like protecting a castle with walls and a moat: Technologies like firewalls and user verification created a perimeter around the castle. However, the landscape has changed with the advent of cloud computing and distributed networks. Data resides in multiple places, and cyber functions rely on multiple partners with varying capabilities. External threats are stealthy, well-funded, highly sophisticated, and global. In some cases, these threats are connected to malicious government agencies. At the same time, the pandemic has made this job harder, driven by greater reliance on remote working and information shared across a wide set of devices and technologies. This development has created new data vulnerabilities. Blockchain, 5G, Distributed Autonomous Organizations (DAOs), and virtual worlds will decentralize information even more. As business models adopt new technologies and platforms, cyber capabilities that build trust are ever more critical.

The technical challenges to bolstering cybersecurity are enormous. We will highlight the nuances of the three-pronged challenge faced by cyber teams when building trust, namely:

- The customer dilemma
- The workforce dilemma
- The partner dilemma

The Customer Dilemma

To deliver richer, more fulfilling human experiences, brands depend on vast quantities of personal data. For example, when Ashley shops for shoes online, she wants to be able to track her orders and revisit past purchases. Amelia is a fan of the time-saving option to start from her past order when ordering pizza for her kids on a Saturday night. Arguably these benefits are basic requirements for a good shopping experience, and they all take quite a lot of personal data.

Deb acknowledges that this poses a dilemma for organizations: "Collection and use of data is now core to business models everywhere, and leaders will need to reevaluate their approach to balancing the risk and value of data. While data can create incredible opportunities to enhance experience, it can also destroy value and erode trust if not properly protected and secured. Forward-leaning leaders are proactively thinking about balancing benefits and risks, working closely with other executives in marketing and experience, risk, legal, IT, and board members to make informed choices." Moreover, customers have grown wary of giving so much information to be monetized by tech giants and others without personal benefit. Most customers will allow brands to collect data, but only if the customers feel it is relevant and useful to them personally. They also want a choice in what data is captured and how it is used. For instance, in our recent study, 68 percent of respondents said they found it helpful when a brand they regularly shopped with provided them alerts when items go on sale. In comparison, 11 percent found these alerts creepy. We can subtract the percentage of customers who find this activity intrusive from the customers who find it helpful to get a "net helpful score." In this case, getting relevant alerts received a net helpful score of 57 percent. At the other end of the spectrum, people reacted negatively when it appeared as though their device was listening to them. You're chatting with a friend about your caffeine craving, and a coffee ad shows up in your social media feed. In this case, 26 percent suggested this interaction was helpful, while an overwhelming 53 percent indicated the interaction was intrusive (net helpful score of negative 27 percent). (See Figure 15.1.)[202]

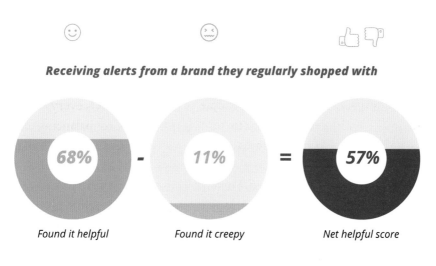

Customer reactions to tracking vary based on relationship with the brand

Receiving alerts from a brand they regularly shopped with

| 68% | - | 11% | = | 57% |
| Found it helpful | | Found it creepy | | Net helpful score |

Receiving alerts that appeared their device was listening

| 26% | - | 53% | = | -27% |
| Found it helpful | | Found it creepy | | Net helpful score |

Figure 15.1

Customers' desire to share data is strongly influenced by their relationship with the organization in question, and the extent to which it benefits them individually.

> *Consumers want their data to be gathered and used intelligently, in a way that benefits them, at the same time as they want their privacy protected.*

To satisfy this demand, organizations must design ways for customers to manage their data dynamically and make those choices visible with easily understood interfaces.

Organizations should also make informed choices about what data to gather and what data *not* to gather. Cyber teams play a critical role in guiding colleagues in marketing and experience about the risks associated with data collection, and which data itself may present the greatest risk relative to the value of the data. Once those choices are made, cyber teams are responsible for protecting and governing the use of that data. Cyber professionals also need to consider how data collection practices are communicated to customers, as well as the level of autonomy given to customers in choosing which data to provide. The level of authority and decision-making varies greatly from organization to organization. In some cases, cyber teams are responsible for these choices, while in others these decisions are driven by the business side. In either case, cyber teams are responsible for the trust built or lost through these actions and must collaborate closely with other teams in the process.

The Workforce Dilemma

Cybersecurity is also critical to worker trust, because the organization is entrusted with an incredible amount of sensitive data from workers—social security numbers, retirement plans, home and family information, tax and health information, just to name a few. That information can be destructive in the wrong hands. Securing that information is as vital as ensuring physical safety was in twentieth-century industrial workplaces.[203]

On the flip side, workers themselves can also present security dilemmas. Today's technologies empower people to work from home, create content and new products and services, analyze data, collaborate inside and outside the organization, communicate, sell company goods and services, and serve customers. Most of that value-added activity requires people to have some level of secure access by way of an identified and authorized identity, making workers one of the single biggest cybersecurity concerns.

In a recent WSJ study, 67 percent of cybersecurity professionals surveyed said they were concerned about malicious employees.[204] However, most breaches are due to human error, and not malicious intent. Researchers from Stanford University and Tessian, a cybersecurity firm, found that approximately 88 percent of all data breaches are caused by an employee mistake.[205]

A recent example is the 2017 breach of one of the U.S.-based credit reporting agencies (CRA), which exposed the personal data of more than 147 million people and resulted in a $425 million settlement. In his congressional testimony, the CEO repeatedly referred to an "individual" in the CRA's technology department who failed to "heed security warnings and did not ensure the implementation of software fixes that would have prevented the breach."[206] It's hard to believe that one careless person could cause so much damage. If this anecdote inspired you to update the software on your laptop right this second, join the club.

In the case of workers, cybersecurity teams need to ensure everyone is accountable for protection through education, training, and enforcement.

The Partner Dilemma

Organizations of all sizes rely on a complex ecosystem of partnerships to bring their goods and services to market in a way that either builds or erodes trust for their consumers. Companies will source materials for production, work with cloud partners on information management and accessibility, work with advertising partners on brand messaging, and rely on shipping companies for delivery, to name just a few examples of partnership. Each of these transactions involves sharing the data and information needed for the task, which must be protected by cyber teams. Sourcing materials might include order quantity and type, as well as payment information. Working with advertisers might involve sharing data on brand perception and consumption. Delivery partners will need access to customer names, addresses, and orders to process shipments. With all of this data sharing required, organizations may only be as strong as the weakest link.

This is one of the reasons why the business functions should be bringing the cybersecurity teams into the decisioning process when it comes to partner evaluation. While cyber teams don't typically make the choice about a business partner, they can help assess the associated risks. Hughes describes choosing partners much like the process for choosing a daycare center for your children. "You would expect your children to be just as safe in daycare as they are at home. The same is true in the cyber realm. Organizations should expect their data to be equally as safe and secure in the hands of a third party as it is when in the organization's own control."

This level of protection and care is critical, because mistakes made by partners can echo throughout the business ecosystem and cause significant harm. We saw this effect in incidents like the 2021 SolarWinds attack, in which malware on the company's system spread through software updates to 18,000 customers, an entire network of business relationships.[207] This incident was a sophisticated attack that impacted a wide range of organizations. According to SEC reports, the breach impacted Fortune 500 companies as well as multiple agencies in the U.S. government. This attack underscores the significant consequences of a security event on an organization's ability to function smoothly and reliably—and the risk that one node (let alone secondary and tertiary relationships) in a network will raise broader network risk. The attack also underscores the point that getting visibility is incredibly hard; one organization could have thousands of vendor relationships, each of which could be a point of attack.

Deb suggests that the SolarWinds attack might represent an inflection point. She says, "Incidents like SolarWinds have created even more scrutiny over supply chains, underscoring that an organization's security is only as strong as the security of partners (and the broader vendor network of those partners as well). Organizations are accountable for safeguarding information and share a responsibility to respond and manage broader network threats in near real-time. This presents a daunting challenge and severe risk for organizations. However, for those organizations that do this well, there is also an incredible opportunity to build and bolster trust."

Cybersecurity Principles for Building Trust

Even with significant advances and a more holistic approach, many organizations are not prepared for the innovative new methods malicious cyber actors use to attack both their data and the data of alliance partners. Cyber threats can spread, only becoming visible when an entire business ecosystem is infected. Simply put, organizations cannot build trust without a strong cyber program.

In order to build trust through cyber, we will discuss four key principles:

- Consider prevention to be aspirational (but not always realistic)
- Be an enabler, not a blocker
- Share intent and allow choice
- Plan for human error

Consider Prevention to Be Aspirational (But Not Always Realistic)

"Protect and prevent" is a mantra familiar to any cyber professional: Protect the organization's data infrastructure from attack and prevent data incidents such as accidental misuse of data by workers. What might be less familiar, though increasingly accepted in the cyber world, is the expectation that prevention is an aspiration, but not a realistic goal on its own.

Given the highly complex and rapidly evolving nature of the cyber landscape, it's reasonable to expect that organizations are facing and managing threats every single day that will impact trust. It is similarly reasonable to expect that some of these attacks will be effective, and that a company should measure success based on how quickly the threat is managed rather than how many threats are avoided. Mike Hughes said, "If a company claims that they don't have any security events and investigations, you should never do business with them because that's an indication that their security isn't strong enough. These minor events must be remediated quickly as they are the beginnings of potential data breaches and large incidents."

A better definition of success is evaluating dwell time, or the elapsed time it takes to detect an attack, in combination with the time it takes an organization to recover. Cyber teams are ultimately responsible for making sure that businesses can go on as usual without cyber interruptions, workers can access the systems needed to do their jobs, and customers can continue to engage, use services, and make purchases. To help us understand what this means for REI, Hughes told us the story of how REI was formed.

It all began with an ice axe. Specifically, there was a brand of ice axe sold in Austria that was difficult and expensive to get in the States. REI's founders realized that collective buying power would enable access to better gear at a cheaper price, so the concept of an outdoor goods co-op was born. Today, REI's goal is still to ensure that everyone gets a taste of how it feels to live life well by enjoying their time outdoors. For Hughes, this means keeping workers and customers safe from attacks and ensuring resilience: "The goal for us is to enable the outdoor adventure lifestyle—that's really what we're designed to do." Imagine someone is planning their summer camping trip but can't access REI's website. They might go somewhere else to make a purchase, or they may forgo the gear, neither of which promotes REI's ambition and brand.

To minimize dwell time (the length of time a cyber attacker is in the system), limit recovery requirements, and ensure smooth operations, Hughes promotes a belt-and-suspenders approach. Companies should build redundant safety procedures to help both contain the threat and manage risk. Increasingly, this means organizations are adding "detect and defend" to the mantra of "prevent and protect." The two strategies work in concert. No prevention program will be perfect, which is why organizations will always need a detect and defend program as well.

Organizations should also place a vigorous emphasis on embedding cyber and trust into their business practices. This adoption will allow them to be better poised to withstand relentless adversaries; strengthen relationships with customers, partners, and employees; and reduce distractions. By proactively anticipating these challenges, while being nimble and resilient to a range of potentially disruptive scenarios, companies can focus on the mission.

Be an Enabler, Not a Blocker

Balancing the opportunities seen by CMOs and CXOs, such as bringing in a new data vendor, and the need to engender trust through data protection and privacy, means there is no room for silos in cyber work. A partnership between marketing (which generally determines what data to collect) and cyber (which guarantees privacy, security, and compliance) is required to deliver a safe, seamless experience to customers and other stakeholders.

Hughes points out that marketing organizations tend to be very optimistic about partnerships. Marketers see the upside in revenue or new customer acquisition. "That kind of optimism makes it easy to ignore warning signs, so my team's job is to work carefully with third parties and understand their strength in privacy, security, governance, and engineering. We need to build a holistic picture for our organization. If there are red flags we'll work with the potential partner, recommending they do a few things differently with their cyber so we can go forward. And if that can't happen, we'll probably tell our sales and marketing people this doesn't look like a good idea."

CISOs enable data owners (CMO/CXO and others) to achieve their strategy safely and in compliance with regulations by providing expertise early in their processes. Building strong relationships based on listening, and finding mutually beneficial solutions to conflicting interests, is the first step. Be prepared to explain consequences of data breaches in terms that your colleagues will understand, such as customer attrition, revenue loss, and degradation of stakeholder trust. If the cyber leader is not especially skilled at explaining scenarios and consequences, someone on their team must be—trust is not earned by blocking others from achieving their jobs but by making your knowledge and judgment contribute to their goals.

Share Intent and Allow Choice

Of course, when you're talking about gaining trust, the most important asset you need to protect is often an individual's data. Organizations should state, in plain language, how and why an individual's data will be used (remember the discussion from Chapter 14 on relevant transparency). To put a finer point on it, this *does not* mean a ten-page legal document designed to protect an organization's interests. It *does* mean helping people to understand why their data is being used and what's in it for them personally.

Trusted organizations are also more willing to give control to individuals by empowering them to choose their own data and privacy preferences. This empowerment is a pathway to higher perceptions of humanity—that the company's cyber practices value a person's individual preferences. It's important to note that humans are highly likely to stick with default settings; if the default is to share a lot of data, and customers have to execute many steps to change the settings, they typically won't do that (or they will do it partially, or unsuccessfully). Organizations should recognize this pattern and carefully consider strategies, such as opt-in and opt-out. A simple example of an opt-in model is when users select what they do and don't want to share, versus an opt-out model, in which users have to figure out what's being gathered and proactively request that the data-gathering stop. In our research, we've seen some of the least trusted brands going for opt-out, giving many users an unpleasant and trust-destroying surprise later when they discover what's been captured.

There can be no doubt that agency is critically important to individuals, and we can look to Apple as an example. In April 2021, Apple introduced a feature allowing iPhone® mobile device[208] users to choose whether advertisers could track their online activity. By December 2021, 89 percent of U.S. iPhone users were running a recent enough version of the software to be presented with the prompts. And of those with the ability, 71 percent chose to opt out of tracking. This decision exposed a significant lack of trust,[209] particularly in social media companies, four of which collectively lost $278 billion of market value as a result of people opting out in this way.[210]

Plan for Human Error

Human error comes with the cyber territory. Everyone plays a role in safeguarding security and reducing risk. While technology can do a lot to help reduce cyber risk, addressing fundamentally human factors is both important and very challenging.

For example, when cybersecurity experts promote complex verification codes without an easy way to use them, they tempt people to create workarounds (like writing down a code or using a nonsecure code file) that defeat the purpose. Getting locked out of one's organization account several times without simple recourse is frustrating and prompts people to think of systems as incompatible with work. They think, "It's too hard to get this done, I'll just use my personal smartphone this time," and you have a breach of security driven by frustration. Security measures are commonly seen as impediments rather than enablers of work, and they can't achieve their full potential without proactive teamwork from all other areas of the business.

Organizations can earn trust and promote desired behavior from workers by establishing "best intent" defaults that enable them to do their work with a minimal chance to expose data in the wrong places. An organization can build trust with workers by assuming that they are taking effective precautions to share data with only the relevant parties, particularly when sharing externally. It is also reasonable, however, to assume that workers make mistakes, so a best intent example in this case would be to have an additional pop-up for every external email with an attachment, asking the sender to be sure that the audience is in fact the intended audience, and that all recipients are authorized to receive this information.

The best cybersecurity teams treat workers as an extension of their practice. Cybersecurity should be the responsibility of every individual in the organization, and it requires collaboration from everyone, including leadership. For example, the C-suite has to make informed decisions around the right balance between security measures that offer protection, and those that are an encumbrance. Together, a CMO and a CISO can understand the implications of data collection choices and work to minimize risks to the customer.

Understanding and planning for human error, and working collaboratively across functions and levels, reduces the potential for cyber risks and increases trust.

At this point, we've explored the ways it is both crucial and challenging to build trust in key functions across an organization, as well as highlighting principles for surmounting those challenges. We turn now to the reason it is incumbent upon every one of us to put these principles into practice. In the next chapter, we discuss why trust matters, why organizations must take up this call to action, and how all of us can get started today, not just in our capacity as leaders but as customers, workers, and, most of all, humans.

Conclusion

In this chapter:
- The urgent need to build trust today
- Why organizations must lead the way
- Principles for building trust

O ur research gives us tremendous hope for the future, because collectively organizations have the resources and power to change the world by creating and maintaining trust.

The Urgent Need to Build Trust Today

Our friend David Kirby of Ford offers this poignant analogy for how essential trust is to the fabric of our society: If you go to a meeting in a conference room, the first thing you do is find an empty chair and sit down at the table. Imagine one day you pull up the nearest chair and plop down. Before you know what happened, you find yourself with an ungraceful landing on the floor, the broken chair upturned beside you. The next day, will you sit down immediately, or will you instead check your chair first?

If you have to check your chair every time you sit, or confirm your bank is holding your money safe, or sniff-test your food every time you eat . . . If you have to wonder if a product will work as advertised, or question whether your employers will keep their promises . . . If you have to do all these things, you won't have time to do much more.

Trust is foundational to human progress. Tens of thousands of years ago, humans lived in small nomadic groups that traveled together, hunted together, and gathered periodically with other groups. Out of this grew tribal culture, and eventually individuals took on specialized roles. Some hunted. Some gathered food. Others made tools and created useful objects. Some raised children, and others tended animals. You didn't steal food from somebody in your tribe because you needed the tools she was making.

As societies evolved, spoken languages developed and were later written down. Much of the earliest writing recorded transactions in a barter economy as a way of preserving records and "enforcing" trust.[211] These ten sheep skins in exchange for those five sharpened blades. There is a practical reason that happened. Humans can maintain about 150 social relationships at a time. After that we need analogues like writing to record and remember information important to relationships.[212]

In this way, implicit trust from within the tribe could be extended to those outside the tribe. Trust was less about whose tribe or family you were from. Instead, trust was replaced by written contracts and laws. Those who were trustworthy relied on a framework of rules (called the "rule of law") to trust people they didn't know. The untrustworthy were forced into some degree of good behavior by threat of punishment.

This is how you codify trust among millions—by creating ways that the trustworthy can continue their lives and work, protected from the untrustworthy by social institutions. Trust in abstractions like "money" grew out of a need to carry on transactions beyond barter.

Now, however, we believe that the world is facing a trust deficit that has a direct impact on national economic performance. In Chapter 2 we shared that economists Paul Zak and Stephen Knack found that a 15 percent rise in a nation's belief that "most people can be trusted" adds a full percentage point to economic growth every year.[213] If you apply the economists' math to the *global* economy at the time of this writing, you find that a 15 percent rise in belief that most people can be trusted would add $847 billion (!) to annual GDP.[214]

Why Organizations Must Lead the Way

Even though trust has eroded, companies and nonprofits are starting from a position of relative strength in society. We believe that gives organizations the opportunity—and responsibility—to revitalize trust. There are three reasons in particular that we want to highlight:

- Demonstrated track record of innovation and agility
- Relative position of strength
- Building trust is an economic imperative

Demonstrated Track Record of Innovation and Agility

Organizations are far more nimble than other institutions when it comes to solving problems. Innovative companies succeed by finding new ways to create experiences and satisfy customers. Modern charitable organizations like the Gates and Skoll Foundations are engines of innovation in nonprofit work. The great innovative movements of recent decades, like agile management and design thinking, find their practical testing in organizations willing to try new things. These organizations are looking for a competitive edge, or more complete fulfillment of their missions.

Organizations, and especially businesses, are capable of changing course when needed. Only a few years ago, auto executives might have said, "Don't talk to me about electric vehicles. They'll never replace the gas vehicle." In 2022, all the major car companies are redesigning their fleets with dozens of new, fully electric models. A few are committing billions to being fully electric within a decade.[215] Some of the world's most powerful business leaders are pushing hard on their organizations and others to take broad action on climate change, arguing that it poses a threat to profits as well as lives.[216]

Relative Position of Strength

Businesses are now the most trusted type of institution. Edelman, a global communications firm, completed their twenty-first study on public trust, surveying more than 33,000 people in over twenty-eight countries. According to their research, businesses earn the highest level of trust (61 percent), closely followed by NGOs (59 percent). Both types of organizations are more trusted than the government (52 percent) and media companies (50 percent), which are perceived as highly divisive.[217]

Not only are businesses more trusted, but they are also increasingly expected to be drivers of positive change. We believe they should shape policy debates about the economy, inequality, and climate change, and improve healthcare and education. And, as we discussed in Chapter 11, workers are looking specifically to *their own* employers. While just over half of U.S. respondents said they trust businesses, almost three-quarters view their own employers as a mainstay of trust.[218]

Increasingly we look to business and NGO leaders to rebuild trust. And if they don't, who else is going to do it?

Building Trust Is an Economic Imperative

Ultimately, business leaders must realize that if their humans don't thrive, their organization won't survive. When humans thrive, traditional metrics thrive as well: long-term profitability, resilience in the face of relentless change, fulfilling a purpose, and enduring shareholder value.[219] This premise has fueled the rise of ESG and stakeholder capitalism to mainstream prominence, discussed in Chapter 11.

Economists will tell you that trust is necessary for ongoing economic relationships. People want to do business with organizations that are not solely interested in maximizing profit with every transaction. Even a purely rational analysis, the kind that dominated economic thinking for hundreds of years, suggests that creating trust matters to organizations who want to last for a significant time because it creates repeat customers.[220]

Behavioral economics remind us that people are not fully rational in their economic decisions. Because people have a limited ability to hold all details of a relationship in mind at once, they revert to making choices based on a "gut feeling." The lesson is: You won't build trust with purely rational arguments. In the famous words of Maya Angelou, what matters most is how people *feel* about their experiences of the Four Factors of Trust.

Principles for Building Trust

We want to leave you with a final word on five principles you can use to turn trust into a discipline that elevates the human experience for your workers, customers, and partners.

- First, humanize *yourself*, modeling trustworthy leadership behaviors to your teams.
- Then measure trust and the component factors of humanity, transparency, capability, and reliability. The HX TrustID questions are free to use, and we hope that you will take them and apply them to your organization.
- Design humanity, transparency, capability, and reliability into your organizational culture so they are part of every interaction.
- Don't go it alone. We hope we have demonstrated through the stories we shared that building trust is a coordinated team effort across every part of the organization and partner ecosystem.
- Finally, lead with transparency by reporting on trust both internally with your teams and externally in your public statements.

It is our ambition to build trust and help leaders positively impact the humans in their ecosystem. And we can do this while continuing to drive profitable growth, which can be a powerful fuel for good. After all, profit is how capital creates both more jobs and better jobs.[221] In nonprofit companies, revenue is the fuel that turns ideas and values into real-world results. After the revenues and profits are earned and put to use, though, the larger questions remain: "Am I improving the world? Am I fulfilling a greater mission? Do I work for more than wealth, power, or fame?"

We are passionate about building trust to elevate the human experience *because it creates the types of organizations we want to belong to, and the type of world in which we want to live.*

Appendix

APPENDIX A
HX TrustID Survey Methodology

Response Scale

We use a 7-point response scale for the HX TrustID Factor and attribute questions.

1	2	3	4	5	6	7
Strongly Disagree	Dis-agree	Some-what Disagree	Neither Agree nor Disagree	Some-what Agree	Agree	Strongly Agree

Customer Survey Questions[222]

The Four Factors of HX TrustID

Please indicate the extent you agree or disagree with the following statements.

1. [Humanity] [Brand] demonstrates empathy and kindness towards me, and treats everyone fairly.

2. [Transparency] [Brand] openly shares all information, motives, and choices in straightforward and plain language.

3. [Capability] [Brand] creates quality products, services, and/or experiences.

4. [Reliability] [Brand] consistently and dependably delivers on its promises.

The HX TrustID Attributes

Please indicate the extent you agree or disagree with the following statements.

1. [Humanity] [Brand] quickly resolves issues with safety, security, and satisfaction top of mind.

2. [Humanity] [Brand] values and respects everyone, regardless of background, identity, or beliefs.

3. [Humanity] [Brand] values the good of society and the environment, not just profit.

4. [Humanity] [Brand] takes care of its employees.

5. [Transparency] [Brand]'s marketing and communications are accurate and honest.

6. [Transparency] [Brand] is upfront about how they make and spend money from our interactions.

7. [Transparency] How and why my data is used is communicated in plain and easy-to-understand language.

8. [Transparency] [Brand] is clear and upfront about fees and costs of products, services, and experiences.

9. [Capability] Products are good quality, accessible, and safe to use.

10. [Capability] Prices of products, services, and experiences are good value for money.

11. [Capability] Employees and leadership are competent and understand how to respond to my needs.

12. [Capability] [Brand] creates long-term solutions and improvements that work well for me.

13. [Reliability] [Brand] can be counted on to improve the quality of their products and services.

14. [Reliability] [Brand] consistently delivers products, services, and experiences with quality.

15. [Reliability] [Brand] facilitates digital interactions that run smoothly and work when needed.

16. [Reliability] [Brand] resolves issues in an adequate and timely manner.

Workforce Survey Questions

The Four Factors of HX TrustID

Please indicate the extent you agree or disagree with the following statements.

1. [Humanity] [My employer] demonstrates empathy and kindness towards me.

2. [Transparency] [My employer] uses straightforward and plain language to share information, motives, and decisions that matter to me.

3. [Capability] [My employer] creates a good work experience for me and provides the resources I need to do my job well.

4. [Reliability] [My employer] consistently and dependably delivers upon commitments it makes to me.

The HX TrustID Attributes

Please indicate the extent you agree or disagree with the following statements.

1. [Humanity] [My employer] values and treats workers with respect.

2. [Humanity] I feel [my employer] cares about my well-being.

3. [Humanity] [My employer] treats everyone fairly.

4. [Humanity] I feel engaged by the culture of [my employer].

5. [Transparency] Important communications are timely and informative.

6. [Transparency] [My employer] is open and communicative about how the business is doing.

7. [Transparency] [My employer] provides visibility into how their actions align with their stated values.

8. [Transparency] The information I need to do my job is easy to find and understand.

9. [Capability] I respect leadership's ability to make good decisions.

10. [Capability] [My employer] provides tools, technology, and resources that allow me to do my job well.

11. [Capability] [My employer] follows through on and achieves its stated goals.

12. [Capability] [My employer] delivers an exceptional work experience.

13. [Reliability] I feel [my employer] is committed to and accountable to its workforce.

14. [Reliability] I can count on [my employer] to improve its policies and procedures in support of its employees.

15. [Reliability] I can depend on [my employer] to support me and address issues that I raise.

16. [Reliability] When an internal crisis or incident occurs, I can count on [my employer] to handle it.

How to Calculate the HX TrustID Score

Now that we have outlined our methodology, let's walk through a more detailed example of how to calculate the HX TrustID score.

1. Define the responses:
   a. Strongly Agree and Agree responses are defined as Positive/High Trust.
   b. Somewhat Agree, Neither Agree nor Disagree, and Somewhat Disagree responses are defined as Neutral Trust.
   c. Strongly Disagree and Disagree responses are defined as Negative/Low Trust.

Negative/Low Trust			Neutral Trust		Positive/High Trust	
Strongly Disagree	**Disagree**	**Some- what Disagree**	**Neither Agree nor Disagree**	**Some- what Agree**	**Agree**	**Strongly Agree**

2. Based on the 7-point scale for humanity, here is an example of how the percentage of respondents broke out across these three buckets for a particular brand.

Humanity

Negative/Low Trust	Neutral Trust	Positive/High Trust
11%	43%	46%

3. To get to this brand's humanity score, we would subtract 11 (the Negative/Low Trust) from 46 (the Positive/High Trust) for a humanity score of 35.

   High Trust (46) – Low Trust (11) = Humanity score **(35)**

4. Repeat this calculation for the remaining Four Factors.

Transparency

Negative/Low Trust	Neutral Trust	Positive/High Trust
7%	45%	48%

Transparency score: 48 − 7 = **41**

Capability

Negative/Low Trust	Neutral Trust	Positive/High Trust
5%	40%	55%

Capability score: 55 − 5 = **50**

Reliability

Negative/Low Trust	Neutral Trust	Positive/High Trust
9%	38%	53%

Reliability score: 53 − 9 = **44**

5. To calculate the brand's composite score, we would take a straight average of the Four Factors.[223]

   Composite HX TrustID score: (35 + 41 + 50 + 44) / 4 = **43**

APPENDIX B

The Demographics
That Matter Most
for Customers

For customers, the following demographics drive trust in descending order:

- *Parenthood:* Parents are more likely to trust brands.
- *Geography:* Urban customers trust more than suburban ones, who trust more than rural customers.
- *Education level:* More educated customers are more likely to trust.
- *Age:* Millennials trust the most, followed by Gen Z, X, Boomer, and Silent.
- *Living situation:* Those living with others (especially married) trust more than those living alone.

Parents are more likely to trust brands than non-parents

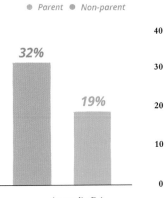

● Parent ● Non-parent

Appendix B.1

Parenthood

Parents are the most likely to be trusting among all groups we surveyed. Parents are about 70 percent more trusting than non-parents. The reasons behind this might not seem obvious when thinking about parenthood as a demographic variable. However, through the lens of *expectations*, the rationale becomes clearer. Most parents will agree that having children wildly alters their expectations. For example, when Ashley had twins, she quickly adjusted to expecting little or no sleep (the twins are now four and this is still true). Additionally, caring for others creates limitations on how and where parents spend their time and resources, further influencing expectations.

Urban customers trust brands more than suburban or rural customers

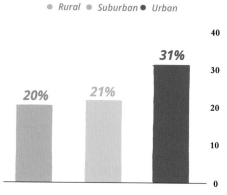

Appendix B.2

Geography

The geographic density of a customer's location showed noticeable correlation with customer trust. Urban dwellers trust most, then suburban, then rural. Urban customers are about 48 percent more trusting than suburban customers and about 55 percent more trusting than rural customers. We believe these three geographic variables show correlation rather than causation. Similarly, it's hard to know whether people move to cities because they trust, or move to rural areas because they distrust, or whether the experience of where you live shapes whether you trust. A similar dynamic might apply to those living in cities. They are near centers of business and commerce, with more customer choices and options. Accordingly, urban customers have more ability to set expectations for what businesses will do for them, and, therefore, more agency to bring about the outcomes they desire.

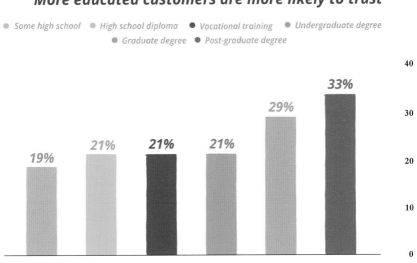

More educated customers are more likely to trust

Appendix B.3

Education Level

As educational attainment increases, we see a clear pattern of increased trust across all Four Factors. On average, those with postgraduate degrees are 61 percent more trusting than those without any graduate degree. Similarly, those with graduate degrees are about 42 percent more trusting than those without. Education contributes to *agency*—to a person feeling more autonomous, with more choices among brands. Greater educational attainment also implies a person has more tools for comparison and choice, including technological and critical thinking skills, as well as a wider range of customer experiences to draw on (similar to workers moving up a job ladder). The more educated are less worried about the potential for disappointing buying decisions and tend to have more choice when buying. Whether the cause is economic advantage, or a sense of empowerment through knowledge, people who are educated have a greater freedom (through agency) to trust a brand.

Millennial customers trust the most, followed by Gen Z, Gen X, Baby Boomer, and the Silent Generation

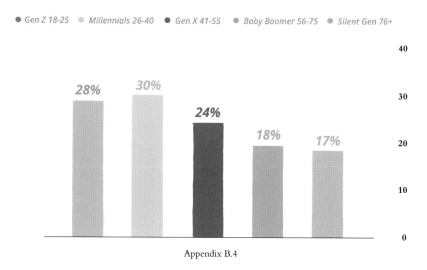

● Gen Z 18-25   ● Millennials 26-40   ● Gen X 41-55   ● Baby Boomer 56-75   ● Silent Gen 76+

Appendix B.4

Age

Our data reveal that Millennials have the highest trust, followed by Gen Z and Gen X, and finally Baby Boomers and the Silent Generation. Millennial customers are about 44 percent more trusting than the average of non-Millennial customer generations. Notably, while age is one of the top variables for customers across all Four Factors of Trust, it didn't rise to the top for workers (see Appendix B.4.) And yet, the contrast is not that surprising. Your age as a customer has more influence over your *agency* and *expectations* than your age as a worker (where job level and role are much more important, even though they often correlate with age). We believe that agency is again the key driver of this difference. Familiarity with technology (among younger generations) makes it easier to have *agency* because people know how to use digital tools to get the answers they need. Many Millennials tell eye-rolling stories about their Baby

Boomer parents asking if they should download a software update every time Microsoft or Apple releases one. Similar stories get told about older generations' slow adoption of services like electronic banking.

Those living with others (especially married) trust more than those living alone

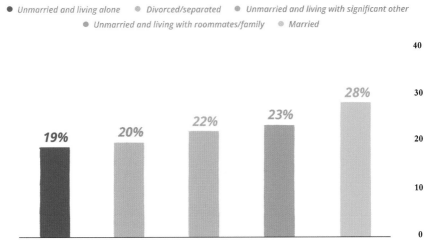

- Unmarried and living alone ● Divorced/separated ● Unmarried and living with significant other
- Unmarried and living with roommates/family ● Married

Appendix B.5

Living Situation

People who are married and living together are 47 percent more trusting than people who are single and living alone. Similarly, those who are unmarried but live with other people (roommates/family or significant other) are on average 19 percent more trusting than those unmarried and living alone. It is hard to know whether people marry and/or live with others because they already trust more, or whether the experience of living with others shapes trust. From our own experience, we know that living with others requires more flexibility (and sometimes patience), and likely this experience may translate to a more flexible trust perspective. It's important to note also that marital status will have a strong correlation with parental status, and per above we know that parents have a higher likelihood to trust.

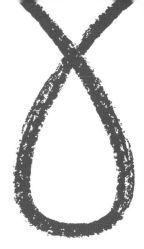

The Demographics That Matter Most for Workers

The top variables associated with trust levels for workers were consistent (but not identical) across all Four Factors.

The most significant variables we found were:

- *Job level:* The more senior you are, the more trusting you are.

- *Flexible working schedule:* Those who have flexibility are more trusting, possibly from a sense of greater agency to influence their work experience.

- *Organization type:* Those who work for privately owned (versus publicly traded companies or the government) are likely to be more trusting.

The more senior a worker is, the more trusting they are

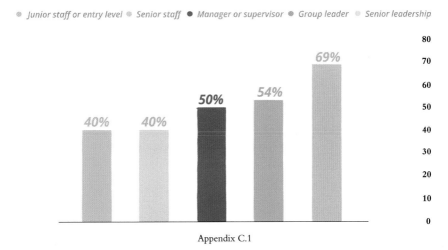

Junior staff or entry level ● Senior staff ● Manager or supervisor ● Group leader ● Senior leadership

Appendix C.1

Job Level

The higher workers move up in job level, the more likely they are to trust their employer. In our research, lower-level staff are only about 70 percent as trusting as executives. The closer workers are "to the top," the more they understand organizational strategy, and the more involved they are in the decision-making process. Seniority gives a worker important positional power. Therefore, when a worker is more senior, he or she has greater agency than those lower in the hierarchy. In addition, understanding the inner workings of an organization gives a worker more informed expectations, as well as greater positional power to get expectations met.

Business leaders overestimate the trust of their workforce

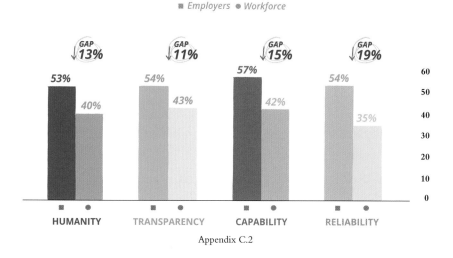

Appendix C.2

It's worth nothing that employers overestimate their workforce's trust level by almost 40 percent.[224] This is a workforce trust gap that mirrors how business leaders' overestimate customer trust (as discussed in Chapter 5). When executives assume everyone in the workforce trusts the organization as much as they do, they are often mistaken, and probably miss opportunities to improve engagement, retention, and performance.

Workers who have job flexibility are more trusting

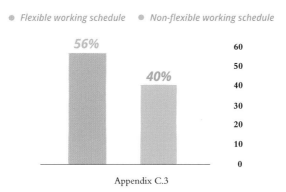

Appendix C.3

Flexible Working Schedule

Flexibility gives agency; lack of flexibility constricts agency. It makes sense that an unmet need for flexibility would trigger lower trust (across all Four Factors). When workers have flexibility, they are about 40 percent more trusting of their employers than when they do not have flexible work schedules.

For-profit workers are the most trusting—driven by the private workforce

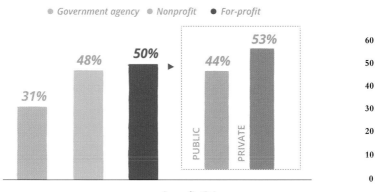

Appendix C.4

Organization Type

Those who work for privately owned versus publicly traded companies are more trusting across all Four Factors, but especially in transparency. Private company workers are about 21 percent more likely to trust than public company workers. This makes sense, as transparency is directly tied to setting expectations for private company workers. In private companies, leaders arguably have more control over the strategic agenda and workforce communications, which may drive workers' perception of transparency.

In comparison, government workers are even less trusting of their employers. Government workers are only 65 percent as trusting as non-profit workers and only about 62 percent as trusting as for-profit workers. Consider that the working environment is likely to play a high role in *expectations*. Government workers may not know what to expect (nor feel like they have much agency) if their roles are tied to the political winds or policy changes. In contrast to the cycle we saw in senior executives of companies, constraints to individual agency might mean that government workers have less power to see their expectations fulfilled.

We also found some interesting nuances and variables that were very important for one or two factors, but not all four:

- *Customer interaction:* Workers who interact with customers weekly or daily are more likely to view their employer as human and transparent.

- *Dependents:* Workers who have a dependent in their household (for example, a child or senior) are more likely to view their employer as reliable.

- *Performance compensation:* Workers whose compensation included performance bonuses (such as bonus pay or stock options) are more likely to view their employer as transparent and capable; transparency includes the sharing of financial performance, and capability is implied in the organization's success.

- *Number of benefits:* Workers with more benefits are more likely to view their employer as capable (for example, more health insurance like vision/dental, life insurance, disability, retirement/flex savings, paid time off, and/or medical leave, among others).

Workers who interact with customers frequently are more likely to view their employer as more human and transparent

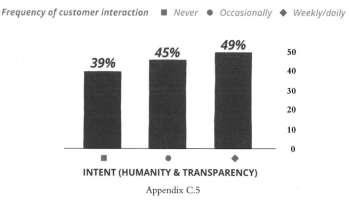

Appendix C.5

Customer Interaction

Workers who interact with customers regularly are more likely to rate their employers high in humanity and transparency. Workers who interact with customers on a weekly basis are about 18 percent more trusting than the average of workers who do not interact with customers on a weekly basis. Frontline workers represent their employer to the outside world and are expected to embody the organization's brand and customer focus. Good experience requires a high degree of humanity and transparency, which the frontline is asked to provide. In turn, these workers likely feel greater ownership in delivering humanity and transparency to customers. They may also have the agency to solve problems and satisfy customers directly.

Dependents

Workers who have a dependent in their household (for example, a child or senior) are more likely to view their employer as reliable. Perhaps workers who have dependents have sought out employers that can provide more holistic coverage and flexibility when it comes to taking care of themselves and their dependents. Perhaps they are more vocal about their needs and expectations with their employer—buying themselves more agency and their employers more trust via reliability. Perhaps employers, either through design or culture, emphasize the things (scheduling, predictable pay) that make them feel more reliable to those with dependents.

Workers who have a dependent in their household are more likely to view their employer as reliable

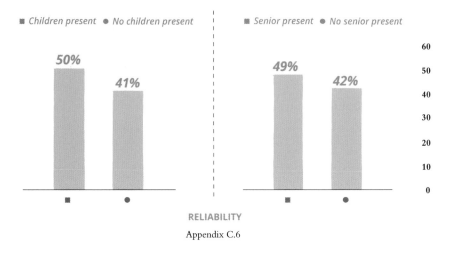

Appendix C.6

Workers with performance compensation are more likely to view their employer as transparent and capable

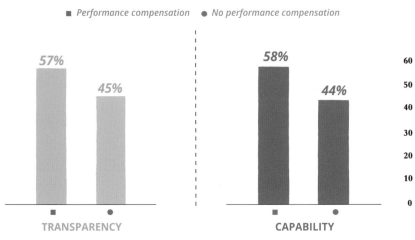

Appendix C.7

Performance Compensation

When it comes to pay, there is a strong relationship among transparency, capability, agency, and expectations. Workers who are compensated based on company performance likely feel greater *agency* over their compensation. By achieving greater performance, they increase their compensation. They likely view their employer as more capable as well, since they themselves are more actively invested in their organization's success (otherwise known as the self-attribution bias).[225]

The direct link between performance and compensation requires transparency in the numbers. In order to motivate workers, and to demonstrate equity, organizations likely need to be very transparent with how worker actions drive organizational performance, and how organizational performance translates to worker compensation. With such clarity, workers likely have more clear *expectations* around their roles and responsibilities, and how they will be compensated for their actions and efforts.

Workers with more benefits are more likely to view their employer as capable

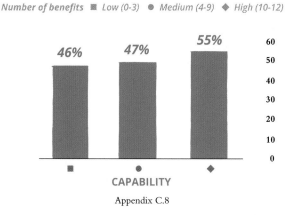

Appendix C.8

Number of Benefits

Workers with more benefits view their employer as more capable, as you can see in Appendix C.8. Types of benefits included in the numerical count are more health insurance (such as vision or dental), life insurance, disability, retirement/flex savings, paid time off, and/or medical leave, among others. A full suite of benefits makes workers feel like they are well-taken care of as whole humans, both at work and at home. Recall from Chapter 1 that a capable employer is one that creates a good work experience and provides the resources for workers to do their job well. It's no surprise that for many workers, this translates to a holistic benefits package. Feeling taken care of as a whole human allows workers to bring their best, most productive selves to work (as discussed in Chapter 13).

Workforce trust scores by ethnic identity (detailed)

Appendix C.9

Identity Demographics

As discussed in Chapter 6, the trust gap between ethnically diverse workers and those who identify as White evened out over the course of our research. See Appendix C.9 for a full demographic breakdown of trust within the workforce. The ethnicity options listed in each of our workforce surveys (May 2020, October 2020, October 2021) were as follows: American Indian or Alaska Native, Asian, Black or African American, Hispanic or Latino, multi-racial/other, Native Hawaiian or Other Pacific Islander, White or Caucasian. Ethnic groups with sample sizes below 50 are not included in Appendix C.9. It is important to note that the sample size for Native Hawaiian or Other Pacific Islander in our May 2020 survey and Multi-racial in our October 2020 survey were between 50 and 100 and may not be statistically significant.

Endnotes

Introduction

1. Sandra Sucher and Gupta Shalene, *The Power of Trust: How Companies Build It, Lose It, Regain It* (New York: PublicAffairs, 2021), 2.
2. Deloitte Human Experience in Uncertainty. Study. May 2020. 16,000 respondents: When asked to rank sources trusted to determine when it is safe to resume normal activities, 9 percent of respondents ranked their employer in their top 3 (as compared with 6 percent ranking local business in their top 3 and 4 percent ranking major business in their top 3).
3. "Public Trust in Government: 1958–2021," U.S. Politics & Policy, Pew Research Center, May 28, 2021, https://www.pewresearch.org/politics/2021/05/17/public-trust-in-government-1958-2021/.
4. Corey S. Powell, "Panic in Space Can Be Deadly. Here's How Astronauts Train to Stay Alive in Emergencies," NBCNews.com, July 19, 2018, https://www.nbcnews.com/mach/science/panic-space-can-be-deadly-here-s-how-astronauts-train-ncna892941. Accessed October 15, 2021.
5. Deloitte's HX TrustID dataset includes over 200K survey responses (customers and workforce), collected between May 2020 and June 2021.
6. As of this writing, a patent for the HX TrustID™ platform is pending.

Chapter 1

7. The competence and intent framework was developed by Deloitte leaders from across the globe and all our businesses in partnership with Sandra Sucher, an HBS professor and leading expert in trust.

8. We identified the Four Factors after extensive qualitative research. We later used our commercial cross-industry dataset (with over 160K responses across 425 company brands) to conduct a linear regression to explain the mean of stated trust rating of a brand using the Four Factors scores calculated for that brand (with a fitted intercept). Stated trust refers to responses to the question: "To what extent do you trust [brand name], on a scale of 0–10, 10 being the highest?" The variance of stated trust explained by the model (r-squared) was 79 percent. Note that not all factors contribute equally.

9. From our cross-industry dataset, 31 percent of the customers who rated brands neutral on humanity had defended the brand after hearing someone's criticism of it. Of the customers who rated brands high on humanity, 66 percent had performed the same action.

10. Lydia Saad, "U.S. Ethics Ratings Rise for Medical Workers and Teachers," Gallup, November 20, 2021, https://news.gallup.com/poll/328136/ethics-ratings-rise-medical-workers-teachers.aspx. Accessed December 14, 2021.

11. Lydia Saad, "Military Brass, Judges among Professions at New Image Lows," Gallup, January 18, 2022, https://news.gallup.com/poll/388649/military-brass-judges-among-professions-new-image-lows.aspx.

12. Physicians spend approximately 16 percent of their time in patient rooms versus approximately 33 percent for nurses; National Institutes of Health, "Estimating Time Physicians and Other Health Care Workers Spend with Patients in an Intensive Care Unit Using a Sensor Network," National Library of Medicine, https://pubmed.ncbi.nlm.nih.gov/29649458/. Accessed December 14, 2021.

13. From our cross-industry dataset, customers who rate a brand high on humanity are 3.5 times more likely to want to give their business to that brand when compared to customers who rate the brand neutral or low on humanity. By comparison, healthcare customers who rate a brand high on humanity are 4.5 times more likely to want to give their business to that healthcare brand, and travel and hospitality customers are 4.3 times more likely. The likelihood factors used in this book are calculated using a ratio of probabilities assuming the events are not independent.

14. In our research we use a seven-point Likert scale where "Agree" includes respondents who answered Agree (6) or Strongly Agree (7), "Disagree" includes respondents who answered Disagree (2) or Strongly Disagree (1), and "Neutral" includes Somewhat Agree (5), neither Agree nor Disagree (4) and Somewhat Disagree (3). See Appendix B for more detail on methodology.

15. Pearson correlation was conducted to evaluate the effect of using an extended range as compared to the decided range (described endnote 14). The extended range included Somewhat Agree (5) in "Agree" and Somewhat Disagree (3) in "Disagree," therefore moving them out of "Neutral." When the scores of each factor (decided range) were correlated with the extended range of the same factor, correlation was high across all Four Factors and the composite score.

	Pearson r: decided vs extended
Humanity	0.98
Transparency	0.97
Reliability	0.97
Capability	0.97
Composite	0.98

This high correlation was found despite the difference in the fraction of "Neutral" responders: decided=66 percent, extended=43 percent. We also conducted a linear regression to explain the mean measured trust rating of a brand using the extended Four Factors scores (with a fitted intercept). The variance of trust explained by this model (r-squared) was 82 percent (compared to 79 percent when neutrals were removed). Given the limited statistical impact, we felt comfortable removing neutral scores. In summary, a simpler calculation that was more focused on the extremes allowed us to maintain both our business goal of simplicity and broad applicability without losing statistical significance.

16. At this point you are probably wondering about the relationship between an organization's customer HX TrustID and worker HX TrustID. For example, "Is an organization with a high worker humanity score more likely to have a high humanity score from its customers?" We are glad you asked because we were curious too. And of course the answer is yes—they are deeply correlated. However, at this point we only had hypotheses, not evidence. We'll address this question specifically in Chapter 7.

17. We conducted a linear regression to explain the mean stated trust rating of a brand using the mean (composite) of the Four Factor scores calculated for that brand (with a fitted intercept); this yielded an r-squared of 74 percent. By comparison, the weighted linear regression to explain the mean stated trust rating of a brand using the Four Factor scores calculated for that brand (with a fitted intercept) yielded an r-squared of 79 percent. The minimal decrease in r-squared value between these two models indicates that equal weighting of the factors has a limited impact on explanatory power. To achieve our business goal of simplicity (including broad applicability and comparability of composite scores across industries), we were comfortable with this minor reduction in accuracy when describing the composite score of the Four Factors.

18. There is a large body of research on trust and we saw many similarities in how researchers defined trust. For example, of the many articles that defined trust in the 1980s and 1990s has become the most influential (Roger C. Mayer, James H. Davis, and F. David Schoorman, "An Integrative Model of Organizational Trust." *Academy of Management Review* 20, no. 3 [1995]: 709–734). Many scholars have adopted their three facets or dimensions of trust (ability, benevolence, and integrity). This work and others informed our own research, and helped us to identify the Four Factors.

19. In order to account for potential bias between what people say versus what they actually do (see more on this in Chapter 2), we designed our research to evaluate the impact of respondents' beliefs on *past* behavior (for example, How often have you chosen [brand] over competitors with similar products or services? Have you paid more for [brand]?). For this first study, all customers were asked to name a brand they trust in a specific subsector. All workers were asked to think about their current, or most recent, employer. The brand's name was used as an input throughout the remainder of the survey questions. Participants were also asked to rate each brand across competence and intent variables.

20. We analyzed nine consumer subsectors in the U.S.: Airlines, Automotive, Hotels/Resorts/Casinos, Restaurants and Food Service, Transportation and Logistics, Other Travel (Rental Car/Cruises/Rideshare), Apparel and Other Retail, Food/Beverage and CPG, and Grocery and Mass Merchant.

21. 79 percent represents the adjusted r-squared (using a fitted intercept); see note 8 for more detail.

22. Industries include Automotive, Transportation and Hospitality, Retail and Consumer Products, Technology, Telecom/Media/Entertainment/Sports, Financial Services, Insurance, Healthcare, Life Sciences, Government and Public Services, and Energy/Resources/Industrials. For this round of research, respondents were provided with a list of brands and asked to indicate those they were current customers of, or currently aware of. "Aware" was defined as being familiar enough with a brand that you could describe it to a friend. Respondents were then asked the series of questions (the Four Factors, attributes, and past behaviors) for brands they were current customers of or currently aware of.

23. Includes two workforce studies, both focused on the U.S.: (1) Deloitte October 2020, Elevating the Human Experience Research, 6K respondents and (2) Deloitte October 2021, HX TrustID Workforce Research, 5K respondents.

24. Reduced dataset to 108 stock ticker brands (including 28 financial services companies and 80 nonfinancial services companies). Conditions met for each company: publicly traded with sufficient financial history, HX TrustID score is collected at a brand level that matches the company's stock ticker.

25. Pulled 13 quarters of financial data, including 300+ features per company (checked the average, max-to-min trend, median, etc. on all 13 quarters but only used data from the final quarter in the analysis).

26. A statistical relation was found between price to book ratio and return on equity ratio, for all companies—with a significant and distinguishable amplification for highly trusted companies. Higher trusted companies are also more vulnerable, as erosion in their returns can conversely result in a 4x higher decrease in their value.

27. For nonfinancial services companies, a linear equation with 8 unique financial metrics multiplied by trust was found to explain more than 63 percent of the analyzed market stock return's variance, while trust score added exploratory power of 1 percent to the equation. The average marginal trust multiplier of the analyzed period is 0.1 percent. For financial services companies, a 1-point increase in trust contributes to an increase in stock return of 0.55 percent times the original trust score. For nonfinancial services companies, it is 0.1 percent times the original trust score. As a marginal average trust multiplier in a linear equation, by definition, expected returns grow as trust grows.

Chapter 2

28. "Confidence in Institutions," Gallup Historical Trends, August 13, 2021, https://news.gallup.com/poll/1597/confidence-institutions.aspx. Accessed December 10, 2021.

29. Lee Rainie and Andre Perrin, "Key Findings about American's declining trust in government and each other" Pew Research Center, May 30, 2020, https://www.pewresearch.org/fact-tank/2019/07/22/key-findings-about-americans-declining-trust-in-government-and-each-other/. Accessed September 22, 2021.

30. Lee Rainie and Andrew Perrin, "Key Findings about Americans' Declining Trust in Government and Each Other," Pew Research Center, May 30, 2020, https://www.pewresearch.org/fact-tank/2019/07/22/key-findings-about-americans-declining-trust-in-government-and-each-other/. Accessed April 19, 2022.

31. Lydia Saad, "Military Brass, Judges among Professions at New Image Lows," Gallup Historical Trends, January 18, 2022, https://news.gallup.com/poll/388649/military-brass-judges-among-professions-new-image-lows.aspx. Accessed April 19, 2022.

32. Jerry Useem, "The End of Trust: Suspicion Is Undermining the American Economy," *Atlantic,* November 24, 2021, https://www.theatlantic.com/magazine/archive/2021/12/trust-recession-economy/620522/.

33. United States current-dollar GDP increased 10.1 percent, or $2.10 trillion, in 2021 to a level of $23.00 trillion (the growth rate is historically high, coming out of the pandemic). The dollar value of adding an additional 1 percent annual growth (from 10.1 percent to 11.1 percent) is approximately $208 billion. Source: "Gross Domestic Product, Fourth Quarter and Year 2021 (Second Estimate)," U.S. Bureau of Economic Analysis, U.S. Department of Commerce, April 5, 2022, https://www.bea.gov/news/2022/gross-domestic-product-fourth-quarter-and-year-2021-second-estimate#:~:text=Current%2Ddollar%20GDP%20increased%2010.1,(tables%201%20and%203).

34. *Friends,* "The One Where Ross and Rachel Take a Break," Season 3, Episode 15.

35. National Academies of Sciences, Engineering, and Medicine, "Understanding Airline and Passenger Choice in Multi-Airport Regions," National Academies Press, January 22, 2014, https://nap.nationalacademies.org/

catalog/22443/understanding-airline-and-passenger-choice-in-multi-airport-regions. Fred Reichheld, *Winning on Purpose: The Unbeatable Strategy of Loving Customers* (Cambridge, MA: Harvard Business Review Press, 2021). Accessed April 19, 2022.

36. Gardiner Morse, "Hidden Minds," *Harvard Business Review,* August 1, 2014, https://hbr.org/2002/06/hidden-minds%20Accessed%20December%20 12. Accessed December 12, 2021.

37. Suzanne Ewing et al., *Architecture and Field/Work* (London: Routledge, 2010), 80.

38. Karlyn Bowman, "The Trouble with Polling," *National Affairs,* 2018, https://www.nationalaffairs.com/publications/detail/the-trouble-with-polling. Accessed April 19, 2022.

39. R. Curtin, S. Presser, and E. Singer, The Effects of Response Rate Changes on the Index of Consumer Sentiment. *Public Opinion Quarterly* 64 (2000): 413–428; J. Goyder, K. Warriner, and S. Miller, Evaluating Socio-economic Status (SES) Bias in Survey Nonresponse. *Journal of Official Statistics* 18 (1, 2002): 1–11.

40. William G. Smith, "Does Gender Influence Online Survey Participation?: A Record-linkage Analysis of University Faculty Online Survey Response Behavior" (dissertation, 2008). Accessed April 19, 2022.

41. "The Story of One of the Most Memorable Marketing Blunders Ever," Coca-Cola Company, https://www.coca-colacompany.com/company/history/the-story-of-one-of-the-most-memorable-marketing-blunders-ever. Accessed April 19, 2022.

42. Tom Huddleston Jr., "Netflix's 'Stranger Things' Revives New Coke. Here's How the Failed Soda Cost Coca-Cola Millions in 1985," CNBC, July 10, 2019, https://www.cnbc.com/2019/07/05/netflix-stranger-things-revives-new-coke-heres-how-the-failed-soda-cost-coca-cola-millions.html. Accessed April 19, 2022.

Chapter 3

43. Organizations might use "likelihood to recommend," for example, but the outcomes they seek are similar.

44. We conducted a Pearson correlation analysis to compare the HX TrustID composite score to NPS: $r=0.81$ ($p<0.00001$).

45. NPS is calculated by taking the percentage of respondents who agree and subtracting the percentage of respondents who disagree to the survey question: *How likely are you to recommend [brand name] to a friend or colleague?* Response options are on a scale from 0 to 10, 10 being the most likely. Promoters are customers who respond with a score of 9 or 10. Passives are customers who respond with a score of 7 or 8. Detractors respond with a score of 0 to 6.

46. We conducted a Pearson correlation analysis to compare the Four Factors to NPS. Humanity score to NPS: $r=0.71$ ($p<0.00001$). Transparency score to NPS: $r=0.7$ ($p<0.00001$). Reliability score to NPS: $r=0.83$ ($p<0.00001$). Capability score to NPS: $r=0.85$ ($p<0.00001$).

47. Fred Reichheld, *Winning on Purpose: The Unbeatable Strategy of Loving Customers* (Cambridge, MA: Harvard Business Review Press, 2022).

Chapter 4

48. Dr. Delos M. Cosgrove, "A Healthcare Model for the 21st Century." *Group Practice Journal,* Volume 60, No. 3, March 2011.

49. Rachel Silver, "Energizer® Sets Record for Longest-Lasting AA Battery Just in Time for the Holidays," Guinness World Records, December 11, 2018, https://www.guinnessworldrecords.com/news/commercial/2018/12/energizer-sets-record-for-longest-lasting-aa-battery-just-in-time-for-the-holida-551165. Accessed December 18, 2021.

50. Marriott International (@MarriottIntl). "A message to Marriott International Associates from President and CEO Arne Sorenson," Twitter, March 19, 2020, 10:00a.m., https://twitter.com/MarriottIntl/status/1240639160148529160? ref_src=twsrc%5Etfw%7Ctwcamp%5Etweetembed%7Ctwterm% 5E1240639160148529160%7Ctwgr%5E%7Ctwcon%5Es1_&ref_ url=https%3A%2F%2Fembedly.forbes.com%2Fwidgets%2Fmedia.html%3 Ftype%3Dtext2Fhtmlkey%3Dcfc0fb0733504c77aa4a6ac07caaffc7schema% 3Dtwitterurl%3Dhttps3A%2F%2Ftwitter.com%2Fmarriottintl%2Fstatus% 2F1240639160148529160image%3Dhttps3A%2F%2Fi.embed.ly%2F1%2F image3Furl3Dhttps253A252F252Fpbs.twimg.com252Fmedia252FETegd-mQWkAA8Lfl.jpg26key3D8804248494c144f5b4765c41f66c6ed5.

Chapter 5

51. Consumer survey methodology: 10-minute online survey of 1,000 adults in the U.S. conducted between June 29 and July 6, 2021. All respondents: Owned a smartphone or mobile phone and used it within the past week; had received a communication from a business within the preceding month by email, text message, messaging app, social media, phone or company mobile app; had shopped for a product or service online or by mobile phone within the preceding month. B2C leader survey methodology: 10-minute online survey of 500 leaders at B2C companies in US between June 29 and July 6, 2021. All respondents: Held a position of director or higher at a B2C company with 1,000 or more employees; held responsibility for one or more of the following: consumer digital communications strategy, messaging, implementation and/or technology; worked in/led one of the following departments: customer service/support/experience, e-commerce, executive leadership or general management, marketing, product development, product management, sales, or web development.

52. This section adapted from Reichheld, et al., "Close the trust gap to unlock business value and improve customer engagement. Actionable insights on consumer perceptions and the business value of trust, based on new research," Deloitte/Twilio, October 2021.

53. Ibid.

54. In statistics, the standard deviation is a measure that quantifies the breadth and variety of values in a dataset (responders' ratings in the context of the current work). A low standard deviation implies a condensed set of responses, or that most respondents answered close to the same value on the scale. A high standard deviation implies that there was a high degree of variety and breadth in the responses, or that respondents consistently answered differently across the scale. Therefore, a high standard deviation can be a proxy for divisiveness, and a low standard deviation can be a proxy for agreement. What a low standard deviation does not inherently indicate is where on the scale (high/low/neutral) that agreement occurs. However, in the case of the *Ambivalent Neutrals*, the responses are condensed around the neutral/central portion of our trust scale. Mean standard deviations of *Ambivalent Neutrals* approximately range between .09 and 1. The mean standard deviation is approximately 1.2, while the highest standard deviations range from over 1.5 to over 1.9.

55. Allan M. Brandt, "Inventing Conflicts of Interest: A History of Tobacco Industry Tactics," National Center for Biotechnology Information, *American Journal of Public Health,* January 2012, https://www.ncbi.nlm.nih.gov/pmc/articles/PMC3490543/.

56. Emma Baccellieri, "What Can We Learn from the WNBA's Vaccination Success?" *Sports Illustrated,* September 20, 2021, https://www.si.com/wnba/2021/09/20/wnba-vaccination-99-percent-daily-cover.

57. Candace Buckner, "WNBA Players' Next Cause: Educating Themselves—and Fans—on Vaccine Safety," *Washington Post,* March 8, 2021, https://www.washingtonpost.com/sports/2021/03/04/wnba-coronavirus-vaccine-safety/.

58. Tim Rea, Chief Experience and Marketing Officer, Edward Jones, Interviewed by Ashley Reichheld, January 24, 2022.

59. "Paid Program: The Future of Financial Advice," *The Wall Street Journal* Custom Content, June 19, 2019, https://partners.wsj.com/edward-jones/future-of-financial-advice/how-financial-advisors-can-redefine-the-client-experience/.

Chapter 6

60. "Social Identities," Northwestern University: Searle Center for Advancing Learning and Teaching, https://www.northwestern.edu/searle/initiatives/diversity-equity-inclusion/social-identities.html#:~:text=Social%20identity%20groups%20are%20usually,%2C%20and%20religion%2Freligious%20beliefs. Accessed April 19, 2022.

61. We looked at how individual demographic variables divide respondents into high, low, or neutral trust across the Four Factors. We measured the degree of separation using a criterion called the Gini index, which gives each variable a ranked probability score at each decision point and picks the optimal one. The decision tree makes a series of decisions based on the demographic data of each of our survey respondents.

62. We used 12 variables in the customer analysis: Ethnicity, Gender Identity, Sexual Orientation, Age Group/Generation, Living Situation, Annual Household Income, Geographic Region, Area/Geographic Density, Education Level, Employment Status, Relationship Status, and Parenthood. We used 23 variables in the workforce analysis: Ethnicity, Gender Identity,

Sexual Orientation, Age Group/Generation, Living Situation, Annual Household Income, Area/Geographic Density, Education Level, Employment Status, Relationship Status, Parenthood, Number of Children, Child in house, Senior in house, Job title, Job level, Customer interaction, Employment duration, Compensation type, Performance compensation (Yes/No), Number of total benefits, Organization type, Company type (if for-profit).

63. Results were the calculated feature importance scores (Gini importance). Classification of each person's trust level was high, neutral, or low across the Four Factors.

64. Core identity demographic variables were ruled out by the decision tree as contributing to the classification of a person's trust level as high, neutral, or low across the Four Factors.

65. The top ~5–6 variables that assist in classifying a person's trust level as high, neutral, or low across the Four Factors were all experience demographic variables.

66. Generation birth years vary by source. We use dates according to the Pew Research Center: Silent Generation (1928–1945); Baby Boomers (1946–1964); Generation X (1965–1980); Millennials (1981–1996); Generation Z (1997–present).

67. Elka Torpey, "Education Pays, 2020: Career Outlook," U.S. Bureau of Labor Statistics, June 2021, https://www.bls.gov/careeroutlook/2021/data-on-display/education-pays.htm. Accessed April 19, 2022.

68. Deloitte, "HX TrustID Survey," October 2021 (n=5,000). Employers estimate their HX TrustID score with their workforce to be 55%, while workers' actual score is 40%. This represents a gap of 15 percentage points or an overestimation by employers of 37.5 (nearly 40) percent.

69. "American Time Use Survey: Bureau of Labor Statistics," U.S. Bureau of Labor Statistics, July 22, 2021, https://www.bls.gov/news.release/pdf/atus.pdf. Accessed April 19, 2022.

70. Although sample sizes for nonbinary respondents are too small to show by industry, trust among nonbinary customers remains significantly lower than trust among men or women; as an aggregate average across industries, nonbinary customers trust about 36 percent as much as women.

71. Daniel Bergner, "The Struggles of Rejecting the Gender Binary," *New York Times,* June 4, 2019, https://www.nytimes.com/2019/06/04/magazine/gender-nonbinary.html.

72. Jessica Contrera, "The End of 'Shrink It and Pink It': A History of Advertisers Missing the Mark with Women," *Washington Post,* June 8, 2016.

https://www.washingtonpost.com/lifestyle/style/the-end-of-shrink-it-or-pink-it-a-history-of-advertisers-missing-the-mark-with-women/2016/06/08/3bcb1832-28e9-11e6-ae4a-3cdd5fe74204_story.html. Accessed December 30, 2021.

73. "CBS News Goes Undercover to Reveal Gender Price Discrimination," CBS News, January 25, 2016, https://www.cbsnews.com/news/price-discrimination-gender-gap-cbs-news-undercover-dry-cleaners/. Accessed April 19, 2022.

74. Meredith Hoffman, "The Pink Tax: How Women Pay More for Pink," Bankrate, January 11, 2021, https://www.bankrate.com/finance/credit-cards/pink-tax-how-women-pay-more/. Accessed April 19, 2022.

75. Steve Tengler, "New 'Pink Tax' Study Shows Women Pay Upwards Of $7,800 More for Car Ownership," Forbes, October 27, 2021. https://www.forbes.com/sites/stevetengler/2021/10/27/new-pink-tax-study-shows-women-pay-upwards-of-7800-more-for-car-ownership/?sh=224d8ead63d8. Accessed April 19, 2022.

76. Alisha Haridasani Gupta, "Crash Test Dummies Made Cars Safer (for Average-Size Men)," New York Times, December 27, 2021. https://www.nytimes.com/2021/12/27/business/car-safety-women.html.

77. Alex Mayyasi, "How an Ad Campaign Made Lesbians Fall in Love with Subaru," Priceonomics, May 23, 2016, https://priceonomics.com/how-an-ad-campaign-made-lesbians-fall-in-love-with/. Accessed April 19, 2022.

78. Russell Heimlich, "Homosexuality and Morality," Pew Research Center, October 20, 2009, https://www.pewresearch.org/fact-tank/2009/10/20/homosexuality-and-morality/; "LGBT Rights," Gallup, February 18, 2022, https://news.gallup.com/poll/1651/gay-lesbian-rights.aspx. Accessed April 19, 2022.

79. Alex Mayyasi, "How Subarus Came to Be Seen as Cars for Lesbians," Atlantic, May 26, 2021), https://www.theatlantic.com/business/archive/2016/06/how-subarus-came-to-be-seen-as-cars-for-lesbians/488042/.

80. Alex Mayyasi, "How an Ad Campaign Made Lesbians Fall in Love with Subaru," Priceonomics, May 23, 2016, https://priceonomics.com/how-an-ad-campaign-made-lesbians-fall-in-love-with/. Accessed April 19, 2022.

81. Denis Flierl, "New Study Says Subaru Customers Are the Most Loyal of All Mainstream Brands," TorqueNews, January 1, 2021, https://www.torquenews.com/1084/new-study-says-subaru-customers-are-most-loyalty-all-mainstream-brands. Accessed April 19, 2022.

82. Although our sample size is too small to quantify how much less workers who identify as nonbinary trust their employers, based on what we do see in our workforce data (coupled with our much larger customer dataset), it is reasonable to assume that nonbinary workers trust their employers far less than those who identify as male or female.

83. Megan Brenan, "Women Still Handle Main Household Tasks in U.S.," Gallup, January 29, 2020, https://news.gallup.com/poll/283979/women-handle-main-household-tasks.aspx. Accessed December 30, 2021.

84. Sonam Sheth et al., "These 8 charts show the glaring gap between men's and women's salaries in the US," *Business Insider,* March 15, 2022, https://www.businessinsider.com/gender-wage-pay-gap-charts-2017-3. Accessed April 19, 2022.

85. Emilio J. Castilla and Stephan Benard, "The Paradox of Meritocracy in Organizations," *Administrative Science Quarterly,* December 2010, https://gap.hks.harvard.edu/paradox-meritocracy-organizations.Accessed April 19, 2022.

Chapter 7

86. Colleen Bordeaux and Stephanie Lewis, "Designing the Workforce Experience with the Human at the Center," September 23, 2021, https://www2.deloitte.com/us/en/blog/human-capital-blog/2021/human-centered-workforce-experience.html. Accessed April 19, 2022.

87. 24 percent lower turnover for high-turnover organizations and 59 percent lower turnover for low-turnover organizations; "State of the American Workplace Report," Gallup, 2017, https://www.gallup.com/workplace/238085/state-american-workplace-report-2017.aspx. Accessed March 7, 2022.

88. Colleen Bordeaux and Stephanie Lewis, "Designing the Workforce Experience with the Human at the Center," September 23, 2021, https://www2.deloitte.com/us/en/blog/human-capital-blog/2021/human-centered-workforce-experience.html. Accessed April 19, 2022.

89. Deloitte, "HX in Times of Uncertainty," May 2020, https://www.deloittedigital.com/us/en/offerings/customer-led-marketing/hx--in-times-of-uncertainty.html. Accessed March 7, 2022.

90. Blake Morgan, "The Un-Ignorable Link Between Employee Experience and Customer Experience," *Forbes,* February 22, 2018. https://www.forbes .com/sites/blakemorgan/2018/02/23/the-un-ignorable-link-between-employee-experience-and-customer-experience/?sh=4ed8934848dc. Accessed April 19, 2022.

91. Colleen Bordeaux and Stephanie Lewis, "Designing the Workforce Experience with the Human at the Center," September 23, 2021, https://www2 .deloitte.com/us/en/blog/human-capital-blog/2021/human-centered-workforce-experience.html. Accessed April 19, 2022.

92. Stock-based compensation is correlated with market cap for all companies—with a significant and distinguishable amplification for highly trusted companies.

93. Ed Bastian, "Protecting Organizations and Their People," interview by Deloitte, posted January 20, 2021, video audio, 0:56–1:15, https://www .youtube.com/watch?v=SKoMuS38IxA.

94. Rachel Y. Tang, "CARES Act Payroll Support to Air Carriers and Contractors," Congressional Research Service, Updated October 22, 2020, https:// crsreports.congress.gov/product/pdf/IN/IN11482. Accessed December 22, 2021.

95. Ed Bastian, CEO, Delta. Interviewed by Ashley Reichheld and Tom Schoenwaelder, February 17, 2022.

96. "Glassdoor Recognizes Delta on 'Best Places to Work' List for Sixth Year," Delta, January 13, 2021, https://news.delta.com/glassdoor-recognizes-delta-best-places-work-list-fifth-year. Accessed on January 12, 2022; "Best Places to Work," Glassdoor, https://www.glassdoor.com/ Award/Best-Places-to-Work-LST_KQ0,19.htm.Accessed March 7, 2022.

97. "Delta: America's most-awarded airline," Delta, https://news.delta.com/ delta-worlds-most-awarded-airline. Accessed April 19, 2022.

98. Deloitte, "Diverse-Owned Small Business (DSB) Banking Study," December 2020. (n=3,600)

99. "The 2019 State of Women-Owned Business Report," Commissioned by American Express, 2019, https://s1.q4cdn.com/692158879/files/doc_ library/file/2019-state-of-women-owned-businesses-report.pdf. Accessed April 19, 2022.

100. For example, Amex and Delta have an exclusive Sky Miles Credit Card partnership. Delta values the benefit of the program at nearly $7 billion annually. As an exclusive partner, Amex says it contributes significantly to its revenue growth as well; "American Express and Delta renew industry-leading partnership, lay foundation to continue innovating customer benefits," Delta, April 2, 2019, https://news.delta.com/american-express-and-delta-renew-industry-leading-partnership-lay-foundation-continue-innovating. Accessed April 19, 2022.

101. Paris Ward, "Why Amex and Delta Extended Their Credit Card Partnership," Credit Karma, April 17, 2019, https://www.creditkarma.com/credit-cards/i/why-amex-delta-extended-credit-card-partnership. Accessed April 19, 2022.

Chapter 8

102. "Psychological monopolies" refers to organizations that commentators and the public view as so dominant in their industry that they are immune from creative destruction, and unlikely to be replaced by competitors. Source: Ryan Bourne, "Is This Time Different? Schumpeter, the Tech Giants, and Monopoly Fatalism," Cato Institute, June 18, 2019, https://www.cato.org/publications/policy-analysis/time-different-schumpeter-tech-giants-monopoly-fatalism.

103. Emily Pidgeon, "The 10 Most Trusted Brands for 2021" *CEO* magazine, April 26, 2021. https://www.theceomagazine.com/business/management-leadership/trusted-brands-2021/. Accessed April 19, 2022.

104. In our research, survey respondents were asked to self-identify as customers of a brand or aware of a brand. "Aware" was defined as being familiar enough with a brand that you could describe it to a friend. Respondents only provided trust scores for brands they were customers of or aware of.

105. Ashley Reichheld et al., "Cruisers Gonna Cruise," Deloitte report, 2020.

106. "Disney Cast Member," Disney Wiki (Disney Fandom), accessed April 19, 2022, https://disney.fandom.com/wiki/Cast_member#:~:text=Cast%20members%20have%20various%20jobs,theatrical%20terms%20for%20park%20operations.

107. Theresa Caragol, "5 Customer Experience Lessons I Learned on a Disney Cruise," LinkedIn, May 9, 2019, https://www.linkedin.com/pulse/5-customer-experience-lessons-i-learned-disney-cruise-theresa-caragol/; Kara Williams, "9 Disney Wish Cruise Experiences That Will Make You Want to Be a Kid," TravelAwaits, October 15, 2021, https://www.travelawaits.com/2703581/disney-wish-cruise-best-experiences/; Emal Hakikat, "How Disney Improved Customer Experience through Putting Employees First," Inside HR, July 2, 2019, https://www.insidehr.com.au/disney-customer-experience-employees-first/; Erica Silverstein, "Royal Caribbean vs. Disney Cruise Line," Cruise Critic, May 11, 2021, https://www.cruisecritic.com/articles.cfm?ID=2393; Gene Sloan, "Cruise Line Showdown: Comparing Carnival, Disney and Royal Caribbean for Families," Points Guy, December 2, 2019, https://thepointsguy.com/guide/comparing-cruise-lines-for-families-disney-royal-caribbean-carnival/; Walt Disney Company, "2019 Annual Report," Walt Disney Company, 2019, https://thewaltdisneycompany.com/app/uploads/2020/01/2019-Annual-Report.pdf.

108. Deloitte #GetOutInFront Global Research Report, December 2020.

109. Janet Phillips and Joanne Simon-Davies, "Migration to Australia: A Quick Guide to the Statistics," Parliament of Australia, January 18, 2017, https://www.aph.gov.au/About_Parliament/Parliamentary_Departments/Parliamentary_Library/pubs/rp/rp1617/Quick_Guides/MigrationStatistics. Accessed February 23, 2022.

110. "Edelman Trust Barometer 2022," Edelman, 2022, https://www.edelman.com/sites/g/files/aatuss191/files/2022-01/2022%20Edelman%20Trust%20Barometer%20FINAL_Jan25.pdf. Accessed April 19, 2022.

111. "Fact Sheet: Putting the Public First: Improving Customer Experience and Service Delivery for the American People," The White House, December 13, 2021. https://www.whitehouse.gov/briefing-room/statements-releases/2021/12/13/fact-sheet-putting-the-public-first-improving-customer-experience-and-service-delivery-for-the-american-people/. Accessed February 23, 2022.

Chapter 9

112. At Deloitte we define purpose as an organization's distinctive role in society and the long-term value it seeks to deliver to all stakeholders through everything it does. Purpose is different from a mission statement, which more commonly describes the "what" of a company—its actions and goals.

Chapter 10

113. YPO, "96% of CEOs Say Building and Maintaining Trust with Stakeholders is A Top Priority," YPO, January 10, 2020, https://www.ypo.org/2020/01/96-of-ceos-say-building-and-maintaining-trust-with-stakeholders-is-a-top-priority/. Accessed April 19, 2022.

114. Jennifer Lee, Mich Galletto, Praveck Geeanpersadh, "The Future of Trust," Deloitte Canada, 4. https://www2.deloitte.com/content/dam/Deloitte/ca/Documents/deloitte-analytics/ca-chemistry-of-trust-pov-aoda-en.pdf. Accessed January 25, 2022.

115. Fortune/Deloitte CEO Survey, "Fortune/Deloitte CEO Survey," The Chief Executive Program (Deloitte, November 2021), https://www2.deloitte.com/content/dam/Deloitte/us/Documents/about-deloitte/us-fortune-deloitte-CEO-survey-fall-2021-highlights-final.pdf. Accessed April 19, 2022.

116. "2022 Edelman Trust Barometer Reveals Even Greater Expectations of Business to Lead as Government Trust Continues to Spiral," Edelman, January 18, 2022, https://www.edelman.com/news-awards/2022-edelman-trust-barometer-reveals-even-greater-expectations-business-lead-government-trust. Accessed April 19, 2022.

117. "Business Roundtable Redefines the Purpose of a Corporation to Promote 'An Economy That Serves All Americans,'" Business Round Table, August 19, 2019. https://www.businessroundtable.org/business-roundtable-redefines-the-purpose-of-a-corporation-to-promote-an-economy-that-serves-all-americans. Accessed January 16, 2022.

118. Alan Murray, "America's CEOs Seek a New Purpose for the Corporation," Fortune, August 19, 2019. https://fortune.com/longform/business-roundtable-ceos-corporations-purpose/. Accessed January 16, 2022.

119. At Deloitte we define purpose as an organization's distinctive role in society and the long-term value it seeks to deliver to all stakeholders through everything it does. Purpose is different from a mission statement, which more commonly describes the "what" of a company—its actions and goals.

120. Fortune/Deloitte CEO Survey, "Fortune/Deloitte CEO Survey," Chief Executive Program (Deloitte, Fall 2021), https://www2.deloitte.com/content/dam/Deloitte/us/Documents/about-deloitte/us-fortune-deloitte-CEO-survey-fall-2021-highlights-final.pdf. Accessed April 19, 2022.

121. Deloitte, "How Purpose Delivers Value in Every Enterprise Function," Deloitte United States, February 2, 2022, https://www2.deloitte.com/us/en/pages/about-deloitte/articles/how-purpose-delivers-value.html. Accessed April 19, 2022.

122. Deloitte, 2021 Diversity, Equity, and Inclusion (DEI) Transparency Report Executive Summary, 2021, https://www2.deloitte.com/content/dam/Deloitte/us/Documents/about-deloitte/dei-transparency-report-executive-summary.pdf. Accessed January 17, 2022.

Chapter 11

123. Brundtland, G., "Report of the World Commission on Environment and Development: Our Common Future" (United Nations General Assembly, 1987), document A/42/427.

124. Riskconnect, "ESG Reporting: Why Companies Should Act Now", https://riskonnect.com/resources/esg-reporting/. Accessed March 2, 2022.

125. Brian Moynihan and Klaus Schwab, "In Stakeholder Capitalism, Good Metrics Will Keep Corporate Leaders Honest," Fortune, January 27, 2021, https://fortune.com/2021/01/27/stakeholder-capitalism-metrics-purpose-leadership/. Accessed March 2, 2022.

126. Deloitte 2022 Consumer Products Outlook.

127. Barb Renner, Michael Bondar, Justin Cook, and Céline Fenech, "2022 Consumer Products Industry Outlook," Deloitte United States (Deloitte, March 29, 2022), 8, https://www2.deloitte.com/us/en/pages/consumer-business/articles/consumer-products-industry-outlook.html.

128. Deloitte HX in Uncertainty Survey, May 2020. (n=16,000 Customers)

129. Michele Parmelee, "The Deloitte Global 2021 Millennial and Gen Z Survey," Deloitte Insights (Deloitte, June 23, 2021), https://www2.deloitte .com/us/en/insights/topics/talent/deloitte-millennial-survey.html. Accessed April 19, 2022.

130. Dean Hobbs et al., "CFOs Find Benefits from ESG Investing," Deloitte Insights (Deloitte, October 30, 2021), https://www2.deloitte.com/us/en/ insights/topics/strategy/cfo-benefits-esg-investment.html. Accessed April 19, 2022.

131. Jim Burton, Sean Denman, April Little, Enzo Santilli, Christopher Schenkenberg, and Marjorie Whittaker, "Values Driving Value: CFOs Looking to Lead on ESG," Grant Thornton (Grant Thornton, 2021), https://www .grantthornton.com/-/media/content-page-files/campaigns/pdfs/adv-2021-CFO-survey-Q3-Executive-Summary.ashx. Accessed April 19, 2022.

132. "Future of Sustainability in Investment Management: From Ideas to Reality," CFA Institute, 2020 https://www.cfainstitute.org/-/media/ documents/survey/future-of-sustainability.ashx. Accessed March 3, 2022.

133. Sophie Kiderlin, "Sustainable Investments Now Total $35.3 Trillion, Roughly a Third of All Global Assets under Management, Report Shows," *Business Insider,* July 19, 2021, https://markets.businessinsider.com/ news/stocks/global-sustainable-investment-alliance-report-esg-assets-responsible-investing-2021-7. Accessed April 19, 2022.

134. "Sustainability Initiative," Sustainability Initiative (Stanford University), accessed April 19, 2022, https://sustainabilityinitiative.stanford.edu/.

135. "ESG and Financial Performance," NYU Stern Center for Sustainable Business (NYU Stern, 2021), https://www.stern.nyu.edu/experience-stern/about/departments-centers-initiatives/centers-of-research/ center-sustainable-business/research/research-initiatives/esg-and-financial-performance. Accessed April 19, 2022.

136. "Not So Risky Business: Mitigating Risk Through ESG Investing," Change Finance, https://change-finance.com/not-so-risky-business-mitigating-risk-through-esg-investing/#easy-footnote-bottom-1-5554. Accessed March 5, 2022.

137. "10 Reasons You Should Care about ESG Investing," Bank of America Securities (Bank of America, January 7, 2020), https://about.bankofamerica .com/assets/pdf/BofA_ESG-10-reasons-you-should-care-about-ESG-Investing.pdf. Accessed April 19, 2022.

138. Ibid.

139. George Serafeim, "The Type of Socially Responsible Investments That Make Firms More Profitable," *Harvard Business Review,* August 12, 2015, https://hbr.org/2015/04/the-type-of-socially-responsible-investments-that-make-firms-more-profitable.

140. Allison Herren Lee, "Public Input Welcomed on Climate Change Disclosures," SEC (U.S. Securities & Exchange Commission, March 15, 2021), https://www.sec.gov/news/public-statement/lee-climate-change-disclosures.

141. Boffo, R., and R. Patalano, "ESG Investing: Practices, Progress and Challenges," OECD Paris, 2020. www.oecd.org/finance/ESG-Investing-Practices-Progress-and-Challenges.pdf.

142. IBD Staff, "100 Best ESG Companies: Top Stocks for Environmental, Social and Governance Values," Investor's Business Daily, November 10, 2021, https://www.investors.com/news/esg-companies-list-best-esg-stocks-environmental-social-governance-values/.

143. Kwasi Mitchell, John Mennel, and Shira Beery, "C-suite Insights: How Purpose Delivers Value in Every Function and for the Enterprise," Deloitte, accessed April 18, 2022, https://www2.deloitte.com/us/en/pages/about-deloitte/articles/how-purpose-delivers-value.html.%20Accessed%20April%2018.

144. Deloitte 2022 Consumer Products Outlook.

145. "ESG as a Workforce Strategy," Marsh & McLennan Advantage, accessed March 2, 2022, https://www.marshmclennan.com/esg-interactive.html.

146. Deloitte, "DEI and Trust," survey, 2021. (n=1,543 Workers)

147. Sean Denham, Enzo Santilli, and Christopher Schenkenberg, "Third Quarter 2021 Values Driving Value: CFOs Spotlight ESG as a Growing Concern," Grant Thornton, January 31, 2022, https://www.grantthornton.com/library/survey-reports/CFO-survey/2022/values-driving-value.aspx. Accessed April 19, 2022.

Chapter 12

148. Katie Deighton, "Some Chief Experience Officers Want to Make Their Jobs Disappear," *The Wall Street Journal,* June 23, 2021, https://www.wsj.com/articles/some-chief-experience-officers-want-to-make-their-jobs-disappear-11624456801. Accessed June 1, 2022.

149. Procter & Gamble was named the top "Brand Marketer of the Decade" among the world's biggest advertisers. Source: Mihai-Alexandru Cristea, "Procter & Gamble Was Named the Top 'Brand Marketer of the Decade' among the World's Biggest Advertisers," Business Review (Business Review, July 8, 2020), https://business-review.eu/business/media-marketing/procter-gamble-was-named-the-top-brand-marketer-of-the-decade-among-the-worlds-biggest-advertisers-211621. Accessed April 18, 2020.

150. Brad Adgate, "Agencies Agree; 2021 Was a Record Year for Ad Spending, with More Growth Expected in 2022," *Forbes,* December 10, 2021, https://www.forbes.com/sites/bradadgate/2021/12/08/agencies-agree-2021-was-a-record-year-for-ad-spending-with-more-growth-expected-in-2022/?sh=6c42f7447bc6. Accessed April 19, 2022.

151. Gigen Mammoser, "Social Media Increases Depression and Loneliness," Healthline (Healthline Media, December 10, 2018), https://www.healthline.com/health-news/social-media-use-increases-depression-and-loneliness#Does-social-media-cause-depression. Accessed April 19, 2022.

152. "Enough Is Enough: Cyberbullying," Enough Is Enough, accessed April 19, 2022, https://enough.org/stats_cyberbullying.

153. Peter Dizikes, "Study: On Twitter, False News Travels Faster Than True Stories," MIT News, March 8, 2018. https://news.mit.edu/2018/study-twitter-false-news-travels-faster-true-stories-0308. Accessed March 20, 2022.

154. Tom Infield, "Americans Who Get News Mainly on Social Media Are Less Knowledgeable and Less Engaged," Pew Trust Magazine, November 16, 2020, https://www.pewtrusts.org/en/trust/archive/fall-2020/americans-who-get-news-mainly-on-social-media-are-less-knowledgeable-and-less-engaged#:~:text=%E2%80%9CThe%20overarching%20finding%2C%E2%80%9D%20she%20says%2C%20%E2%80%9Cis%20that%20U.S.,events%20and%20broad%20political-knowledge%20questions%20about%20the%20U.S.%E2%80%9D.

155. Gene Demby, "Combing through 41 Million Tweets to Show How #BlackLivesMatter Exploded," NPR (NPR, March 2, 2016), https://www.npr.org/sections/codeswitch/2016/03/02/468704888/combing-through-41-million-tweets-to-show-how-blacklivesmatter-exploded. Accessed April 19, 2022.

156. Ibid.

157. "Her Story," Black Lives Matter, accessed April 19, 2022, https://blacklivesmatter.com/herstory/.

158. "Managing and Measuring Marketing Spending for Growth and Returns," The CMO Survey (Deloitte/Duke Fuqua/American Marketing Association, August 2021), https://cmosurvey.org/wp-content/uploads/2021/08/The_CMO_Survey-Highlights_and_Insights_Report-August_2021.pdf. Accessed April 19, 2022.

159. Duncan MacRae, "CMOs Lack Data Capabilities Needed to Hit Growth Targets," MarketingTech, January 24, 2022, https://marketingtechnews.net/news/2022/jan/24/cmos-lack-data-capabilities-needed-to-hit-growth-targets/. Accessed March 19, 2022.

160. The transformation was sweeping, from customer service to systems, and the case is well worth studying. Source: Ryan W. Buell, Robert S. Huckman, and Sam Travers, "Improving Access at VA," Harvard Business School, December 2, 2016. Case # 9-617-012.

161. Cookieless describes a way of marketing in which marketers are less reliant on third-party cookies—bits of data collected by web browsers that contain customer personal identifiers. Source: "What Is Cookieless?," Adobe Business Glossary (Adobe Experience Cloud), accessed April 19, 2022, https://business.adobe.com/glossary/cookieless.html.

162. David Cutbill et al., "Meeting Customers in a Cookieless World," Deloitte Insights (Deloitte, October 19, 2021), https://www2.deloitte.com/us/en/insights/topics/marketing-and-sales-operations/global-marketing-trends/2022/the-future-of-marketing-in-a-third-party-cookieless-world.html. Accessed April 19, 2022.

163. James Manyika, Jake Silberg, and Brittany Presten, "What Do We Do About the Biases in AI?" Harvard Business Review, October 25, 2019. https://hbr.org/2019/10/what-do-we-do-about-the-biases-in-ai. Accessed March 20, 2022.

164. Diana O'Brien, Jennifer Veenstra, and Timothy Murphy, "The Makings of a More Confident CMO: Three Ways to Increase C-Suite Impact," Deloitte Insights (Deloitte, September 18, 2019), https://www2.deloitte.com/us/en/insights/topics/leadership/redefined-cmo-role.html. Accessed March 21, 2020.

165. Christine Cutten et al., "Building the Intelligent Creative Engine," Deloitte Insights (Deloitte, October 19, 2021), https://www2.deloitte.com/us/en/insights/topics/marketing-and-sales-operations/

global-marketing-trends/2022/finding-unconventional-talent-to-redesign-your-marketing-strategy.html. April 19, 2022.

166. Nat Ives, "Average Tenure of CMO Slips to 43 Months," *The Wall Street Journal*, June 6, 2019, https://www.wsj.com/articles/average-tenure-of-cmo-slips-to-43-months-11559767605. Accessed March 21, 2022.

167. Diana O'Brien, Jennifer Veenstra, and Timothy Murphy, "The Makings of a More Confident CMO: Three Ways to Increase C-Suite Impact," Deloitte Insights (Deloitte, September 18, 2019), https://www2.deloitte.com/us/en/insights/topics/leadership/redefined-cmo-role.html. Accessed March 21, 2020.

168. Ibid.

169. Phillip Britt, "Cio-CMO Collaboration Drives Better CX and Growth," CRM Magazine, December 8, 2021, https://www.destinationcrm.com/Articles/CRM-Insights/Insight/CIO-CMO-Collaboration-Drives-Better-CX-and-Growth-150491.aspx. Accessed April 19, 2022.

170. Colin Mitchell, "Selling the Brand Inside," *Harvard Business Review*, January 1, 2002, https://hbr.org/2002/01/selling-the-brand-inside. Accessed April 19, 2022.

171. "Robert A. McDonald Profile," Robert A. McDonald, Former U.S. Secretary of Veterans Affairs (Veterans Affairs), accessed March 21, 2022, https://www.robertmcdonald.com/leadership/veterans-affairs/.

172. Jennifer Warnick, "How Starbucks Plans to Use Technology to Nurture the Human Spirit," Starbucks Stories & News (Starbucks, January 10, 2020), https://stories.starbucks.com/stories/2020/how-starbucks-plans-to-use-technology-to-nurture-the-human-spirit/. Accessed April 19, 2022.

173. Ibid.

Chapter 13

174. Tiffani Bova, "Tiffani Bova," December 2, 2021, https://www.tiffanibova.com/. Accessed April 19, 2022.

175. Deloitte HX TrustID Survey October 2021. (n=5,000)

176. Interview with Charlie Buchanan, Michael Stephan, and Janine Zucker of Deloitte, July 22, 2021.

177. Jennifer Moss, "Beyond Burned Out," *Harvard Business Review*, February 10, 2021, https://hbr.org/2021/02/beyond-burned-out. Accessed April 19, 2022.

178. "2022 Financial Resolutions Study," Fidelity Investments, 2022, https://www.fidelity.com/bin-public/060_www_fidelity_com/documents/about-fidelity/2022_Fidelity_FinancialResolutionsSheet.pdf. Accessed April 19, 2022.

179. Patrick Thomas, "The Hardest Job to Recruit For: Other Recruiters," *The Wall Street Journal,* November 22, 2021, https://www.wsj.com/articles/the-hardest-job-to-recruit-for-other-recruiters.11637582401?mod=Searchresults_pos4&page=1. Accessed February 4, 2022.

180. "Job Openings and Labor Turnover Summary February 2022," U.S. Bureau of Labor Statistics, March 29, 2022, https://www.bls.gov/news.release/jolts.nr0.htm. Accessed April 19, 2022.

181. Sky Ariella, "27 US Employee Turnover Statistics [2022]: Average Employee Turnover Rate, Industry Comparisons, and Trends," Zippia, December 6, 2021, https://www.zippia.com/advice/employee-turnover-statistics/. Accessed April 19, 2022.

182. Liana Loewus, "Why Teachers Leave—or Don't: A Look at the Numbers," Education Week, January 10, 2022, https://www.edweek.org/teaching-learning/why-teachers-leave-or-dont-a-look-at-the-numbers/2021/05. Accessed April 19, 2022.

183. Tim Walker, "Survey: Alarming Number of Educators May Soon Leave the Profession," National Education Association, February 1, 2022, https://www.nea.org/advocating-for-change/new-from-nea/survey-alarming-number-educators-may-soon-leave-profession. Accessed April 19, 2022.

184. Roderick M. Kramer, "Rethinking Trust," *Harvard Business Review,* June 1, 2009, https://hbr.org/2009/06/rethinking-trust. Accessed April 19, 2022.

185. Ibid.

186. Prasad Setty, "The Results of Our Global Hybrid Work Survey," Google Cloud Blog, November 15, 2021, https://cloud.google.com/blog/products/workspace/insights-from-our-global-hybrid-work-survey. Accessed April 19, 2022.

187. "Future Forum Pulse Survey: Inflexible Return-to-Office Policies Are Hammering Employee Experience Scores," Future Forum, April 2022, https://futureforum.com/pulse-survey/.

188. Ben Wigert, "The Future of Hybrid Work: 5 Key Questions Answered with Data," Gallup, March 15, 2022, https://www.gallup.com/workplace/390632/future-hybrid-work-key-questions-answered-data.aspx. Accessed April 19, 2022.

189. Prasad Setty, "The Results of Our Global Hybrid Work Survey," Google Cloud Blog, November 15, 2021, https://cloud.google.com/blog/products/workspace/insights-from-our-global-hybrid-work-survey. Accessed April 19, 2022.

190. Jen Fisher and Anh Phillips, *Work Better Together: How to Create Strong Relationships to Maximize Well-Being and Boost Bottom Lines* (New York: McGraw-Hill, 2021). 204–206, 216.

191. We aren't advocating blind trust; there are bad apples in any organization of size. Giving trust is not the same as being naïve; see the chapter on cybersecurity for more.

192. "The Pygmalion Effect," Decision Lab https://thedecisionlab.com/reference-guide/management/the-pygmalion-effect. Accessed April 19, 2022.

193. Emilio J. Castilla, "Achieving Meritocracy in the Workplace," MIT Sloan Management Review, June 13, 2016, https://sloanreview.mit.edu/article/achieving-meritocracy-in-the-workplace/. Accessed April 19, 2022.

194. Almost 70 years after the Equal Pay Act of 1963, women generally earn 84 percent of what men earn for doing the same job. There are many reasons for this, including profession, part time versus full time, and seniority, among others. But the compensation difference is a reality that destroys trust in the system, even if individuals feel fairly compensated. Notably, the Economic Policy Institute points out that minimum wage laws and other labor market policies mean the gender compensation gap is smaller at the bottom of the pay scale (92 percent) than at the top (74 percent). Source: Elise Gould, "What Is the Gender Pay Gap and Is It Real? The Complete Guide to How Women Are Paid Less than Men and Why It Can't Be Explained Away," Economic Policy Institute, October 20, 2016, https://www.epi.org/publication/what-is-the-gender-pay-gap-and-is-it-real/. Accessed February 5, 2022.

195. Kathleen Davis, "An Easy Fix for the Great Resignation? Pay Transparency," Fast Company (Fast Company, November 30, 2021), https://www.fastcompany.com/90692823/an-easy-fix-for-the-great-resignation-pay-transparency. Accessed April 19, 2022.

196. Tonja Jacobi and Dylan Schweers, "Female Supreme Court Justices Are Interrupted More by Male Justices and Advocates," *Harvard Business Review,* July 19, 2017, https://hbr.org/2017/04/female-supreme-court-justices-are-interrupted-more-by-male-justices-and-advocates. Accessed April 19, 2022.

197. Adam Grant, "Who Won't Shut up in Meetings? Men Say It's Women. It's Not," *Washington Post,* February 18, 2021, https://www.washingtonpost .com/outlook/2021/02/18/men-interrupt-women-tokyo-olympics/. Accessed April 19, 2022.

Chapter 14

198. L. Ceci, "Time Spent on Average on a Smartphone in the U.S. 2021," Statista, February 25, 2022, https://www.statista.com/statistics/1224510/ time-spent-per-day-on-smartphone-us/. Accessed January 24, 2022.

Chapter 15

199. Sources: "Twitter by the Numbers (2022): Stats, Demographics & Fun Facts," Omnicore, February 2, 2022, https://www.omnicoreagency.com/ twitter-statistics/. Accessed February 11, 2022; Nick Galov, "How Many Emails Are Sent per Day in 2022?," Review42, March 7, 2022, https:// review42.com/resources/how-many-emails-are-sent-per-day/. Accessed February 11, 2022; "Worldwide Texting Statistics," Vermont.Gov, https:// shso.vermont.gov/sites/ghsp/files/documents/Worldwide%20Texting% 20Statistics.pdf. Accessed February 11, 2022.

200. Paul Balsom, "The Surprising Things You Don't Know about Big Data," Adeptia, February 3, 2022, https://adeptia.com/blog/surprising-things-you-dont-know-about-big-data#:~:text=An%20exabyte%2C%20 finally%2C%20is%201%2C024,storage%20grew%20annually%20by%20 23%25. Accessed April 19, 2022.

201. Jennifer Lee, Nick Galletto, and Praveck Geeanpersadh, "The Chemistry of Trust," Deloitte Insights, https://www2.deloitte.com/content/ dam/Deloitte/ca/Documents/deloitte-analytics/ca-chemistry-of-trust-pov-aoda-en.pdf?icid=ca-chemistry-of-trust_popup_pdf_en. Accessed April 19, 2022.

202. Ashley Reichheld et al., "Designing a Human-First Data Experience," Deloitte Insights, October 19, 2021, https://www2.deloitte.com/us/ en/insights/topics/marketing-and-sales-operations/global-marketing-trends/2022/using-customer-data-to-build-trust-helpful-or-creepy.html. Accessed April 19, 2022.

203. Physical safety in the face of known and new threats is an ongoing concern and will always be a trust issue.

204. Rob Sloan, "Companies Name One of the Biggest Cybersecurity Threats: Their Employees," *The Wall Street Journal,* June 21, 2020, https://www .wsj.com/articles/companies-name-one-of-the-biggest-cybersecurity-threats-their-employees-11592606115. Accessed February 11, 2022.

205. "Psychology of Human Error: Could Help Businesses Prevent Security Breaches," CISO, September 12, 2020, https://cisomag.eccouncil.org/ psychology-of-human-error-could-help-businesses-prevent-security-breaches/. Accessed February 11, 2022.

206. Tara Siegel Bernard and Stacy Cowley, "Equifax Breach Caused by Lone Employee's Error, Former C.E.O. Says," *New York Times,* October 3, 2017. https://www.nytimes.com/2017/10/03/business/equifax-congress-data-breach.html.

207. Isabella Jibilian and Katie Canales, "The US Is Readying Sanctions Against Russia Over the SolarWinds Cyber Attack," *Business Insider,* April 15, 2021, https://www.businessinsider.com/solarwinds-hack-explained-government-agencies-cyber-security-2020-12. Accessed February 2, 2022.

208. iPhone is a registered trademark of Apple Inc., registered in the U.S. and other countries and regions; *The Four Factors of Trust: How Organizations Can Earn Lifelong Loyalty* is an independent publication and has not been authorized, sponsored, or otherwise approved by Apple Inc.

209. "The impact of iOS 14+ & ATT on the Mobile App Economy," Appsflyer, https://www.appsflyer.com/resources/reports/ios-14-att-dashboard/. Accessed February 12, 2022.

210. Stephen Warwick, "Apple Privacy Changes Wipe $278 Billion Market Value From 4 Companies," iMore, Feb 3, 2022, https://www.imore.com/ apple-privacy-changes-wipe-278-billion-market-value-4-companies. Accessed February 12, 2022.

Conclusion

211. "The World's Oldest Writing," *Archaeology,* May–June 2016, https:// www.archaeology.org/issues/213-1605/features/4326-cuneiform-t. Accessed January 6, 2022.

212. Robin Dunbar, "Dunbar's Number: Why My Theory That Humans Can Only Maintain 150 Friendships Has Withstood 30 Years of Scrutiny," Conversation, May 12, 2021, https://theconversation.com/dunbars-number-why-my-theory-that-humans-can-only-maintain-150-friendships-has-withstood-30-years-of-scrutiny-160676. Accessed January 6, 2022.

213. Jerry Useem, "The End of Trust: Suspicion Is Undermining the American Economy," *Atlantic,* November 24, 2021, https://www.theatlantic.com/magazine/archive/2021/12/trust-recession-economy/620522/.

214. Global GDP increased 6.1 percent, or $5.17 trillion, in 2021, from a global GDP of $84.75 trillion in 2020. Source: "World Economic Outlook," IMF, April 2022, https://www.imf.org/en/Publications/WEO. The dollar value of adding an additional 1 percent annual growth (from 6.1 percent to 7.1 percent) is approximately $847 billion. Source: "GDP," World Bank, 2020, https://data.worldbank.org/indicator/NY.GDP.MKTP.CD.

215. Mike Colias, Nick Kostov, and Peter Landers, "Auto Makers Supercharge Move Into Electric Vehicles," *The Wall Street Journal,* January 5, 2022. https://www.wsj.com/articles/auto-makers-supercharge-move-into-electric-vehicles-11641420382?mod=Searchresults_pos2&page=1. Accessed January 6, 2022.

216. Dawn Lim, "Larry Fink Wants to Save the World (and Make Money Doing It)," *The Wall Street Journal,* January 6, 2022. https://www.wsj.com/articles/larry-fink-wants-to-save-the-world-and-make-money-doing-it-11641484864?mod=hp_lead_pos10. Accessed January 6, 2022.

217. "Edelman Trust Barometer 2022," Edelman (Edelman, 2022), https://www.edelman.com/sites/g/files/aatuss191/files/2022-01/2022%20Edelman%20Trust%20Barometer%20FINAL_Jan25.pdf. Accessed April 19, 2022.

218. Ibid.

219. Greg Milano, Michael Chew, and JinBae Kim, "Companies That Do Well Also Do Good," CFO, May 15, 2019, https://www.cfo.com/governance/2019/05/companies-that-do-well-also-do-good/. Accessed January 6, 2022.

220. Niko Matouschek, "Trust in Transactions: An Economist's Perspective," Trust Project, Kellogg School of Management, https://www.kellogg.northwestern.edu/trust-project/videos/matouschek-ep-1.aspx. Accessed September 21, 2021.

221. This is not new. The great management thinker Peter Drucker believed the same. See "The Profit Motive." Drucker Institute, November 30, 2010.

Appendixes

222. The HX TrustID Four Factor and attribute questions are based on an assigned brand or organization. For customers, [Brand] is to be replaced with the assigned brand or organization. For workforce, [My employer] is to be replaced with the assigned organization. In-line labels (for example, [Humanity]) are for reference only, not to be included in the respondent view of the survey. The order of the Four Factors and attributes should be randomized for each respondent to minimize the impact of survey bias (as discussed in Chapter 1).

223. The composite HX TrustID score is intentionally unweighted to maintain simplicity and broad applicability across industries. Recall from Chapter 1 that simplicity was one of our original goals when developing the metric. Also recall from Chapter 1 that the relative importance of each factor by industry varies. Although a composite HX TrustID score is comparable across industries as a single metric, how organizations take action against the Four Factors will and should be highly variable depending on their industry and individual organizational context.

224. Deloitte, "HX TrustID Survey," October 2021. (n=5,000)

225. "Self-Serving Bias," Decision Lab, https://thedecisionlab.com/biases/self-serving-bias. Accessed March 5, 2022.

Acknowledgments

Ashley thanks her family and friends, and especially her partner, Marijke, for her infinite patience and love. She also thanks her friend and co-author Amelia for the "human" touch she brings to our work.

Amelia thanks her friends and family, and particularly her husband, Andrew, for his support and love. She also thanks her friend and co-author Ashley for all that she teaches her about how to build trust.

We'd both like to thank our parents, for engendering confidence, for teaching us to value our own intellect and insights, and for encouraging us to write. And we both thank our incredible and trusted team, including the inimitable Emily Werner, without whose tireless efforts and thought partnership we would not have been able to complete this project.

We are indebted to Ambar Chowdhury and Steve Goldbach for telling us to run and "run fast" on this important topic of trust. We want to thank our friends and partners, including Christina Bieniek, Karen Bowman, Todd DeBasio, Dan Helfrich, Nishita Henry, Stacy Janiak, Suzanne Kounkel, Scott Mager, John Peto, Dounia Senawi, and Anthony Stephan. We are grateful to the Deloitte Insights and Future of Trust teams.

We want to thank our research and methodology team for helping us to design, test, and study the HX TrustID, including Mark Allen, Evie Cheung, Jeff Ganis, Brandon Keelean, Lily Kim, Casey Lafer, Shant

Marootian, Deanna Mostowfi, Robert Nix, Deirdre O'Connell, Mat Scholtec, Andy Sussman, Jeffrey Tull, and Rebecca Weidler.

We want to thank our talented designers: Ana Santos for the beautiful book imagery, and Maggie Gosiger and Brad Stapleton for our brand design. For their insights and precision, we want to thank our data scientists, including Ran Bergman, Daniel Capellupo, Ido Cohen, Jingjing Guo, Tal Kaso, Sunil Kumar, Michael Laclavik, Tomer Livne, Olena Bagno Moldavsky, Eli Moore, Dor Sklar, and Denver Stokes.

For keeping us organized and on-track, we want to thank our program management team, including Abigail Winn Farley, Alyssa Hiraoka, Connie Hua, Alberto Masliah, Regan Mizrahi, Nina Pantin, Ashley Perkins, Shreya Raghunandan, Divya Saha, Andrew Stowe, and Joyce Zhou. For helping us to test and study the HX TrustID platform in-market, we want to thank our client delivery team, including Jack Alexander, Enzo Azarcon, Rasika Chakravarthy, Jennifer Daily, Jonathan Epstein, Nicole Gallagher, Lauren Teegarden, and Matt Varraveto.

We want to thank our functional and industry experts for their "how-to" input and expertise, including Colleen M Bordeaux, Charlie Buchanan, Keri Calagna, Terri Cooper, Christine Cutten, Aryn Wood Erwin, Brian Frank, Maggie Gross, Andy Haas, Andy Austin Ho, Joshua Knight, Dorsey McGlone, Michelle Christian McGuire, Emily Mossburg, Tom Schoenwaelder, Maribeth Sivak, Michael Stephan, Jody Stidham, and Janine Zucker. For reading and editing we thank Jessica Barzilay, Doug Hardy, Andrew Krivak, and Bill Marquard. And finally, we are grateful to our editor Zach Schisgal and the entire team at Wiley.

About the Authors

Ashley Reichheld is the creator of the HX TrustID platform and a principal at Deloitte LLP. Ashley is deeply passionate about building trust and elevating the human experience and has helped organizations to reimagine brands and experiences for over 20 years, shaping the moments that matter to their customers, workforce, and partners.

Ashley has lived and worked on nearly every continent and in over 40 countries. She speaks and publishes frequently, and her ideas have been featured in publications and at conferences on the topics of trust and human experience. Ashley graduated from Wellesley College with a dual degree in psychology and women's studies. Ashley lives in Holliston, Massachusetts, with her partner and two children.

Amelia Dunlop is the chief experience officer for Deloitte Digital and is a principal at Deloitte LLP. She is the author of *The Wall Street Journal* bestseller *Elevating the Human Experience: Three Paths to Love and Worth at Work*. Amelia is an advocate for how the HX TrustID helps people and organizations elevate experience.

Amelia speaks and publishes frequently on the topic of human experience, strategy, and innovation. She received *Consulting* magazine's Top Women in Technology award for Excellence Innovation in 2020. She holds a degree in sociology from Harvard University, a master's in theology from Boston College, and an MBA from Cambridge University. Originally from London, England, Amelia lives in Somerville, Massachusetts, with her husband and three children.

Index

A Word From the Authors

Thank you for going on the journey with us to explore *The Four Factors of Trust*. We are passionate about the topic of trust because it creates the types of relationships we want to build, the type of organizations we want to belong to, and the type of world we want to live in.

We hope this book has helped you to learn more about how to measure, predict, and build trust so that you can elevate the experience of your workforce, customers, and partners. To support your trust journey, we hope you take advantage of the **free resources** available at TheFourFactorsOfTrust.com including:

- A dynamic tool that lets you explore our data, including the potential **value of improving your brand's trust score**

- A short video of us talking about our most critical, actionable insights about trust

- A downloadable chapter of *The Four Factors of Trust* you can share with your team

We look forward to seeing you online at TheFourFactorsOfTrust.com.

Ashley Reichheld   Amelia Dunlop